TALLEYRAND

by

DUFF COOPER

GROVE PRESS
New York

First published in Great Britain by Jonathan Cape in 1932

This paperback edition is published with the permission of Phoenix, a division of Orion Books Ltd., London, and was originally printed in 1997.

Printed in the United States of America

FIRST GROVE PRESS EDITION

Library of Congress Cataloging-in-Publication Data

Cooper, Duff, Viscount Norwich, 1890–1954.
    Talleyrand / Duff Cooper.
        p.   cm.
    Includes bibliographical references and index.
    ISBN 0-8021-3767-9
    1. Talleyrand-Pârigord, Charles Maurice de, prince de Bânâvent,
1754–1838. 2. Statesmen—France—Biography. 3. Diplomats—France—
Biography. I. Title.

DC255.T3 C75 2001
944.06'092—dc21
[B]   00-049447

Grove Press
841 Broadway
New York, NY 10003

01 02 03 04   10 9 8 7 6 5 4 3 2 1

Contents

Chapter One

THE OLD REGIME

I

THE childhood of a French nobleman in the eighteenth century was not usually the period of his life upon which he looked back with either affection or regret. The doctrine that parents exist for the sake of their children was not then accepted, and the loving care and hourly attention bestowed upon the children of to-day would have appeared ridiculous to sensible people. When Rousseau, the first man of sentiment, abandoned all his children, one after the other, to be brought up as unknown foundlings, his conduct was thought odd but not vile. The heir to the richest dukedom in France describes how his education was entrusted to one of his father's lackeys who happened to be able to read, how he was dressed in the prettiest clothes for going out but how at home he was left naked and hungry, and how this was the fate of all the children of his age and class. The modern method reflects greater credit on the parents; but evidence is not yet sufficient to prove that it produces a superior type of individual.

Family feeling, however, which has always existed more strongly in France than in England, was certainly as prevalent and as powerful at that period as it is to-day. It was a sentiment that cared more for the interests of the family as a whole than for the interests of the separate members of the family. The individual was expected, and often compelled, to make sacrifices in order that the family might benefit.

The Bastille, which, under the Old Regime, played such an exaggerated part in the imaginations of the ignorant, was principally used to enable indignant parents to obtain from their children that measure of obedience which they considered that the interests of the family decreed.

Charles-Maurice de Talleyrand-Périgord, who was born in Paris on 2nd February 1754, was in his earliest years a victim of these two apparently contradictory tendencies, parental neglect and family pride. He has set it upon record that, during his whole life, he never spent one week under the same roof as his father and mother; and an accident, which occurred to him in infancy while boarded out in the house of a poor woman in the suburbs of Paris, rendered him permanently lame, and therefore unfitted him, in the opinion of his parents, to inherit his father's many titles, which, it was then arranged, should devolve upon his younger brother.

Yet it is not necessary to assume that these parents were inhuman; they were merely following the fashion of their time. They were most anxious to promote the interests of every member of their family, but they did not believe that the future welfare of a man depended upon constant supervision of his childhood. They desired, and sought to obtain, wealth and honour for each of their children, and they knew of only two channels through which wealth and honour could come to a gentleman—the Army and the Church. But a cripple could not be a soldier, and a priest could not hand on his name and titles to his son, and they therefore decided that the second son should be the future head of the family and that the eldest son should enter the Church.

Soon after the occurrence of this accident, which was to exercise so fateful an influence upon his life, the child was sent upon a visit to his great-grandmother, the Princess de Chalais, who resided upon her estates in the province of Périgord. The months that followed were the happiest of his childhood. He found himself living in a period that had already passed away. The old Princess maintained a state of simple, feudal dignity, which the nobility of France had forgotten since Richelieu taught them to live at Court and to look for all preferment to the King. The independence of the aristocracy had vanished, but the quick-witted little boy was permitted to behold at Chalais, as he sat on a stool at the great lady's feet, a survival of the feudal system, and a vision of what France had been more than a hundred years before.

Every Sunday the principal gentlemen from the surrounding country would come to accompany the old lady to church. After the ceremony all the poor and the sick would collect in the hall of the château and they would be received singly by the Princess. Two sisters of charity would interrogate them as to their symptoms and prescribe the remedy. The Princess would then say where it was to be found and one of the gentlemen in attendance would proceed to get it. The château was full of medicines and unguents freshly prepared every year in accordance with ancient recipes. The sick people would take away also some herbs for their ptisan, some wine and other comforts, but what they valued most were the kind words of the lady who helped them and who felt for their sufferings.

Remembering the scene years afterwards he wrote: 'More thorough and scientific medicines employed, even equally free of charge, by doctors of the first reputation, would not have brought nearly so many poor people together and, above all, would not have done them so much good. There would have been lacking the main instruments of healing—prevention, respect, faith, and gratitude. Man is composed of a soul and a body and it is the former that governs the latter. The wounded who have received consolation, the sick who have been persuaded to hope are already in a state to be cured; their blood circulates better, their nerves are strengthened, sleep returns, and the body revives. Nothing is more efficacious than confidence; and it is at its fullest force when it springs from the care and attention of a great lady, around whom are gathered all ideas of power and protection.'

These enlightened views on the relative importance of mind and matter were not all that he took away from his visit to Chalais. For the first time he was treated with real affection and for the first time he felt proud to belong to an ancient family which through long service had earned respect and love. 'If I have shown, without too much familiarity, some affectionate and even tender sentiments; if I have retained in changing circumstances some dignity without any haughtiness; if I respect and love old people, it was at Chalais and from my grandmother that I derived all the good feelings with which I saw my family was regarded in that province.' He parted from the old Princess in tears. She had been born when James II was King of England; he was to die in the reign of Queen Victoria.

When he arrived in Paris after a journey that had taken seventeen days, the child of eight was sent direct to school at the Collège d'Harcourt, without even being permitted to pay a visit to his parents on the way. Henceforth his relations with them were limited to a weekly dinner, to which he was conducted by his tutor, and which he never left without receiving the same admonition—'Be a good boy and do as Monsieur the Abbé tells you.' But he was not unhappy at school. The shadow of the future had not yet fallen upon him. He was popular with his school-fellows, and already gave proof of that adaptability to circumstances and power of pleasing his contemporaries, which were to stand him in such good stead throughout his career.

It was during a period of convalescence after an attack of smallpox, which left him unmarked, that he first began to wonder upon what lines his parents had decided that his life was to proceed. He was not to be left long in doubt, and from the first announcement his whole nature, which had so little of the spiritual about it, revolted against the prospect of becoming a priest. In the hope that the pomp and splendour, inseparable at that time from an episcopal residence, might captivate his youthful imagination, he was sent to stay with his uncle at the Archbishopric of Rheims, where no pains were spared to impress upon him what a fine and pleasant thing it was to rise to a high position in the Church. But he remained unimpressed and, after a year spent in these surroundings, it was only out of weariness and in the conviction that to oppose the wishes of his family was impossible, that he finally consented to enter the seminary of Saint Sulpice, with a view to eventually taking Orders.

Here, where he remained for three years, he was no longer popular. His fellow students found him haughty and reserved, whereas in reality he was only unhappy. Readers of *Le Rouge et le Noir* will remember what Julien suffered at the seminary of Besançon, and it does not need the imagination of a Stendhal to conceive all the bitterness, the impatience, the despair, that must pass through the soul of a full-blooded, worldly, intelligent, and ambitious youth during the long days and nights of adolescence in an ecclesiastical college.

In the depression that weighed so heavily upon him the young student discovered two sources of distraction, both of which were to prove of value to him throughout his life. The first was the college library into which he plunged hungrily, reading principally the works of historians and biographies of statesmen, and feeding his hopes for the future upon the record of the past. The other distraction— more intimate and more personal—he found in his first love affair—the first of many. A chance encounter in a church, an offer to share his umbrella in the rain, led to an intimacy that lasted for two years. She was a young actress whom her parents had forced to go upon the stage against her will; he against his will was in process of becoming a priest. Different as were the roads selected for them by parental authority, they found a bond of union in the fact that they were both dedicated to a profession that they had not chosen; and the priest who could not love the Church found consolation in the arms of the actress who hated the stage. It is odd that his first romance, like that of Sir Walter Scott, should have begun under an umbrella.

2

The coronation of Louis XVI at Rheims, which Talleyrand attended in 1775, was the occasion of his first introduction into the great world, where he was to play so prominent and so prolonged a part. He was now twenty-one years of age, and although there awaited him still four years of preparation before entering the priesthood, he returned no more to Saint Sulpice, but became a student at the Sorbonne, leading a life of complete liberty in Paris.

Wordsworth found it bliss to be alive at the dawn of the French Revolution, and to be young then was, he said, 'very heaven.' But Talleyrand, whose ideas of bliss and of heaven differed considerably from those of the poet, preferred a slightly earlier period, and asserted that nobody could appreciate the pleasure of living who had not lived *before* 1789. He was well qualified to speak with authority on the subject of pleasure, and his tireless pursuit of it was not hindered by the fact that he was to become a priest, nor by his ordination, which took place in the year 1779.

His ordination, and the livings which he subsequently acquired, and which carried no duties with them, enabled him to be independent of his parents, and to afford a manner of living which became his rank rather than his calling. His first preferment is said to have come to him as the result of a witticism that he let fall in the drawing-room of Madame Dubarry, where he complained that in Paris the ladies were more easily to be won than the Abbeys. But the story is unlikely, for by the time that Talleyrand was frequenting the salons of Paris, Madame Dubarry had ceased to have any Abbeys at her disposal.

As soon as he was in a financial position to do so, he acquired a small but comfortable house in a quiet and leafy corner of Paris, where he collected a library of precious volumes and entertained a select and brilliant circle of friends. It became a habit for three or four of them to call there every morning for the purpose of conversation, and to remain to luncheon. The dearest of these to Talleyrand, or rather to the Abbé de Périgord, as he was usually called at this time, was Auguste de Choiseul, the nephew of Louis xv's Minister. They had first met as boys at the Collège d'Harcourt and an intimate friendship, which was never troubled by the shadow of a quarrel, united the two men throughout their eventful lives. 'He was,' said Talleyrand, 'the man that I most loved.'

The name of Louis de Narbonne was at the time often associated with those of the other two as forming a trio distinguished throughout the fashionable world of Paris for their wit, their wickedness, and their conquests. The coterie, of which these three were the centre and heart, included amongst its members all those who were most intelligent, most free thinking, most free speaking, and most free living in Paris.

Never before, perhaps, and never since has a society existed so well equipped to appreciate all the pleasures both of the senses and of the intellect. The restraints upon

liberty of thought and action which man had constructed
for himself in the past were falling away, and those with
which he has since replaced them were not yet invented.
It was a period of feverish excitement, of daring speculation,
of boundless hope. It was the entr'acte between two epochs,
and the group that met in the foyer, provided by the house
of the lame young Abbé at Bellechasse, were well aware
that the next act would differ considerably from the one
they had already witnessed. They were sufficiently far-
sighted to foresee, and bold enough to speculate upon and
to accept, the lines along which the drama would develop;
but meanwhile they had only to flirt, to gamble, and to
chatter, until called to their several places by the ringing of
the bell that should announce the rise of the curtain.

It was the apogee of the philosophical period and, as was
fitting, the patriarch of philosophy arrived in Paris, to
receive the adulation of his disciples before it was too late.
Voltaire, now a very old man, was welcomed with more
than royal honours, and one of the last acts which he performed was solemnly to bestow his blessing upon the Abbé
de Périgord, who knelt at his feet, amid the loud applause
of the company.

It is too commonly supposed that the French aristocracy
before the Revolution was haughty and exclusive, but the
barriers that had hitherto opposed the entry into society of
men of humble birth, were already disappearing. Talleyrand himself bears witness, not without regret, to the changed
conditions beginning to prevail. The love of gambling and
the admiration for witty conversation were, in his opinion,
the principal causes of this development. Gambling is a
great leveller, and a good talker can soon make an
audience forget his lack of heraldic quarterings. The
Revolution was to proclaim 'the career open to talent' as a
new gospel, but a social career in Paris was already open,

if not to talent, at any rate to the bold punter and the ready tongue.

This was the age of conversation, of free and unfettered discussion upon every subject in heaven or on earth. To talk well was then considered the highest attribute that any person could possess. It was the one art at which all endeavoured to excel, the one channel into which all talent was directed. Such conversation as was then audible in Paris had never, perhaps, been heard since certain voices in Athens fell silent two thousand years before. Nor has it been repeated. To every human development there is, it seems, a limit set. The days of the age of conversation were already numbered. The age of events was at hand.

There was one quality that was novel in this conversational period, and which distinguishes it from similar periods in the past. Neither Aspasia nor Xanthippe take any part in the dialogues that Plato has recorded. But in the Paris of Talleyrand's youth the great ladies were the leaders of talk as well as of fashion. They were the arbiters not only of elegance, but of ethics, of politics, and of all the arts. No man could rise to prominence except against the background of a salon, and over every salon a woman ruled.

The years that have since elapsed have witnessed what is called the enfranchisement of woman, but neither from the polling booth nor from her seat in Parliament has she as yet succeeded in exercising the same control over the lives of men and the fate of nations as was hers while she remained merely the centre of a select circle in her own drawing-room.

Already, in the earlier part of the century and in the two centuries before, queens and mistresses of kings had played great parts in public life, but for the first time 'Society,' to use the word in the sense in which Talleyrand himself employed it, began to represent an important body of opinion, independent of, and in opposition to, that of the Court.

In feudal times the king had had to reckon with a free and powerful nobility, living upon their own land, and relying upon the support of their own adherents. The struggle between king and landed aristocracy had resulted in France in the defeat of the aristocracy, just as in England it had resulted in the defeat of the king. And just as in England the king had been allowed to retain all the outward trappings of sovereignty after he had lost the reality of power, so in France the aristocracy retained all their old privileges and the glitter and glamour of greatness long after they had ceased to take any important part in the government of the country.

For a hundred years and more the monarchy in France had been absolute and popular. It was beginning now to lose both power and prestige. A sinister symptom of what was to follow appeared when the higher ranks of society began to lose their respect for the sovereign. It started when Louis xv selected as his principal mistress a member of the middle-class, it continued when he chose her successor from the streets. When the feud between Madame Dubarry and the Duke de Choiseul ended in the dismissal of the minister, the road to Chanteloup, his country house, was crowded with carriages, while familiar faces were absent from the Court at Versailles. For the first time in French history the followers of fashion flocked to do homage to a fallen favourite. People wondered at the time, but hardly understood the profound significance of the event. The king was no longer the leader of society. Kings and Presidents, Prime Ministers and Dictators provide at all times a target for the criticism of philosophers, satirists, and reformers. Such criticism they can usually afford to neglect, but when the time-servers, the sycophants, and the courtiers begin to disregard them, then should the strongest of them tremble on their thrones.

The prestige that Louis xv had lost Louis xvi did not recover. It is true that at the opening of the new reign all the auspices were favourable. A young and virtuous king in place of an old and vile one; a young and beautiful queen in place of a horde of mistresses. Unpopular ministers were dismissed and popular ones replaced them. And it is interesting to remember that Talleyrand in his memoirs remarks that the epithet 'popular' began for the first time to be associated with ministers. The popularity of ministers was beginning to be a matter of importance.

The new King and the new Government were popular, which means that they were liked by the people. But fashionable society, which was at this time strongly liberal in sentiment and to whom, as to all Liberals, 'the People' was an abstract term rather than a number of individuals, fashionable society, dissolute in morals, elegant in manners, pagan at heart, could show no allegiance to a youthful monarch who was neither intelligent nor elegant, but merely a clumsy, courageous, shortsighted Christian, desperately anxious to do right.

Liberal and progressive politics were professed, with or without sincerity, by a large number of those whose words and actions carried weight in the great world of the day. Nor was there lacking a rallying point around which the most reckless and most radical elements in the aristocracy could gather. Apart from the King's own children and brothers, the Duke of Orleans, although a distant cousin, was the next heir to the throne. His wealth was prodigious, his intelligence was not mean, his character was despicable but not unamiable, and he made of the Palais Royal, which was his home, a centre for all those who were inclined to criticise the Government, to laugh at the King, to repeat gossip about the Queen, to air revolutionary theories, and to indulge without restraint in all the dissipations that wealth and power and privilege could provide.

Choderlos de Laclos was an intimate member of the Orleans circle, and he has left, in his famous novel, an impressive picture of the corruption of the world in which he lived. Talleyrand soon became a member of that world, and considerable were the attractions which it provided for a young, ambitious, and already slightly embittered man. Here was to be found all that was most amusing and all that was most alluring in Paris. The great wits and the great ladies gave equally of their best. And a young man, whose intelligence forbade him from thinking that love and laughter were the whole of life, could feel that in this particular coterie, while he was enjoying himself enormously, he was also upon the fringe of politics and on the outskirts of public life.

There is a school of historical writers who will represent the whole of the French Revolution as the result of an Orleanist plot, whereas others deny that the Duke of Orleans was anything but a misguided nonentity exercising no influence whatever upon the events that took place. It is not proposed here to examine the theories or the evidence of either school, but it may be stated in general terms that the Palais Royal before the Revolution represented, in a country where parliamentary government was unknown, the headquarters of what in England would be called the Opposition. It was therefore natural that a young man with capacity and without preferment should drift towards that centre, even if it had not possessed so many additional attractions.

3

It is difficult to form in the mind a definite picture of the personal appearance of any individual whom we shall never see. Of Talleyrand we know that he was about the middle height, that he had a slightly retroussé nose, which enhanced a haughty and even insolent expression, and that he walked with a limp. Barras, who hated him, asserts that he strikingly resembled Robespierre; Arnault, who did not love him, said that he concealed the heart of a devil under an angel's face. Whether or not he could be described as handsome, there is no doubt that his wit and charm of manner made amends for any physical shortcomings, and his numerous successful love affairs were acknowledged, condemned, and envied.

It would be an ungrateful and a graceless task to rummage among the printed libels of the past in the hope of ascertaining exactly what his relationship may have been with one or another of the many women with whom his name was at different times connected. Let it suffice to say that in that gay and gallant world to which his birth admitted him, he assumed immediately a position almost of leadership, that he loved many women and that many loved him, and that those who loved him were admittedly the most intelligent, the most beautiful, and the most influential. Let it be said also, for fear of falling into panegyric, that in an age of universal latitude and easily condoned licence, his conduct incurred severe condemnation, and that he acquired notoriety even before he acquired fame.

Two incidents connected with this period of Talleyrand's life throw light both upon the epoch and the individual. The Countess de Brionne, daughter of a Prince of Rohan and wife of the Master of the Horse, was one of the most influential and most beautiful women of the day. So much was she impressed by the qualities of the Abbé de Périgord, that she designed to procure for him at the age of thirty, no less an honour than a cardinal's hat. For this purpose she wrote to the King of Sweden, a Protestant but a very good friend of the Pope's, whose acquaintance she had made a few years previously during his visit to Paris. Gustavus III no doubt did his best and might have succeeded had not a still more powerful protagonist entered the lists from another quarter. The Austrian Government naturally carried more weight at the Court of Rome than any Lutheran monarch, and the Austrian Government was found to be strongly opposed to the candidature of the Abbé de Périgord. To a modern mind it may seem remarkable that the King of Sweden and the Emperor should be so closely concerned in the fortunes of an undistinguished French abbé. The King's reasons for intervention have been referred to, and the Emperor's were not dissimilar. His sister was Marie Antoinette, Queen of France, and there had recently been an ugly scandal connected with the purchase of a diamond necklace by a Cardinal, who had been persuaded that the Queen was in love with him. The name of the Cardinal was Rohan, which was also the maiden name of the Countess de Brionne, who had warmly espoused her cousin's cause throughout the affair. Marie Antoinette had not forgiven her. Word was sent through the Austrian Ambassador at Versailles to the Court of Vienna that the Austrian representative at the Vatican was to oppose the claims of any candidate supported by the Countess de Brionne, the Cardinal de Rohan, or the King of Sweden. The Austrian Ambassador carried out his orders and the Abbé de Périgord was not promoted.

It seemed to Talleyrand, having failed to acquire a cardinal's hat, that a bishop's mitre should be his for the asking, and when he was confidently expecting one it came to him as a rude blow to find that once again his claims had been overlooked. The reason for his failure to obtain preferment upon this occasion must have caused savage sarcasm and bitter mirth amongst the society of the Palais Royal. The young King had, it appeared, acquired from somewhere the absurd idea that a bishop should be a man of virtuous life, and as the open licence of the private life of the Abbé de Périgord was becoming a scandal, His Majesty took the view that another man would be a more suitable occupant of the vacant see.

Subsequently, however, when another bishopric fell vacant, the King was approached on behalf of the Abbé de Périgord from a quarter and in a manner that he was unable to resist. Talleyrand's father was dying. In his youth he had been personal equerry to the father of Louis xvi. He had neglected and disinherited his eldest son, but he could not bear to die without seeing him a bishop. Louis xvi could be obstinate, but he could not refuse the request of a dying man who had been a friend of his father's. So Talleyrand, despite, it is said, the protest of his own mother, who like others, deplored his way of living, became Bishop of Autun in the year 1788.

4

A life of idle pleasure, even such pleasure as eighteenth-century Paris could provide, is incapable of satisfying the aspirations of a very intelligent man. And the reason of this is that work is a form of pleasure, and that a man who has never worked has missed one of the greatest pleasures of life. Talleyrand, into whose lap all the simpler pleasures were beginning to fall, realised in good time that his intellect would demand a kind of satisfaction that his senses could never give. Appointed in 1780 to the position of Agent-General of the Clergy, he determined at once to make the most of the appointment. It was one of those many positions, which exist to-day as they existed then, where a man will be excused for doing nothing, and will probably be blamed for doing much.

Talleyrand worked hard in an office that might have been a sinecure, and, despite his gay life in the great world, he succeeded in making a deep impression upon his contemporaries as a man of affairs and a practical reformer. Two instances may be quoted of the kind of thing that this dissolute Abbé attempted to do in pre-revolutionary France. He had travelled in Brittany. A love affair had taken him there, but he had not been too busy to attend to a grievance that had been brought to his notice. Amongst that seafaring folk the wives whose husbands did not come back from the sea were not allowed by the rules of the Church to consider that their husbands were dead. They had to live out the rest of their lives neither maids, nor wives, nor widows. Talleyrand attempted to change this system and to permit the unfortunate women to assume, after a reasonable interval, the death of their husbands. He failed. His memorandum on the subject was thrown into the fire by the Bishop of Arras, and, as he himself remarks in his memoirs, there had to be a revolution before these poor Breton women were allowed to re-marry, and many of them had grown rather old in the interval.

As Agent-General of the Clergy, solicitous of the interests both of Clergy and people, he suggested one other reform of an equally practical and popular nature. The State was rapidly going bankrupt, the Church was still extremely rich. One important source of State revenue was the government lottery. Talleyrand, we may assume, had no strong moral objection to gambling, since throughout his life he was a devotee both of the stock exchange and of the card table. But he realised, as every economist has realised, that, for the welfare of the State, the gambling instinct should be discouraged, and, as a member of the Church, he saw how that body could gain prestige, and at the same time assist the Government and benefit the community. He suggested that the Church should purchase from the Government for a large sum the right of raising lotteries and should then abolish them. In the light of subsequent events it appears an admirable suggestion, but such suggestions, however admirable, fall upon deaf ears when revolutions are impending.

The duties of Agent-General of the Clergy were not, however, sufficient to satisfy Talleyrand's appetite for political activity. Already his mind was attracted towards questions of external policy and already he was dabbling in subterranean diplomacy. Calonne had recently taken charge of the finances of France. He was a statesman with whom Talleyrand found it easy to be friends. A courtier first, he would reply to any request of the Queen: 'Madam, if it is possible it is done, if it is impossible it shall be done.' Behind a completely frivolous appearance he concealed ability, and was able to detect it in others. Talleyrand saw in his friendship with the Minister an opening into the world of foreign affairs of which he was quick to avail himself.

One of the principal subjects of political discussion at the time was the Commercial Treaty concluded in 1786 between France and England, which established something like free trade between the two countries. It was criticised at first in France on the ground that it seemed to be working too favourably for England. Talleyrand defended it. They were living in the age of reason and what could be more reasonable than to abolish tariffs between an agricultural and an industrial country, the one receiving freely the manufactured goods and the other the natural products of the neighbour? So it seemed to the young politician in 1786 who hoped that an era of free exchange was approaching, and a better understanding between the two countries, now that the unhappy events of the American War of Independence were forgotten. Calonne was one of the authors of this policy which Talleyrand supported now and clung to for the rest of his life.

There could not have existed a greater contrast to the suave, rosy, and smiling Calonne than the terrific, frowning, passionate, pockmarked Mirabeau. Yet Talleyrand was equally intimate with both, and persuaded the one to employ the other. Mirabeau, who was, as ever, in urgent need of money, was glad to accept a secret mission to Berlin, there to find out how long the dying Frederick was likely to live, and what would be the policy of his successor. Mirabeau, however, was never meant for a diplomatist, and the mission proved singularly lacking in result. All his reports were addressed to Talleyrand, who communicated them to Calonne.

Mirabeau, while he was in Berlin, began to suspect that Talleyrand was betraying him. A man of violent passions and the greatest orator of the age, for any mood that was upon him he found memorable words: 'The Abbé de Périgord,' he wrote, 'would sell his soul for money; and he would be right, for he would be exchanging dung for gold.' A report that in his absence Talleyrand was making love to his mistress may have been responsible for the vigour of this denunciation, and, in spite of it, the two men became again, almost immediately afterwards, the firmest of friends.

Thus, upon the eve of the Revolution, the Bishop of Autun was already a man of considerable importance in Paris. Thirty-five years of age, celebrated for his wit, his profligate life, and his practical ability, he had already achieved an ascendancy in the salon and a secure footing in the political arena. Noble birth, influential connections, and a powerful intelligence, supported by high ambition and unburdened by scruples, all seemed to designate him as a worthy successor to the great ecclesiastical statesmen who in the past had controlled the destiny of France.

Chapter Two

THE REVOLUTION

I

IN 1789, with bankruptcy staring the Government in the face, Louis xvi took the momentous decision to summon the States-General. This meant nothing less than the calling together of representatives of the whole people. Upon the face of it the step was fraught with danger. Changes in method of government should be gradual. For a hundred and fifty years France had been the most autocratic, as England was the most democratic, state in Europe. Yet at this crisis in her affairs it was decided to bring together for purposes of consultation a body far more democratic than the House of Commons as it then existed or than any contemporary assembly in the world.

The States-General had not met since 1614, and anyone born, as Talleyrand was, in 1754, must have grown up in the belief that they would never meet again. But the unexpected happened; and for those men, who were still young, who were conscious of their abilities and spurred by their ambition, but whose activities had hitherto been, of necessity, confined to backstair diplomacy and Court intrigue, there opened suddenly a new, broad, and honourable roadway to political preferment and power.

At Rheims, in 1783, Talleyrand had met in his uncle's house the young William Pitt, who was by five years his junior, who had already been Chancellor of the Exchequer, and was shortly to become Prime Minister of England at the age of twenty-five. His French contemporaries, obsessed as many of them were with democratic notions of government and the fashionable anglophilism which was particularly prevalent at the Palais Royal, must often have reflected that, given similar opportunities and conditions in their own country, they would certainly have distinguished themselves as rapidly as the morose and sickly young Englishman had done. Now the opportunity was at hand.

The first thing was to secure a constituency. Three Orders were to be represented, the Clergy, the Nobility and the Third Estate. There was no hereditary chamber, each order elected its own representatives. Many of the Clergy and of the Nobility were elected to represent the Third Estate, but the clearly indicated constituents of the Bishop of Autun were the clergy of his own diocese, and, in order to make sure that there should occur no hitch in an arrangement so obviously right and proper, the Bishop decided to tear himself away from Paris and to visit, for the first and last time in his episcopal career, the centre of his see.

His sojourn at Autun lasted for a month, and during that time he did everything in his power to acquire the support and good will of the local clergy. All witnesses are agreed as to the exceptional powers which he possessed of rendering himself agreeable to those whom he wished to please. He who had already conquered the salons and the alcoves of Paris found it a simple task to charm and to convince the Burgundian priesthood. Throughout his life he was an epicure of the table as well as of other pleasures, and he was able to entertain his future constituents as they had never been entertained before.

Nor were the inducements which he held out for their support limited to the excellence of his table and the brilliance of his conversation. More solid reasons for approval were provided for those who demanded them. To the assembled clergy of the diocese he delivered a speech, in which he boldly stated what he considered to be the principal abuses that then existed, and drew up a whole programme of practical reforms. It was the custom for those who were represented at the States-General to furnish their representatives with a memorial of their complaints and grievances, and in the old days the representative, who had been little more than the agent of his constituents, had hardly any other duty to perform than to transmit this memorial or 'cahier' to the Sovereign after it had been incorporated in a general 'cahier' for the whole estate.

The clergy of Autun when they came to compile their 'cahier' upon this occasion found that they could not do better than transcribe, almost word for word, the address that had been delivered to them by their Bishop. And so Talleyrand, not for the last time in his career, received, before departing upon a mission, instructions of which he was himself the author.

Some idea of his political opinions at that time may be obtained from a brief summary of this address. He is in favour of regular sessions of the States-General and of codification of the law. No law should be passed and, above all, no taxation should be imposed, without the consent of the people. Public order, he maintains, is based upon two foundations—property and liberty. Property is sacred, but—and there follows a very far-reaching and far-sighted limitation to the doctrine—it may be necessary to inquire whether the term 'property' has not come to be applied to certain objects which could only come under it by a violation of the laws of nature, and also whether in some cases it is not still applied although the causes of its original application have disappeared. He seems here to be leaving himself a loophole for consenting to the nationalisation of Church lands.

Liberty of the subject is to be guaranteed by trial by jury and by *habeas corpus*. Freedom of speech and of the press is to be allowed, and private correspondence is to be inviolable. Education and financial reform are advocated. The latter is to be accomplished without fresh taxation by the abolition of fiscal privileges, by the establishment of a national bank, and, if necessary, by the sale of Crown lands, the raising of loans, and the introduction of a sinking fund. The doctrine of free trade is supported, the persistent heresy of the single tax is denounced, and it is laid down that it should be the duty of wise and enlightened legislation to assure to everybody the right to work, which is described as 'the only possession of those who have no property.'

That this should have been the political programme of an eighteenth-century bishop belonging to the oldest French nobility may surprise a modern reader. Almost as striking, however, as the modernity of the views expressed in this address, is the absence from it of any of those emotional appeals to sentiment, or vague statements of political theory, which at that time were even more popular than they are to-day, and which were particularly noticeable in similar addresses prepared by other adherents of the Orleanist faction. Talleyrand, here as ever, confines himself to what is practicable, and he is careful not to commit himself to any opinion with regard to the future Constitution of the country, for his views upon this subject were not those that were generally popular.

Talleyrand left Autun in the early morning of Easter Sunday, 12th April 1789. It was said that he was afraid to officiate in the Cathedral upon so solemn an occasion as his knowledge of Church ceremonial was quite inadequate, and he had already in the conduct of such duties committed blunders that had shocked his subordinates. But there were stronger reasons, once his work at Autun was accomplished, why he should not delay his return to the scene of all his activities and all his pleasures. Already that scene was being set for the production of one of the greatest dramas in history, and we may be sure that as he sped along the road to the north he threw back no regretful gaze upon the red roofs of the picturesque little town he was leaving, for it was with the future that his thoughts were occupied, and he knew that those spring days were pregnant with events.

2

The opening of the States-General took place at Versailles in the early days of May 1789. The first question that engaged their attention was one of procedure, but upon its settlement the whole future depended. There were three Orders—the Clergy, the Nobility, and the Third Estate, who at first, in imitation of the English, were inclined to style themselves the Commons. The question was, should the three Orders sit together in one assembly, and vote by head, or should there be three separate assemblies, each assembly having one vote? The Third Estate out-numbered the other two Orders put together. Upon the decision of this question, therefore, depended whether the Third Estate was to be the dominant and decisive factor, or whether it was to remain an impotent minority of one to two.

It is astonishing that the Government should not have foreseen that this question was bound to arise, should not have appreciated its vital importance, and should not have been prepared with a policy to meet it. The Estates were left to settle it for themselves. No suggestion, no advice, no guidance was given or offered by the Government until it was too late. From the first the Third Estate stood for the principle of one assembly, and refused to proceed further until it was admitted. The Nobility, despite the presence of a small minority of Liberals, were almost equally solid on the other side. The Clergy wavered. They included among their numbers many representatives of the minor Clergy, whose lot was as hard and whose grievances were as numerous as were those of the Third Estate. This was the weak spot in the ranks of the two privileged Orders, and it proved their undoing. Members of the minor Clergy united themselves with the Third Estate and their example was gradually followed by more distinguished members of the hierarchy.

When it became apparent that the victory of the Third Estate was assured the King attempted to intervene. One morning when the deputies came to their accustomed meeting-place, they found that the doors were shut against them. They met in the nearest convenient building, a tennis court, where they took an oath that they would not separate until their work was accomplished. It was at this juncture that the King for the first time informed them that the Three Orders should sit separately. His authority, which might have prevailed earlier, was now powerless. The Third Estate, who had already assumed the title of National Assembly, had won the day from the moment that the Clergy yielded. The example of the Clergy was finally followed by the Nobility. The command of the King was disregarded and the Revolution was a fact.

In this controversy Talleyrand took no open part. While in favour of reform he was opposed to revolution, and he saw plainly what the result must be if the Third Estate obtained control. He would have liked to set up a two-chamber system on the English model, giving to the Third Estate the powers of the House of Commons, and creating another body composed of the more powerful members of the Nobility and the heads of the Church, which should exercise the control over legislation that was still retained at that time by the House of Lords.

Talleyrand was not among the first of the Clergy, nor even of the Bishops, to throw in his lot with the Third Estate. He did so only when the trend of events became obvious and further resistance would have been useless. His friend and ally at this period was once more Mirabeau, who already dominated the Assembly and who shared his enthusiasm for constitutional monarchy. These two men would have liked to form a Government under such a system and to have become the Pitt and Dundas of a slightly less obstinate and distinctly more progressive George III. One day Mirabeau was descanting upon the particular qualities which a minister in such circumstances should possess, and had enumerated nearly all his own characteristics when Talleyrand interrupted with: 'Should you not add that such a man should be strongly marked by the small-pox?'

Events, however, were rapidly passing out of the control of moderate leaders. Even Mirabeau was powerless to arrest them. Exactly how far either he or Talleyrand was now or later in the counsel or the pay of the Court is difficult to determine, but it is certain that they both offered the King advice and that he did not take it.

Talleyrand's chief channel of communication with Louis XVI was the latter's youngest brother, the Count d'Artois, who exercised some influence both upon the King and upon Marie Antoinette. His last interview with the Count took place in July. It was after the fall of the Bastille. Talleyrand visited him in the dead of night and implored him to urge upon his brother that the last hope for the monarchy lay now in the dissolution by royal authority of the Estates and the resort, if it became necessary, to force.

So impressed was the young Prince by the force of Talleyrand's reasoning, that, having already gone to bed, he dressed again, obtained an audience of the King, and endeavoured to prevail upon him. But Louis would listen to no plan that might entail bloodshed. The next morning the Count d'Artois left France, leading the emigration of the nobility. He was not to meet Talleyrand again for twenty-five years, when he returned in the wake of the victorious allied forces, to take over the restored kingdom on behalf of his brother Louis xviii. Talleyrand sent him a messenger on that occasion to remind him of the midnight interview. D'Artois remembered it perfectly and the first act of the restored dynasty was to take the advice of the statesman whom they had so disastrously disregarded. If the Bourbons had learnt nothing else during a quarter of a century of exile they had at last come to realise that the counsels of Talleyrand were not to be neglected.

3

Realising now that the preservation of the Monarchy was no longer possible, Talleyrand determined to preserve himself. To so clear-sighted an observer of events only two courses remained open. Either he must throw in his lot with the emigrating nobility or else he must wholeheartedly support the Revolution. For the King, who refused to fight, no hope remained. Revolutions can be suppressed by force, but they can never be tricked or bribed into submission.

Talleyrand refused to emigrate although he was urged to do so by the Count d'Artois and others. His own country, to which throughout his life he was devoted, still presented a tempting field for his activities, and one in which he felt capable of accomplishing much. His political views had always been pronouncedly liberal. The reforms which he had advocated at Autun were still to be completed. The zeal of the reformers had only to be kept within bounds, the disorders which had already arisen had only to be suppressed, and the great work of regeneration and reconstruction in which the idealists of 1789 so fervently believed might be brought to a splendid and peaceful conclusion.

Talleyrand was not an idealist, but he was a reformer, and the reforms to which he was committed were those of which his country stood in urgent need. How great a rôle awaited him in the coming years he could not tell, but when he measured his own capabilities, of which he was an accurate judge, with those of his colleagues in the Assembly he could feel confident of his superiority. So long as a career remained open to him in France he refused to leave it, and for more than three years after the fall of the Bastille and the beginning of the emigration he continued to play an important part in the events that were engaging the world's attention.

He had already acquired a reputation for intelligence and for profligacy. He increased both during the years that followed. Oratorical abilities, which were the type best calculated to impress the Assembly, he lacked, but he possessed an impressive manner, a singularly deep voice, and he never spoke except when he had something of importance to communicate.

On 10th October 1789 he brought forward a motion for the transference to the State of all ecclesiastical property. This was one of the acts of his life which provoked the deepest indignation at the time, and was subsequently to be the most frequently quoted against him. The suggestion itself appeared in the eyes of the faithful to be flagrantly sacrilegious, and the fact that it came from a churchman and from a bishop magnified its enormity beyond bounds. It

should, however, be remembered that the Church was rich
and that the State was bankrupt, and that the proposal, as
put forward, was not intended to inflict any real hardship
upon the Church, for the State was to take over the whole
maintenance of the Church, to provide adequately for all
the clergy and to administer such charities as the Church
had hitherto administered. In modern parlance the Church
was not to be robbed but to be nationalised. The proposal
was welcomed by the Assembly, and the position of Talleyrand was strengthened.

   Financial reform and the introduction of universal and
compulsory education were the two other matters which
principally attracted his attention. Both were vital to the
success of the Revolution and the future welfare of France.
He was in favour of a national bank; he was strongly opposed to the reckless issue of *assignats* and spoke against it
in the Assembly. The concluding words of his speech
epitomised the financial argument in a sentence: 'You can
compel a man to accept an *assignat* for a thousand francs
in payment of that sum of money, but you can never compel
a man to give you a thousand francs in coin in return for an
assignat. . . . It is for that reason that the whole system will
fail.'

   His *Report on Public Education*, the reading of which to
the Assembly occupied three days, is admittedly a document which marks an epoch in the history of this subject.
Talleyrand's most violent detractors are unable to withhold
from it their admiration, and have therefore been compelled
to fall back on the assertion that Talleyrand was not the
author. He acknowledges himself that he sought assistance
from all who were most qualified to give it, none of whom
subsequently claimed to have done more than contribute
advice. The present system of public education in France,
which is frequently held up as a model to other countries,

owes much to this report including the creation of the National Institute.

The abolition of the royal lottery, the emancipation of the Jews, a proposed Anglo-French Conference for the stabilisation of weights and measures, these are the suggestions, all severely practical, with which we find the name of Talleyrand associated at a period when his colleagues of the Assembly were wasting in windy declamations about the brotherhood of mankind those precious days that might have been devoted to the reconstruction of France.

When, however, criticism of the Assembly, which was beginning to lose its popularity, grew loud, Talleyrand came forward as its champion, and delivered a speech, which from an oratorical point of view was his most successful, and in which he justified all that had hitherto been accomplished and exhorted his audience to continue their laborious task. In the same month, February 1790, he was elected President of the Assembly, defeating the Abbé Sieyès, who was the other candidate, by a large majority.

4

Meanwhile the difficulty of combining in one individual the positions of ecclesiastical dignitary and revolutionary leader was continually increasing. On 14th July 1790 the Feast of the Federation took place in Paris. It was the Bishop of Autun who was selected to celebrate mass at the altar erected in the Champ de Mars in the presence of the King and Queen, the members of the Assembly, the National Guard, and an enormous crowd of spectators. All present swore a solemn oath of fidelity to the Nation, the Law, and the King. Lafayette, Commandant of the National Guard and popular hero of the moment, was the first to swear. As he did so the reverend Bishop whispered to him: 'Don't make me laugh.' When the ceremony was over the Bishop hurried off to a gambling saloon, where he succeeded in breaking the bank.

The fact that a prelate of such notoriously bad morals should have been selected to perform such an office upon such an occasion, proves the difficulty that the Revolution was already experiencing in finding respectable people to do its work. Talleyrand's passion for gambling and specula- tion was at this time the cause of greater scandal than even the other forms of pleasure in which he indulged; and he found himself obliged to publish a denial of certain rumours which were current as to the large sums that he had recently won. Yet upon an occasion of such great national import- ance, because a bishop was needed, the authorities were compelled to apply to the Bishop of Autun.

Already, in May of the same year, the Assembly had adopted the measure known as 'the Civil Constitution of the Clergy.' This was in effect the logical sequel of the nationalisation of Church property. It placed the Church under democratic control, re-organised its establishment, allowed for the popular election of bishops and curés, and set at defiance the authority of the Vatican. In June Talley- rand was the only bishop who continued to sit in the Assembly.

At the end of the year the Assembly went further and decreed that the clergy themselves must swear allegiance to their new Constitution. The vast majority, including, of course, all those who were the most sincere and generally respected, refused the oath. Only four prelates, of whom Talleyrand was one, were found willing to accept it.

This act in itself practically constituted a breach with the Church, but in the following January (1791) he went further and formally resigned his bishopric on the ground that he had been elected one of the administrators of the

Department of Paris, and that it would be impossible for him in the future to devote himself to the affairs of his diocese.

It would have been better for Talleyrand's reputation had his connection with the Church terminated with his resignation, but unfortunately there remained one further function in which he was persuaded to take part. The Assembly, who had no intention at present of departing from Christianity, were faced with the task of finding recruits to fill the places of those ecclesiastics who had lost their livings rather than violate their consciences. The difficulty proved not insurmountable, although the new priesthood had little odour of sanctity about it, and carried small weight in the minds of religious people.

When, however, it came to appointing substitutes for the non-juring bishops, the additional obstacle presented itself that the law of apostolic succession demanded that any new bishop should be ordained by one who already held that position. Now, in the case of each of the other three prelates who had taken the oath, reasons existed why they could not perform this ceremony of consecration; therefore recourse was once more had to Talleyrand, who, although he had already resigned his see and was in almost open revolt against his Church, consented to undertake the task, and performed the extremely sacred ceremony of ordination for the benefit of three of the newly appointed bishops, who were thus enabled subsequently to ordain their colleagues.

The oath of allegiance to the Civil Constitution of the Clergy, given as it had been in open disobedience to the instructions of the Pope, brought upon Talleyrand the anathema of Rome. In April he was formally excommunicated. He offered no excuse and no defence, but wrote to the Duke de Biron, one of his companions in pleasure and colleagues in politics: 'Have you heard that I have been excommunicated? Come and console me by having supper with me. Every one must refuse me fire and water, so this evening we will have cold meat and iced wine.'

Shortly afterwards, when the question was debated in the Assembly whether those priests who had refused the oath should be allowed to perform religious services, Talleyrand spoke eloquently on their behalf. It was non-sense, he contended, to limit the doctrine of freedom of opinion to a man's private thoughts. If in the new era of liberty men were to be allowed to think as they pleased, they must also be allowed by their actions to show what they thought. For himself, he was glad that he had taken the oath, although it had brought excommunication upon him. He believed that the Constitutional Church repre-sented the purest form of the Catholic religion. Whatever the present Pope might do, that Church would remain attached to the Holy See, and would await with confidence a change of opinion either in him or in his successors.

The speech was characteristic of one who at times of violent commotion was capable of taking calm and long views, and who under personal affront was strangely incapable of bearing malice.

5

There was at this time living in Paris an American gentleman named Gouverneur Morris. He was a man of considerable intelligence, some experience of public affairs, especially of their financial side, and having warmly es-poused the cause of the colonists in the American War of Independence, he retained a cynically aristocratic view of life and a profound contempt for democratic theories. He was also a man of courage and resource. Later on, when Jefferson left Paris for a safer place, Morris was appointed American Minister, and he was the only foreign representative who remained at his post throughout the worst days of the Terror. On one occasion when he found himself the centre of a hostile mob in favour of hanging him on the nearest lamp-post as an Englishman and a spy, he unfastened his wooden leg, brandished it above his head, and proclaimed himself an American who had lost a limb fighting for liberty. The mob's suspicions melted into enthusiastic cheers, but, as a matter of fact, he had never fought for liberty nor for anything else, and had lost his leg as the result of a carriage accident.

Gouverneur Morris loved pleasure as much as he loved business—and he also loved the beautiful Countess de Flahaut. She was a young woman, the wife of an old husband, the daughter of a former mistress of Louis xv and herself the acknowledged mistress of Talleyrand. She lived in an apartment in the ancient palace of the Louvre which had come to her as the reward of her mother's frailty; and here she almost daily entertained her admirers.

We are inclined when we think of the French Revolution to imagine Paris in a state of continual turmoil and confusion, with angry mobs prowling the streets and tearing aristocrats in pieces, from the taking of the Bastille in the summer of 1789 until the end of the Terror in the summer of 1794. In reality, however, during the first three years of this period the life of the ordinary Parisian continued to be very much the same as usual. The shadow of the Revolution hung over everything, the glamour of the Court had gone, the rumour of great events was in the air, but there were still dinner-parties and dances, gambling and love-making and political intrigue, and the general atmosphere must have been very similar to that which prevailed in London during the Great War. Lady Sutherland, the British Ambassadress, wrote from Paris in December 1790: 'The tranquillity of France is but little disturbed notwith-

standing the wonderful changes that have of late happened. . . . In short this world is grown very dull.'

Of this life, as it was lived by those who pursued both
politics and pleasure, we can obtain a very vivid picture
from the diary which Gouverneur Morris kept from day
to day. From the same source we are provided with an
intimate sidelight upon the life of Talleyrand, for the two
men met regularly in the apartment of the woman they
both loved.

Talleyrand was in the stronger position of these two
lame lovers, for he had been first in the field and the lady
had already borne him a son, who had indeed been recognised
by her husband, but as to whose parentage nobody then or
afterwards ever entertained the slightest doubt. This son
became in course of time an aide-de-camp to Napoleon, the
lover of the Queen Hortense, the father by her of the Duke
de Morny, the husband of an English heiress, and the
grandfather of the fifth Lord Lansdowne. He died in 1870
on the eve of the battle of Sedan.

The first reference to Talleyrand in the diary is dated
14th October 1789—'Go to dine at Madame de F.'s. She
receives a note from the Bishop of Autun. He is to dine
with her at half-past five. She insists that I shall leave her
at five. I put on a decent show of coldness . . . we are to
dine *a trio* with the Bishop to-morrow.' Henceforth 'the
Bishop' appears almost daily in the record of Gouverneur
Morris's life. Sometimes he is spoken of with bitterness
as the object of jealousy, at others with satisfaction as being
subject to it himself. But upon the whole it is plain that
Madame de Flahaut achieved that rare and difficult triumph
so dear to the heart of the intelligent coquette, she made her
two lovers not only tolerate but like one another, and was
able to pass her time agreeably in the presence of both.
'Madame de Flahaut's countenance glows with satisfaction

in looking at the Bishop and myself as we sit together, agreeing in sentiment and supporting the opinions of each other. What a triumph for a woman. I leave her to go home with him.'

On 9th November of the same year he dined at the house of Monsieur Necker, the celebrated Minister of Finance and father of Madame de Staël, to whom, at this time, Talleyrand was making advances. Morris sat next to her at dinner. 'Much conversation about the Bishop d'Autun,' he records. 'I desire her to let me know if he succeeds, because I will, in such case, make advantage of such intelligence in making my court to Madame de F. A proposition more whimsical could hardly be made to a woman.'

At this time Talleyrand was still envisaging a ministerial portfolio, a prospect that was frustrated by a resolution of the Assembly which forbade its members to accept office. Morris advises him with regard to his speeches in the Assembly, and finds him reluctant to act upon the advice, for: 'He has something of the author about him; but the tender attachment to our literary productions is by no means suitable to a minister.' This evidence is interesting in the light of accusations frequently made later, that Talleyrand always made use of others in the composition of his speeches and despatches.

At the beginning of 1790 Morris meets 'the mother of the Bishop d'Autun. She is highly aristocratic; she says that the great of this country who have favoured the Revolution are taken in, and I think that she is not much mistaken in that idea.'

In January 1791 we find Madame de Flahaut 'complaining bitterly of the Bishop of Autun's cold cruelty. . . . He treats her ill. His passion for play has become extreme and she gives me instances which are ridiculous.' Nevertheless a few days later, being engaged in the matter of consecrating the new bishops and in serious fear of his life, he made a will in favour of Madame de Flahaut and left it with her, to her great alarm, on the eve of performing the ceremony.

After an intimate acquaintance of some three years, Morris's considered opinion of Talleyrand is summed up in a semi-official letter addressed to Washington. He has just mentioned the names of Narbonne and Choiseul, and he adds to them that of Talleyrand: 'These three are young men of high family, men of wit and men of pleasure. The two former were men of fortune but had spent it. They were intimates all three and had run the career of ambition together to retrieve their affairs. On the score of morals neither of them is exemplary. The Bishop is particularly blamed on that head; not so much for adultery, because that was common enough among the clergy of high rank, but for the variety and publicity of his amours, for gambling, and above all for stock jobbing during the ministry of M. de Calonne, with whom he was on the best of terms, and therefore had opportunities which his enemies say he made no small use of. However, I do not believe in this, and I think that, except his gallantries and a mode of thinking rather too liberal for a churchman, the charges are unduly aggravated.'

6

In June 1791 the royal family attempted to escape from France. They were recognised at Varennes and reconducted to Paris. Such an event might have been expected to entail the immediate downfall of the monarchy; but the time was not yet ripe for a republic. The upper and middle class supporters of the Revolution began to be alarmed. A new club, the Feuillants, came into existence. It represented the moderate element and sought to counterbalance the Jacobins. Talleyrand was a member. They were few in number but

strong in talent and it seemed at first that they were likely
to prove victorious. The newspaper of Marat was suppressed, many of the extremists went into hiding, Danton,
the brazen-lunged apostle of audacity, fled the country.
The Assembly decreed a new Constitution in which the
power and the prestige of the King were increased rather
than diminished. Amid scenes of enthusiasm the King
accepted the Constitution: the Constituent Assembly, its
work accomplished, was dissolved, and none of its members
were permitted to belong to the new Legislative Assembly
which took its place.

Talleyrand having ceased to be a member of the Assembly
and still debarred from accepting office under the crown,
now found himself unemployed in a Paris where it was no
longer pleasant to be idle. A Feuillant Government was in
power and his friend Narbonne was Minister for War, so
that he had every reason to expect that some use would be
found for his services. Gouverneur Morris advised him to
apply for the post of Ambassador at Vienna, suggesting that
as the link of communication between Marie Antoinette
and her brother the Emperor, he would be 'in the straight
road to greatness.'

But Talleyrand had other views both regarding the road
to greatness and the orientation of French diplomacy.
In April 1791 Mirabeau, exhausted by excess of work and
excess of dissipation, had died, and Talleyrand, who had
been with him to the last, and had pronounced his funeral
oration, felt that the mantle of his friend had fallen upon
him. It might have been the mission of Mirabeau to carry
into the conduct of foreign affairs the true spirit of 1789
which was a spirit of peace rather than of war. He had seen
plainly that the great task of reconstruction at home could
be accomplished only if peace were maintained abroad, and
he had been prepared to adopt, as the guiding principle of

his foreign policy, the welfare of the people rather than the ambition for territorial expansion. He had favoured from the first an alliance with England, realising that there can never exist security for either country except upon the basis of permanent and solid friendship.

Talleyrand belonged to the same school of political thought. Child of the eighteenth century and disciple of Voltaire, he loved the substantial blessings of peace, and despised the fustian heroics of war. The necessity of an understanding with England was as evident to his clear vision as the rumours about Pitt's spies were absurd. The desire for peace, and the promotion of an Anglo-French alliance as the surest way of obtaining it, provide the main clue to consistency throughout a long career that has become a by-word for tergiversation. The glamour of Napoleon's conquests, which still exercises so powerful a fascination over romantic minds, was powerless to excite the enthusiasm of a philosophical statesman who travelled over the field of Austerlitz on the morrow of the battle with feelings only of horror and disgust. As early as 1786 he had welcomed the Commercial Treaty between England and France, and fifty years later his last public service was to secure an understanding between the Governments of Louis-Philippe and William IV. In a letter to the Minister for Foreign Affairs, at the period with which we are now dealing, he wrote: 'Two neighbouring nations, one of which founds its prosperity principally upon commerce and the other upon agriculture, are called upon by the eternal nature of things to have good understanding and mutually to enrich one another.'

Meanwhile the Revolution was moving daily in the direction of war. The same policy recommended itself to the various parties for different reasons. The extremists wanted, in the words of Merlin de Thionville, 'to declare

war on the kings and peace with the nations'—the Girondins
believed that war would mean the downfall of the King and
the logical fulfilment of the revolutionary ideal. The
Feuillant Government hoped that war—a nice, small war
directed if possible only against the Elector of Trier for
having been too kind to the *émigrés*—would restore their
credit, enable them to remove the King from Paris and continue to carry on his Government with the assistance of the
army. The King and Queen, who were now very near to
despair, saw in the advent of a foreign invader the last
hope of deliverance from the hands of their own people.

Narbonne and de Lessart, a nonentity who was now
Minister for Foreign Affairs, were, however, fully alive to
the importance, which doubtless Talleyrand impressed upon
them, of securing the neutrality of England or, if possible,
an alliance, before engaging in any Continental complications. It was in order to achieve this object that in January
1792 Talleyrand departed upon a mission to London.

Owing to his having sat in the Assembly he was still
precluded from receiving any official status. He was, however, provided with the necessary letters to members of the
British Government calculated to assure him a reception
and a hearing. Officially the object of the mission was the
purchase of horses for the French army and the head of it was
Talleyrand's intimate friend the Duke de Biron.

Biron, who is better known under his earlier title of
Lauzun, had a reputation for gallantry which exceeded that
of all competitors. His name had been associated with those
of the Empress of Russia and the Queen of France, and
English readers may be interested to remember that it was
for this handsome Frenchman that the beautiful Lady
Sarah Lennox, who had turned the young head of George
III, formed so passionate an attachment that she was prepared to leave her husband on his behalf. He was as brave

a soldier as he was adventurous a lover. Having fought for American independence and having always proclaimed liberal sentiments, he embraced the cause of the Revolution from the first, commanded one of the earliest revolutionary armies, and perished by the guillotine, going to his death as gaily as he had gone through his life, and sharing a bottle of wine with his executioner.

Two more aristocratic representatives of a revolutionary Government could hardly have been imagined than the pair that arrived in Golden Square on the evening of 24th January 1792. They appeared, upon the surface, to possess all the qualities which were likely to recommend them to the fashionable society of the day; but their mission was foredoomed to failure.

The French Revolution was never popular in England, nor was its unpopularity restricted to the wealthy and the privileged class. It was new, it was strange, it was foreign, it was irreligious, and it was French. After the execution of Louis XVI in the following year, outbursts of feeling in England led to riots that endangered the lives and property of the upper and middle-class Radicals who were the only friends of the Revolution in the country. Then the Jacobin, like the modern Bolshevik, became an object of contempt to the healthy, and a bogey of fear to the nervous part of the nation. Already the greatest of political pamphlets had been launched against the Revolution, and had made an instantaneous and ineffaceable appeal to all who could read or think. Burke's *Reflections* were written before any of the worst excesses, which he prophesied, had occurred, and neither the cheap rhetoric of Tom Paine nor the reasoned dullness of Sir James Macintosh could wipe out the deep impression it had made.

Readers of Burke had met in London many members of the French nobility, who had fled early from the wrath to come. Their courage and gaiety in misfortune had won for them friends and supporters who, while still able to sympathise with the poor peasantry of France, whom misery had goaded into rebellion, could feel nothing but loathing and contempt for renegades and profligates such as Talleyrand and Biron, who seemed to have been false to their King, their religion, and their caste.

It was doubtless owing to the machinations of his fellow countrymen that Biron shortly after arrival found himself arrested for debt, a predicament into which the heroes of English eighteenth-century fiction are continually falling, and from which, as readers of that fiction are aware, extrication was fraught with difficulties. The mission being unofficial, Biron possessed no diplomatic status which would have protected him, and Talleyrand had considerable trouble before he succeeded in securing the release of his friend.

The social position of the mission which had begun badly was thus rendered worse. The English people never gave much for a foreign Duke, and such a Duke emerging from a sponging house lost any hope of consideration in their eyes. Later in the year when it was known that the members of the French Legation had arrived at Ranelagh all ways were cleared at their approach, people shrank from them as though they bore the plague, and the situation became so unpleasant that they were compelled to retire, when it was noticed that Talleyrand was the only member of the party who betrayed not the slightest sign of confusion.

The failure of the mission was as complete in the political as in the social sphere. France had nothing to offer—although Talleyrand was later empowered to suggest certain colonial concessions, such as the island of Tobago—and England had everything to give. In fact, the neutrality which Talleyrand hoped to secure was exactly the policy which Pitt was determined to pursue, but he was equally determined to keep a free hand, and not to make any rash commitments to a Power which, according to the generally accepted diplomatic opinion of the day, was not likely, owing to its internal disorders, to play any important part in Europe for many years to come.

George III received Talleyrand and was barely civil; the Queen received him and turned her back. This virtuous couple, who were scandalised by the private life of Fox and shuddered at the name of Wilkes, were hardly likely to accord a hearty welcome to one who was not only a notorious libertine, but also a supporter of revolution and an excommunicated priest. Pitt received him and was as stiff as only Pitt could be, although he condescended to remember early days when they had met as youths in the house of Talleyrand's uncle, the Archbishop of Rheims. Finally, he was received by Grenville, the Secretary of State for Foreign Affairs, who listened in silence to all he had to say.

The British Foreign Office has always been shy of the semi-official, and the task of Talleyrand, bearing only the dubious credentials of a tottering Government, was hopeless from the first. For nearly an hour he talked to Grenville, endeavouring to persuade him that accounts of the disorders in France were much exaggerated and that the present Government was firmly established; reminding him that it was not for England to condemn revolutions, and eagerly disavowing all intention of political propaganda.

He even resorted to the *argumentum ad hominem*, and said that, while he would hesitate to make such an appeal to an older minister, Grenville's youth—he was only thirty-two— encouraged the hope that he would take an enlightened view of the situation, which would redound to his future glory. Talleyrand did not know that Grenville had never been young, and that glory was not sufficiently substantial to from one of the objects of his ambition.

He ended by proposing that the two Governments should mutually guarantee all one another's territorial possessions, both European and colonial, hoping in this way to provide Great Britain with a valuable reassurance with regard to Ireland, which at that time represented the weak spot in British defence. He suggested that Grenville should not answer him immediately, but should think over what he had said and receive him again, to which Grenville agreed. At a second interview he was informed that, while the British Government had no intention of departing from their policy of neutrality with regard to France and were filled with the best intentions towards her, they could not enter into any definite undertakings or even negotiate with an envoy who was not properly accredited.

Talleyrand had not made a good impression either in public or private. Grenville considered him deep and dangerous, and those who met him were struck by the cold impassivity and haughty reserve of his manner. The English expect a Frenchman to be gay and animated, just as the French expect an Englishman to be morose and taciturn. The English resent a silent Frenchman and the French distrust a loquacious Englishman.

Despite his failure Talleyrand was not discouraged. He avoided Court and Government circles in which the reception accorded him by the King and Queen had set the fashion, but continued to frequent the Opposition, making friends particularly with Lord Shelburne, a statesman whose breadth of mind and length of vision commanded his respect, and whose aristocratic exclusiveness, in combination with advanced liberal opinions, provided exactly the atmosphere in which Talleyrand was most at home.

He still believed firmly in the possibility of an Anglo-French alliance, felt confident that with time he could achieve it, and wrote home urging that a fully accredited representative should be sent as the titular head of the mission who would in reality act under his instructions. In order to press his views more forcibly upon Ministers he returned to Paris early in March, only to find on his arrival that the Government had fallen, that the Minister for Foreign Affairs was accused of treason, and that the Girondins were in power.

7

The new Minister for Foreign Affairs was Dumouriez, an intelligent adventurer to whom the Revolution seemed to offer a last opportunity of retrieving the failure of his life. Dumouriez had a more definite, and a more practicable, foreign policy than his predecessor. He was determined to strike at Austria, the ancient enemy of France and the modern opponent of the Revolution. He had decided to strike at her through the Belgian provinces, which were now an Austrian possession, and he realised that, if he were to do so successfully, he must first secure at least the neutrality of England. He was sufficiently acquainted with European history and politics to appreciate that any inter-ference with the Low Countries was bound to arouse immediately the anxious attention of England; but he had worked out in his own mind a reconstituted map of Europe in which an independent state of Belgium should afford Great Britain a safer guarantee of neutrality than the Austrian provinces could ever do, and in which a firm alliance between the two great western Powers based upon their common form of government, constitutional monarchy, and cemented by a commercial treaty, should provide the world with a guarantee of peace. The vision of Dumouriez became a fact in the course of time, but not until he himself had disappeared from the scene, and only as the result of twenty years of warfare.

The question of appointing a representative in London arose immediately. Talleyrand was plainly designated for the post and was anxious to return to it. Paris was already becoming a dangerous habitation for a man of his antecedents. Dumouriez had no liking for Talleyrand, whom he felt to be his intellectual as well as his social superior, and would rather have appointed some obscure creature of his own who would have acted as an unquestioning tool of the type with which he proceeded to fill the French chancelleries throughout Europe. But circumstances were too strong for him, and he reluctantly consented to Talleyrand's return. He took with him as the official head of the mission the youthful Marquis de Chauvelin, and the pair of them arrived in London at the end of April. Meanwhile France had declared war on Austria.

The situation in which Talleyrand now found himself was even more difficult than that in which he had been placed at the beginning of the year. Pitt was as anxious to avoid war as he had ever been; Talleyrand was as sincere in his repudiation of all forms of propaganda and in his assurances as to the pacific intentions of the French Government. But already the 'war on kings' had been declared in the Assembly; already the missionary spirit was abroad in the streets of Paris and finding noisy utterance in the press; already the first soldiers of the revolutionary crusade had crossed the frontier into the Low Countries; and already the English people were irritated, indignant, and alarmed. Wise and moderate individuals were still struggling for peace, but ignorant and passionate mobs were sweeping all obstacles before them as they surged irresistibly forward to their own destruction in war.

The reception which George III accorded to Chauvelin was hardly warmer than that which Talleyrand had received. The King knew how much weight to attach to a letter from

Louis XVI which the new Minister brought with him; and
the publication of the text of this letter in the French press
before its presentation only increased the contempt of
English official circles for the manner in which the French
Government now conducted their foreign relations. On
25th May, however, the British Government officially
announced their determination to maintain a neutral attitude with regard to the hostilities that had broken out
between France and Austria. This declaration might have
been accounted a triumph for Talleyrand. Dumouriez
accepted it as such and conveyed his warm congratulations
to Chauvelin. But in fact neither Talleyrand nor Chauvelin
were in any way responsible for the policy upon which Pitt
had long been determined, and which he would have pursued with the same tenacity whoever had been representing
France at the Court of St. James's.

In Paris events were moving with increasing rapidity.
Louis, on the advice of Dumouriez, dismissed his Girondin
Ministers, and Dumouriez transferred himself from Foreign
Affairs to the Ministry of War and thence to the command
of the troops in the field. The Girondins, furious at their
dismissal, joined with the Jacobins in planning insur-
rection, and at their instigation the mob invaded the Tuileries, when only the cool courage of the King preserved himself and his family from massacre. The position abroad of
the representatives of a king who had lost all semblance
of authority in his own capital became increasingly difficult,
and at the beginning of July Talleyrand returned once more
to Paris.

The days of the monarchy were now numbered. On 10th
August the Tuileries were invaded for the second time, the
Swiss Guards were massacred, and the royal family took
refuge with the Legislative Assembly, who finally imprisoned them in the Temple. The stern disapproval with

which these developments were naturally regarded by all the monarchical Governments of Europe aroused consternation in those revolutionary leaders who were capable of appreciating the dangers attendant upon the isolated position into which France was gradually drifting. In these circumstances the pen of Talleyrand was employed to draw up a reasoned defence of the events of 10th August for communication to foreign Powers. The line adopted in this document was to lay the blame for what had taken place upon Louis himself. He was accused of having betrayed the new Constitution and of having bribed others to do the same.

It was indeed the case that Louis had never considered himself bound by the oaths which he had given under compulsion and from any observance of which he had been absolved by the Pope. It was true also that he had made secret payments to many politicians, including, in all probability, the new Minister for Justice, Danton, who did not, however, attain even to the Tammany definition of an honest man, as he was not one who would 'stay bought.'

By lending his hand, however, to the drafting of this justification Talleyrand committed himself further than he had ever done before, or was to do again, to the advanced stages of the Revolution. He used to plead in later years that, so tremendous was the excitement of these times, men were hardly responsible for their actions. It would indeed have required more than ordinary courage to refuse to undertake this task when requested to do so by the Government. The life of a former bishop and a born aristocrat, most of whose relatives had already emigrated, was not too secure in Paris on the morrow of the assault on the Tuileries and on the eve of the September massacres.

It may have been at the request of Danton, the real head of the new Government, that Talleyrand undertook the task. In any case it was to Danton that he now turned for assistance in the vital matter of leaving the country. It was from Danton's own hand, in the Ministry of Justice, which stood then where it stands to-day, in the Place Vendôme, that Talleyrand received his passport at one o'clock in the morning of the first of September. On the following day the massacres began.

Chapter Three

EXILE

I

On the road that runs from Leatherhead to Dorking there stands an eighteenth-century residence which, although it has undergone considerable alterations, still bears the name of Juniper Hall. Here, in the summer of 1792, was formed the nucleus of a small society of French refugees. The Constitutionals—the Liberals—those members of the aristocracy who if they had not welcomed the Revolution had at least tried to make the best of it, and who, only after the fall of the monarchy and under the shadow of the Terror, abandoned their country in order to save their lives, found at Juniper Hall a brief haven of refuge. They were all poor; temporarily they were all ruined; they had all suffered, and were still suffering the loss of friends and relatives by massacre or execution, and yet they contrived for some months in this quiet Surrey residence to lead a life of such charm, gaiety, and elegance that those of their neighbours who were admitted into their circle felt that they were obtaining a glimpse of a civilisation superior to anything that contemporary England could show.

The Princess d'Hénin, who had enjoyed with her young husband the reputation of being the handsomest couple ever seen at the Court of Versailles, was one of those who dispensed hospitality at Juniper Hall. She had been lady-in-waiting to the Queen, and together with three other intimate friends, the Princess de Poix, the Duchess de

Biron, and the Princess de Bouillon, had formed a coterie
in Paris which, owing to their position, their intelligence,
and their unwavering loyalty to one another, had exercised
for a period the most powerful influence in French society.
Although she was now middle-aged she was still beautiful,
and her faithful lover Lally Tollendal, whom she eventually
married, was seldom absent from her side.

Here also was the witty Countess de la Châtre, who, in the
words of the Chancellor Pasquier, was not a lady 'whose
austerity was oppressive,' and who had come to England in
order to be with the Marquis de Jaucourt, who had played
a distinguished part in the earlier days of the Constituent
Assembly, and who was to act as Minister for Foreign
Affairs in Paris when Talleyrand was taking part in the
Congress of Vienna.

And here also for a short period came Madame de Staël
with Narbonne, whom she loved, and whom by her courage
and devotion, together with the discreet exercise of her
diplomatic privileges, she had delivered from the hands of
the patriots of Paris when they were hunting for him under
her roof.

In this society Talleyrand was, of course, welcome. He
took a small house in Woodstock Street, Kensington, where
Madame de la Châtre presided, but he was a frequent
visitor at Juniper Hall, and we can learn the impression
that he made upon a stranger and a foreigner at this period,
thanks to the facile pen of Fanny Burney.

Not far from Juniper Hall there resided in the village of
Mickleham one of the many daughters of Dr. Burney, the
teacher and historian of music, who was a familiar figure
in most social and intellectual circles of the time. To Mrs.
Susanna Phillips and her unmarried sister Fanny, who was
frequently staying with her, the advent of this remarkable
French colony was an event of importance. The world was

filled with rumours of the strange and terrible things that were happening in France. Diaries and letters of the time prove that events in Paris formed then the principal subject of conversation and of correspondence. And suddenly there descended upon these rural, almost surburban, surroundings a flight of astonishing and charming people, bearing the most magnificent titles, who not only came direct from the scene of the great drama, but who had also, themselves, played leading parts in it.

Mrs. Phillips lost no time in calling upon them, and wrote enthusiastic and detailed accounts of their witty and charming conversation to her sister Fanny, mentioning particularly a certain Monsieur d'Arblay, who possessed from the first a romantic interest in the eyes of the sisters, from having served as Adjutant-General under the still popular hero Lafayette. Fanny hastened down to Surrey in order to share in the delights described, and sent to her father and other correspondents reports as rapturous as those of Susanna. 'There can be nothing imagined more charming, more fascinating than this colony'; 'a society of incontestable superiority'; 'these people of a thousand'; 'they are a marvellous set for excess of agreeability'; 'English has nothing to do with elegance such as theirs.' She can think and write of nothing else and her testimony to the unusual charm which these people exercised is of value, for she was not a fool, she was no longer in her first youth, she had seen the best society and heard the finest conversation of her time. She had been often in the company and had earned the approval of Dr. Johnson.

She was prejudiced against Talleyrand before she met him, for already his wickedness was becoming a legend. 'Monsieur de Talleyrand,' she writes, 'opened last night with infinite wit and capacity. Madame de Staël whispered to me: "How do you like him?" "Not very much," I answered. . . . "Oh, I assure you," cried she, "he is the best of the men." I was happy not to agree.'

But a few days later: 'It is inconceivable what a convert M. de Talleyrand has made of me. I think him now one of the finest members and one of the most charming of this exquisite set. Susanna is as completely a proselyte. His powers of entertainment are astonishing, both in information and in raillery. . . .'

And here is a little picture that is worth preserving, drawn by the pen of Susanna Phillips. Lally Tollendal, 'large, fat, with a great head, small nose, immense cheeks . . . *un très honnête garçon*, as Monsieur de Talleyrand says of him, *et rien de plus*'—Lally Tollendal had written a tragedy, *La Mort de Strafford*. It was to be read aloud to the company after dinner. Dinner was very gay but at the end of it Monsieur d'Arblay unaccountably disappeared. 'He was sent for after coffee several times that the tragedy might be begun; and at last Madame de Staël impatiently proposed beginning without him: '*Mais cela lui fera de la peine*,' said M. de Talleyrand good-naturedly, and as she persisted, he rose up and limped out of the room to fetch him; he succeeded in bringing him.'

While Susanna watched with eyes of guileless admiration the kindly Bishop limping out to fetch his friend, may we be permitted to wonder whether there was not underlying the action a spice of malice which was hidden from that innocent gaze? It may be that neither Talleyrand nor d'Arblay, the one a card-player, the other a soldier, was looking forward with enthusiasm to an evening spent in listening to Lally Tollendal reading his tragedy aloud. But Talleyrand was determined that if he were captured, d'Arblay was not going to escape. And so with ironic courtesy—a species of humour in which he excelled—he made sure that the tragedy should not begin until d'Arblay was in his place.

Indeed there was much that went on at Juniper Hall to which the sisters Burney were remarkably blind. Prim little figures, they had wandered out of the sedate drawing-rooms of *Sense and Sensibility* and were in danger of losing themselves in the elegantly disordered alcoves of *Les Liaisons Dangereuses*.

Dire was their distress and deep their indignation when the benevolent Dr. Burney first sounded a warning note. Fanny's enthusiasm for Madame de Staël, a fellow authoress and one of world-wide reputation, had been received with the most appreciative tenderness by that large-hearted lady, and there had been an invitation to stay for two or three weeks which had dutifully been referred to Dr. Burney before acceptance. The Doctor did not forbid, but neither did he encourage it. 'Madame de Staël,' he wrote, 'has been accused of partiality to M. de Narbonne—but perhaps all may be Jacobinical malignity.'

Fanny was inexpressibly shocked. 'I do firmly believe it a gross calumny,' she writes. 'She loves him even tenderly, but so openly, so simply, so unaffectedly, and with such utter freedom from all coquetry, that, if they were two men or two women, the affection could not, I think, be more obviously undesigning. She is very plain, he is very handsome; her intellectual endowments must be with him her sole attraction. She seems equally attached to M. de Talleyrand. . . . Indeed I think you could not spend a day with them and not see that their commerce is that of pure but exalted and most elegant friendship. I would, nevertheless, give the world to avoid being a guest under their roof, now I have heard even the shadow of such a rumour.'

As all the ladies at Juniper Hall had been living from the first quite openly with their lovers, Madame de Staël was naturally perplexed by the sudden coolness which succeeded Fanny's fervent admiration. But the little coterie was soon dispersed, all except M. d'Arblay, whose intentions proved honourable and were rewarded, so that he remained to live in England as the husband of Miss Burney.

2

One cause that may have hastened Talleyrand's departure from France was the knowledge that when the Tuileries were sacked on 10th August there had been discovered a carefully concealed iron box which contained the secret correspondence of the King. The only evidence that was produced which would implicate Talleyrand was a letter from a third party stating that he was anxious to place his services at the King's disposal, and that he had authorised the writer to say so. This, however, was sufficient to secure his condemnation by the Convention on 5th December 1792, a sentence against which he despatched a vehement protest that was duly printed in the *Moniteur*.

Before it reached France there appeared in the same publication another and equally energetic defence of Talleyrand over the initial 'D.' Who his defender may have been remains uncertain, but there is strong reason to suppose that it was no less a person than Danton himself. Amongst other arguments that the writer in question produces to prove the innocence of Talleyrand is the statement that on the very day of his condemnation the Ministry for Foreign Affairs had received from him, from London, a political memorandum which expressed the 'purest revolutionary principles.' Now it so happens that among Danton's papers, after his death, there was found such a memorandum, signed by Talleyrand, and dated 25th November.

The contents of this document are of profound interest to the student of Talleyrand's foreign policy, and provide an invaluable testimony to the perspicacity of his vision and the

consistency of his views. The new France that has been
created by the Revolution must, he maintains, adopt a new
policy which will be in accordance with the philosophy of
her Constitution. The basis of this policy must be the
abandonment of the old ambition to be the greatest Power
in Europe and of the old endeavour to acquire aggrandisement of territory. 'We have learnt, a little late no doubt,
that for States as for individuals real wealth consists not in
acquiring or invading the domains of others, but in develop-
ing one's own. We have learnt that all extensions of territory,
all usurpations, by force or by fraud, which have long been
connected by prejudice with the idea of 'rank,' of 'hege-
mony,' of 'political stability,' of 'superiority' in the order of
the Powers, are only the cruel jests of political lunacy, false
estimates of power, and that their real effect is to increase
the difficulty of administration and to diminish the happiness
and security of the governed for the passing interest or for
the vanity of those who govern. . . . France ought, therefore, to remain within her own boundaries, she owes it to
her glory, to her sense of justice and of reason, to her own
interest and to that of the other nations who will become
free.'

Remembering that these were, and remained, the sincere
opinions of Talleyrand, we shall find it easier to understand
why it became impossible for him to act as the faithful
Foreign Minister of Napoleon.

He goes on, in the same paper, to discuss what alliances
it will be desirable for France to conclude. In future, all
such alliances should be of a purely defensive character,
and should be restricted to those states upon her own
borders which, following her example, will have adopted a
free Constitution. The alliance with England, which he considered so important in the past as a counterweight to the
family interests of the Bourbons, will be less needed in the

future, and the two countries should concentrate upon
industrial and commercial agreements. Their main object
should be free commerce between both countries and their
respective colonies. Already he has realised the potential
markets for European goods that the development of these
colonies will offer, and the vision inspires him with the
further ambition to liberate the vast Spanish possessions in
South America, and to impose upon them the policy of the
open door.

'The vessels,' he writes, 'of France and of England
united will throw open to free trade that vast part of the
western world which lies in the Pacific Ocean and in the
South Seas.' This was the very policy towards which Castlereagh was gradually moving at the time of his death, thirty
years later, and which Canning subsequently crystallised in
an historic phrase when he claimed to have 'called the new
world into existence in order to redress the balance of the
old.'

3

In London Talleyrand moved in a restricted circle. He
had been careful to make it plain to the Government upon
arrival, that he no longer held any, even semi-official,
appointment. But he had a reputation for depth and
cunning, so that he was regarded with suspicion in official
quarters. Socially, he was still the object of hostility to all
the earlier-arrived emigrants; and fashionable society, slow
to realise the full importance of the events that had taken
place in the summer of 1792, continued to regard him as
one who had taken part in the Revolution and who had
recently come to England as its representative. 'Did I tell
you,' writes Lady Stafford to Granville Leveson-Gower,
'that the Évêque d'Autun is here, by the name of Mons.
Talleyrand-Périgord? He is a disagreeable-looking man,

has a baddish, tricking character, and supposed not very upright in disposition or heart.' And Gouverneur Morris on a visit to London enters in his diary: 'The Duchess of Gordon asks my opinion of Bishop d'Autun, who is, she is told, a very profligate fellow.'

But although feeling with regard to France was running high, and although the majority of the Whigs had lost all their enthusiasm for the Revolution, there were still some who, in the words of a letter which Talleyrand wrote to Lord Shelburne in the October of this year, remained 'faithful to Liberty, despite the mask of blood and dirt with which certain atrocious scoundrels have hidden her features.'

Lord Shelburne himself, with that belief in popular government and contempt of popular opinion which distinguished him, was the most prominent of those who refused to allow their settled opinions to be affected by terrible events. Steering always a middle course, he was drawing closer to Fox and further from Pitt at this time, and it was in his house that Talleyrand, a welcome guest, was able to meet some of the leaders of the Opposition.

Towards the end of the year Talleyrand was obliged to move from Woodstock Street into Kensington Square for greater economy, and to sell the whole of his library which, despite the fact that he had been proscribed as an emigrant, he succeeded in having transferred from Paris to London. The sale realised £750, which was all that remained to him to live on. Many of his friends were living in equally straitened circumstances. Madame de Flahaut, who had followed him from Paris, and had found lodgings in Half Moon Street, sought to augment her income by her pen, and produced a novel of which Talleyrand corrected the proofs.

Another companion in misfortune was Madame de Genlis, mistress of the Duke of Orleans and governess of

his children, who, censorious of weakness in others and
indulgent of it in herself, made more enemies than friends
on her way through life. When she came to write her
memoirs, Talleyrand, one of the best-hated men of his age,
is one of the few of whom she has nothing but good to
record. Poor as he was, he offered to assist her with a
considerable sum of money, and he was a regular guest in
the humble dwelling where she was educating the sister of
the future Louis-Philippe and the mysterious and beautiful
Pamela, who became in course of time the tragic bride of
Lord Edward Fitzgerald. He put life and gaiety into their
little supper-parties of two or three, and always praised, with
that affectionate irony which even those who distrusted
him found endearing, the 'estimable frugality' of the fare
which was all that his hostess could afford. On one occasion,
however, owing presumably to an unexpected windfall,
she was able to offer a sumptuous feast to a large number of
friends. Talleyrand, arriving with the others, whispered
in her ear: 'I promise not to look surprised.'

Old Horace Walpole, still writing letters in Berkeley
Square, informs Lady Ossory that 'that scribbling trollop
Madame de Sillery,' by whom he means Madame de
Genlis, 'and the viper that has cast his skin, the Bishop of
Autun, are both here, but I believe little noticed, and the
woman and the serpent I hope will find few disposed to
taste their rotten apples.'

All the eventful year of 1793, which witnessed the
execution of Louis xvi and the outbreak of the war
between France and England, the decline of Danton and
the rise of Robespierre, was passed quietly by Talleyrand in
London. It was probably during this year that he wrote the
treatise on the Duke of Orleans which forms part of his
published memoirs. He offers no defence for, and indeed
strongly condemns, the character and conduct of Philippe-

Égalité, but acquits him of any responsibility for the outbreak or the course of the Revolution. 'If historians strive
to discover the men to whom they can give the honour or
attribute the blame of having caused, or directed, or modified
the French Revolution, they will be wasting their time. It
had no authors, nor leaders, nor guides. The seed was
sown by writers who, in a bold and enlightened age, wishing
to attack prejudice, overthrew the principles of religion and
of social life, and by incompetent Ministers, who increased
the embarrassment of the treasury and the discontent of the
people.' Whether Talleyrand wrote these words in 1793
or at a later date they can be taken as giving his considered
opinion, the soundness of which few historians will be
inclined to dispute.

At the end of January 1794 Talleyrand was suddenly
informed, without any previous warning, that he must leave
England immediately. The Government were taking action
under the powers conferred upon them by the Aliens Act
which had been passed in the previous month. They were
not obliged to give any reason for their decision, and no
reason was ever given. Talleyrand wrote a dignified protest to Pitt which that Minister had not the civility to
answer, despite the fact that he had been as a young man
received with hospitality by Talleyrand's uncle, and that
he had himself two years earlier received Talleyrand as a
representative of the French Government. Letters which he
addressed to the King and to Lord Grenville remained
equally without reply.

According to the standards of the eighteenth century the
treatment accorded to Talleyrand was harsh, although in
the twentieth century, which has a more ruthless method of
waging war, he would have considered himself extremely
fortunate to escape internment. He was an alien enemy,
he had supported the Revolution up to the very moment

of his arrival in England, he had written a justification of the 10th of August, and he had been on the best of terms with Danton, who had provided him with the passport which enabled him to leave France. If the French Government had wished to maintain a secret agent in England they could not have found amongst their twenty-five millions one better qualified for the post, and, a few years later, when he wished to return to France, he allowed it to be stated in his defence that he was actually in the service of the French Government at this time. He had explicitly stated the opposite in writing to Lord Grenville on his arrival, and he was probably speaking the truth; but while we may regret that he should not have met with greater courtesy from British Ministers, it must be admitted that there was no individual in the country at the time to whom the terms of the Aliens Act could with greater justice have been applied.

He sailed from the Thames at the beginning of March, and had an anxious moment in the Channel when, owing to the weather, it seemed likely that the vessel would be obliged to seek refuge in a French port. Eventually, however, she put in at Falmouth, where he went ashore and sought refreshment at an inn. The innkeeper informed him that there was an American general staying there, who shortly afterwards appeared, and with whom Talleyrand had some conversation. Finally he asked whether he could give him letters of introduction for America. 'No,' replied the General, 'I am perhaps the only American who cannot give you letters for his own country.' The General who dared not say his name was Benedict Arnold. 'I must confess,' said Talleyrand, 'that I felt extremely sorry for him. Political puritans will blame me but I am not ashamed of the sentiment because I have been a witness of his punishment.' After all, in Talleyrand's eyes, Arnold's crime, or blunder,

was only that while fighting on the winning side he had
believed in the victory of the other, and, at the wrong
moment, had transferred his allegiance. It was a melancholy
encounter—Arnold, broken, disgraced, ashamed; Talleyrand an exile, first from his own country and now from
Europe, ruined in pocket, tarnished in reputation, with
nothing to hope for from the victorious Revolutionaries,
and even less from the defeated Bourbons. The unknown
and largely undiscovered continent of America offered little
scope to the particular talents that he possessed, little use
for the knowledge and experience that he had acquired.
He appeared to be beginning life all over again in far less
favourable circumstances —and he was forty years of age.

4

We may judge of the mood in which Talleyrand now
regarded the future from the fact that on arrival in the
Delaware river, after thirty-eight monotonous days at sea,
he had so little appetite for landing, so little curiosity to
visit a new continent, that he attempted, without going
ashore, to take passage on a vessel that was sailing immediately for India. There was, however, no berth available so that he was compelled to land and to proceed to
Philadelphia, where he soon discovered a number of French
acquaintances.

He had brought with him a letter of introduction from
Lord Shelburne to Washington, which he lost no time in
presenting, but which did not secure for him the interview
that he desired. Washington was deeply engaged in the
difficult task of keeping free from those entangling alliances
which he always dreaded for his own country. In the circumstances he thought it wiser not to receive a man who had
just been expelled from England, and who was denounced

by the French representative in Philadelphia as the enemy
of France. We cannot blame him. His letter of refusal was
couched in terms of the greatest civility. What, after all,
did the reception of one French emigrant matter in comparison with the future of the United States?

In default of meeting Washington he made friends with
an American who, it may be permitted to think, was then
the most remarkable man in the whole of that continent.
Alexander Hamilton was a man whom Talleyrand could
both love and respect. They had much in common. Where
they differed the advantage was wholly upon Hamilton's
side. They were both by breeding and in outlook aristocratic, and both without the prejudices that aristocracy too
often connotes. They were both passionately interested in
politics, and both of them looked at politics from a realistic
standpoint and despised sentimental twaddle whether it
poured from the lips of a Robespierre or of a Jefferson.
The terrorist sobbing over humanity or the slave-owner
spouting about freedom were equally repulsive to these two
practical statesmen who attempted to see things as they
were. Both loved pleasure, both rejoiced in that embroidery
of life which we call elegance; neither was impervious to
the charms of women. But while the Frenchman became a
byword for lack of principle in an unprincipled age the
American had principles for which he would have died.
While Talleyrand saw in politics a path to riches, Hamilton
would sooner have picked a pocket than made a penny out
of his political position. Talleyrand frankly—for in such
matters he was always frank—could not understand why
Hamilton, fallen from office, was obliged to go back to the
Bar in order to make a living. He could not even admire a
lack of self-interest, which seemed to him foolish. Yet the
two were friends. Years afterwards Aaron Burr, who had
killed Hamilton in a duel, left a card upon Talleyrand in

Paris. The major-domo was instructed to inform Monsieur Burr when he called again that over Talleyrand's mantelpiece there hung the portrait of Alexander Hamilton.

At Philadelphia Talleyrand found a small French colony, the centre of which was a bookshop kept by Moreau de Saint Méry at number 84 First Street. Here almost nightly took place animated reunions of French refugees, who discussed over their host's Madeira the past, the present and the future of their country. More than one of them had, like Talleyrand, sat in the Constituent Assembly. Moreau de Saint Méry himself had been there, as had the Vicomte de Noailles, who had won fame by proposing the voluntary resignation of all privileges on the part of the nobility. The Marquis de Blacons and the Duke de La Rochefoucauld-Liancourt had also been members, and the latter, like Talleyrand, had reached Philadelphia via England and had made some impression upon Miss Burney on the way.

Another emigrant was the Count de Moré, who had visited America on a previous occasion when he had come to fight for the cause of Independence. But liberty was a blessing that he desired for other countries rather than his own, and he emigrated at the outset of the Revolution; consequently he distrusted and disliked those of his own class who had not done likewise. His memoirs, written long afterwards when he was an old man, contain references to his fellow-countrymen whom he found in Philadelphia at this time. He has little good to say for any of them, and in many cases his statements can be shown to have been untrue. It is to him that we owe the story that Talleyrand outraged the susceptibilities of the Philadelphians by his open admiration for a woman of colour with whom he frequently appeared in public. There is no corroboration of this statement, and the writer himself renders it difficult of belief by adding that Talleyrand's 'company was much sought after, for he was an amusing companion and had plenty of wit of his own, though many witticisms of other persons were often ascribed to him.'

A more sympathetic portrait is to be found in the memoirs of Madame de la Tour du Pin who with her husband and child was living in the country near Albany. She was a beautiful woman of Irish origin, by birth a Dillon. She had recently, after a series of thrilling and romantic adventures, escaped from Bordeaux with the aid of Madame Tallien, and was throwing herself with energy into the task of working on a farm. One morning as she was engaged in the courtyard of the farm with a hatchet in her hand, making the necessary preparations for the day's dinner, she heard a deep voice behind her exclaim: 'It would be impossible to cut up a leg of mutton with greater majesty.' Turning she saw Talleyrand who had come out from Albany with an invitation from General Schuyler to return with him to dinner and to spend the night.

Madame de la Tour du Pin was as good as she was beautiful. 'She has made a great impression on the ladies of Boston,' Talleyrand wrote to Madame de Staël. 'She sleeps with her husband every night and they have only one bedroom. Warn Mathieu (de Montmorency) and Narbonne of this. Tell them it is essential in order to have a good reputation in this country.' It was difficult for such a woman to have a high opinion of Talleyrand, but while she disapproved she found it impossible to dislike. She wrote of him upon this occasion: 'Monsieur de Talleyrand was kind, as he has always and invariably been to me, with that particular charm in conversation which nobody ever possessed as he did. He knew me from my childhood and therefore had a slightly paternal manner with me which was singularly delightful. One couldn't help regretting that there were so many reasons for not thinking well of him,

and after listening to him for an hour one was compelled to
banish the recollection of everything one had heard against
him. Worthless himself, he hated, strangely enough, what
was bad in others. Listening to him without knowing him,
one could believe that he was virtuous. Only his exquisite
good taste prevented him from saying in my presence things
that would have shocked me, and if, as sometimes happened, some remark of the kind did escape him, he would
quickly correct himself and exclaim: 'Ah—it's true—you
don't like that sort of thing.'

He performed many kind and useful services for Madame
de la Tour du Pin, both at this time and later in the course
of her long, eventful, and tragic life.

When they returned to Albany on the evening of the day
of this visit, General Schuyler had important news for them.
Robespierre had fallen, the Terror was over, the dangerous
phase of the Revolution was at an end. By the same post the
news arrived that among the very last batch of victims who
had fallen under the guillotine on the same morning that
Robespierre was being defeated in the Convention, was
Talleyrand's young sister-in-law, the mother of three
children. Sincerely as he mourned her, his mind that
night must also have been full of speculation as to how his
own future would be affected by these events. Although
he had found plenty to occupy him in the United States,
and had entered into various financial transactions which
had brought him profit, he was desperately anxious to return
to his country and to collect the broken fragments of his
career.

The first step was to secure the erasure of his name from
the list of emigrants whose liberties and lives were still in
danger if they returned to France. With this end in view
he turned for assistance to Madame de Staël, who worked
for him with ardour and devotion, as she always worked for

any friend who needed her help. Years afterwards, when they were no longer friends, Napoleon asked Talleyrand whether it was true that Madame de Staël was given to intrigue. 'To such an extent,' replied Talleyrand, 'that if it were not for her intrigues, I should not be here now.' 'She seems, at any rate, to be a good friend,' was Napoleon's comment. 'She is such a good friend,' said Talleyrand, 'that she would throw all her acquaintances into the water for the pleasure of fishing them out again.'

Talleyrand himself drew up a formal petition which he forwarded to the Convention, while Madame de Staël characteristically persuaded the mistress of Marie - Joseph Chénier to sing pathetic ballads to him about the sorrows of exile. Chénier, the brother of the poet, was at the moment one of the most powerful speakers in the Convention. The ballads did their work, and the orator did his.

'Pride of soul and principle made him a republican'— it was thus that he described Talleyrand in his speech to the Convention, 'and it is in the bosom of a republic, in the fatherland of Benjamin Franklin, that he has sought the contemplation of that imposing spectacle—a free people.' The motion for his erasure from the list of emigrants was passed with acclamation, and at the beginning of November 1795, Talleyrand received the good news in New York.

Despite his anxiety to return to Europe, he delayed his journey for six months. Nobody in the eighteenth century would undertake the crossing of the Atlantic in winter if it could possibly be avoided. He thus spent over two years in the United States of America. The impressions he received are recorded in his memoirs and in a lengthy letter that he wrote to Lord Shelburne at the time.

The cause of the Revolution was still extremely popular in America. Cheers for France and Liberty, groans for England and Tyranny, were the order of the day. There was a vociferous section of the people in favour of intervention in the war on the side of the Republic. But so profound an observer as Talleyrand was not deceived by what was apparent on the surface. He assures Lord Shelburne that, despite these manifestations, the country is at heart English, and that it is England more than any other country that stands to benefit from the rapidly increasing prosperity and population of her former colonists. It is not a question of sentiment but of necessity. Only England can provide those industrial products which the new country demands, only English finance can afford the long-term credits which are at present essential for her development.

The only obstacle that he foresees to the rapid improvement of relations between the two countries is the incredible folly of the British Government, in doing everything that could possibly offend the susceptibilities and alienate the affections of the Americans. Their diplomatic representatives are treated with contempt in London, and England is represented in America by men who are known for the fervour of their opposition to the cause of independence or else by minor officials of no importance.

'Would the superiority of England be diminished,' he pleads, 'if you were to send here as Minister some great nobleman, a young man with pleasant manners? If you knew what the vanity of a new people is, when they are still embarrassed as to their position in the world, if you knew the Americans, you could have no doubt as to what the general effect throughout the country would be of so simple a manœuvre. The Americans would be flattered and the day that they are flattered they are won. Two years ago Prince Edward (the Duke of Kent) was at Boston and there was a ball. This year people still talk with gratitude of how he did not refuse an invitation, and of his kindness and good nature. The woman who danced with him from joy, embar-

rassment, or respect, fainted and had an attack of nerves.
If Lord Wycombe (Lord Shelburne's son) has forgotten
how long he stayed in the various towns of America that
he visited, and the names of the people with whom he dined
or had tea, I shall be well able to remind him; those things
are not forgotten here. They are entered on the family
register.'

He ends the letter by saying: 'My conclusion is that the
Americans will remain independent, that they will be more
useful to England than to any other Power, and that this
utility will increase in proportion as the English Government gives up its present haughtiness of demeanour in all
its relations with America.'

Before Talleyrand left America he had an interview with
William Cobbett. Two more strangely contrasted individuals never met. Cobbett was at this time earning his living
in Philadelphia by teaching English to French emigrants.
He had also plunged recently into political journalism which,
for him, meant always bitter polemics and violent personal
abuse. Although he had left England under a cloud, failing
to appear as the prosecutor of officers under whom he had
served as a private soldier and against whom he had brought
charges of peculation, now that England was at war the
profound patriotism of his nature prompted him to set his
pen at her service and to denounce the iniquities of all her
enemies. So for a short period he was loud in praise of King
and Constitution and pitiless in exposure of republicans,
revolutionaries, and atheists. There was nobody whom he
had attacked more violently than Talleyrand whom, he says
himself, he had called 'an apostate, a hypocrite and every
other name of which he was deserving.' He was the more
surprised therefore when he heard that Talleyrand wished
to meet him. The meeting was arranged, and Cobbett,
whose idea of calling on an enemy was to do it with a thick

stick, confesses that he was completely bewildered when
Talleyrand addressed him with the greatest civility and
complimented him upon his wit and learning. When
Talleyrand proceeded to inquire whether it was at Oxford
or at Cambridge that he had been educated, Cobbett, who
had never seen the inside of school or college, could bear it
no longer. With that suspicion, which never leaves the
ill-educated even when they are brilliantly intelligent, that
the man of higher culture is making a fool of them, Cobbett
burst out with the typically vigorous and bucolic assurance
that he 'was no trout, and consequently not to be caught by
tickling.'

Cobbett suspected that Talleyrand had come to purchase
his support, for he was convinced that Talleyrand was an
agent in the pay of the French Government, just as many
people in Philadelphia were convinced, and with better
reason, that Cobbett was an agent in the pay of the Government of Great Britain. He was incapable of understanding
what was probably the real reason of Talleyrand's visit—
curiosity to meet a remarkable man—just as he was incapable of believing, in his blunt and honest way, that a
man could feel no resentment against one who had called
him an apostate and a hypocrite.

Cobbett was wrong in his belief that Talleyrand was
in the pay of the French Government. There is no shred of
evidence to support the theory. It was, however, the same
suspicion that had doubtless been responsible for his exile
from England. And it was not an unnatural suspicion.
Possibly his conduct encouraged it.

It is one thing to be a paid spy, it is another to be an
intelligent traveller anxious to acquire any information that
may be of value to your country and, incidentally, to yourself. His eyes were ever turned towards Paris, his mind
ever busy with plans for his return. That return would be

vastly facilitated if he could bring with him or send on in advance some proof of his zealous attachment to the Government that was now in power. Mr. Kipling has devoted one of his short stories to this period of Talleyrand's life, and while there is no reason to suppose that the episode that he imagines ever took place, the story itself probably contains the true answer to the question whether Talleyrand was working for the French Government or not. Fiction is often an aid to history, and the penetrating eye of genius can discern much that remains elusive to the patient researches of the historian.

Chapter Four

THE DIRECTORY

I

SAILING from the Delaware River on a Danish vessel in the middle of June, Talleyrand reached Hamburg at the end of July. He had not yet disembarked when a messenger arrived bearing a letter from Madame de Flahaut. She was in Hamburg, and was receiving the attentions of a wealthy Portuguese, Monsieur de Souza, whom it was her firm intention to marry. The arrival of Talleyrand, whom every one knew to have been her lover and the father of her son, might, she feared, seriously interfere with her matrimonial arrangements. She therefore suggested that instead of landing he should return immediately by the same ship to America. Talleyrand was always ready to help a friend, but this particular request went a little beyond what he considered the obligations of friendship. He took no notice of it, tactfully avoided the courting couple, and the projected marriage subsequently took place with the happiest results.

Another old friend whom he had last seen in London and found again in Hamburg was Madame de Genlis. The beautiful Pamela was still with her, now the bride of Lord Edward Fitzgerald, who was filling the house with Irish rebels plotting the rebellion of 1798.

There were other French refugees in Hamburg, all with separate plots and separate parties. One desire only they had in common, and that was to return to France. Conditions there remained so unsettled, the situation so volcanic, that even for Talleyrand, whose name had been removed from the list of emigrants, Paris was not without danger. When he arrived there he was to discover that having been denounced in England and America as a French spy, in Paris he was suspected of being in the pay of a foreign Government. It is therefore not surprising that he waited a month at Hamburg, and another fortnight at Amsterdam, before finally putting his head into the lion's mouth and returning to his native city.

Many and far-reaching were, we are taught to believe, the results of the French Revolution; the immediate and actual result, however, so far as France was concerned, was the creation of a Government the most inefficient, corrupt, and contemptible with which any great country has ever been cursed. The Directory, which ruled France for four years, from November 1795 to November 1799, had only one principle—to protect in their existing situation the large number of people who had made substantial profits out of the Revolution. The Directory was therefore afraid of two things—on the one hand the return of the Bourbons, on the other a fresh revolution which would entail a redistribution of national property and the submersion of those particular revolutionaries whom chance, and no other conceivable agency, had recently thrown to the top of the melting-pot.

There were five members of the Directory, and, by the Constitution, one of them was replaced each year. Of the thirteen individuals, who at different times were Directors, ten were little better than nonentities. Carnot, who was a member during the first two years, had character and ability, although his hands were stained with all the blood that had been shed under the Terror. Sieyès, who refused office in the first days of the Directory and accepted it in the last, made some impression on his contemporaries as a political philosopher, but he was both conceited and a coward, an unfortunate combination of qualities which rendered it equally difficult for him either to accept the policy of others or to impose his own.

The soul of the Directory was Barras, who was the only member to remain in office from the beginning to the end. Barras, unlike his colleagues, had some pretensions to being a gentleman. He was also the only one of them who succeeded in not looking quite ridiculous in the elaborate fancy dress that David, the painter, had designed, and which the Constitution decreed that the Directors should wear upon ceremonial occasions. He was a Gascon and had served in the army. He possessed bravado rather than courage, cunning rather than cleverness, joviality rather than humanity, and swagger rather than elegance. He was the only Director who did not appear rather ashamed of himself. He was in fact shameless, and, having collected money with both hands for four years, he finally departed in peace with one last colossal bribe in his pocket.

It was the duty of the Directory to appoint Ministers and it was no easy business to find in Paris men who were fit for ministerial posts. From the supply of talent usually available there had to be deducted, first the emigrants, secondly the armies—there were four in the field at this time—and thirdly the two Chambers, whose members were forbidden by the Constitution to hold office. What the Directory most needed was experience and ability, and these were the very qualities that Talleyrand had to offer. It is therefore less surprising than it at first appears that, arriving in Paris in September with no resources and no friends in power, an ex-noble and an ex-bishop, he should have found himself in the following July promoted at a leap to the position of Minister for Foreign Affairs.

Of the steps that led up to this appointment we have two accounts. One is contained in the memoirs of Barras and the other in the memoirs of Talleyrand. Neither rings true. According to Barras it was Madame de Staël who first introduced Talleyrand to him and then pestered him with repeated visits urging him to give Talleyrand a post. Finally, according to this version, she arrived one day in a state of violent emotion with the announcement that unless Talleyrand was promoted at once, he was determined to commit suicide. Barras insinuates that Madame de Staël conveyed to him at this interview that there was no sacrifice that she was not prepared to make on behalf of her friend. He adds that he resisted the advance and rejected the appeal, but the weak feature of his story is that while he insists with pride upon his firmness in refusal he gives no explanation as to why he finally capitulated, and, at some difficulty to himself, forced Talleyrand upon his reluctant colleagues.

Talleyrand himself says that, much against his will, he was persuaded by Madame de Staël to dine with Barras at a villa on the banks of the Seine. Shortly after his arrival, before dinner had been served and before Barras had appeared, news was brought that a young man who served Barras as secretary, and to whom he was particularly devoted, had been drowned while bathing in the river. Barras was overcome with grief and was unable to come down to dinner. Talleyrand dined alone, and afterwards went up to his host's room where he did his best to console him. So tactful and sympathetic was Talleyrand's behaviour that Barras was completely conquered. The two drove back to Paris together the best of friends, and the appointment to the Ministry for Foreign Affairs was the result.

Barras further relates an unconvincing story of how Talleyrand received the news. He was at the opera with his friend Boniface de Castellane. It was Benjamin Constant, now the lover of Madame de Staël, who was sent to inform him. Talleyrand, overcome with delight, insisted on going off at once to thank Barras. Seated between Castellane and Constant in the carriage, pressing both their knees in his excitement, he kept muttering to himself how much money he hoped to make out of his new position. '*Une fortune immense, une immense fortune,*' are the words he is supposed to have repeated. On arrival he almost over-whelmed Barras, who was about to retire for the night, with expressions of gratitude, and on leaving could hardly be restrained from embracing the servants. Of this story it is sufficient to say that Talleyrand was famous throughout his life for complete self-control and composure in all circum-stances. It was coarsely, if concisely, put by one of his contemporaries, who said that he could be kicked a dozen times from behind without his face betraying the fact to those who were in front of him. Barras was a notorious liar and when he wrote his memoirs he had every reason for hating Talleyrand. That part of the story which he did not actually witness was reported to him by Madame de Staël who had it from Benjamin Constant. Both of them were by profession writers of romance.

Any reader is at liberty to believe as much or as little of contemporary accounts as he desires, and indeed half the fascination of studying the memoirs of the past is the endeavour, by making allowance for the prejudices and predilections of the writer, to sift truth from falsehood. All that we can say for certain about this particular intrigue, for an intrigue it was, is that Talleyrand succeeded in obtaining office through the assistance of Barras, and that the agent who brought the two men together was Madame de Staël.

2

The Paris in which Talleyrand found himself Minister for Foreign Affairs in 1797 was a very different town from that which he had known in the happy days before the Revolution. Symptomatic of the wretched condition into which France had fallen were the rivers of mud which flowed through the principal streets of the capital, the dilapidated houses, the broken monuments, the plundered and forsaken churches. But although little effort had yet been made to set upon foot the work of reconstruction, the one indestructible quality of the Parisian had already reasserted itself, and the town, though neither so clean nor so comely as it had been, was as gay as ever. Indeed, the reaction from the gloom and misery produced by the Revolution was an outburst of enjoyment which took the form of almost frenzied revelry and unbridled licence.

Dancing appeared to be the main interest of the population, and the deserted palaces of the great, the empty monasteries and convents, even some of the former churches were converted into resorts where this prevailing passion could find satisfaction. Hither, clad in transparent muslin, with bare legs, sandals, and rings upon their toes, their hair cut short and curled in what they believed to be the ancient Roman fashion, came the fair pleasure-seekers of the day to tread a measure with their cavaliers. Among the latter it was the singular mode to wear clothes which were carefully designed not to fit, to pull their hats down to their eyebrows, and to swathe their necks in vast cravats which concealed the chin and fringed the lower lip.

The outward forms of the Revolution were still observed, the new calendar and the new jargon. Toy dogs were trained to growl at the name of aristocrat, every tenth day was décadi and the excuse for a gala, at which Monsieur and Madame addressed one another with equal politeness as Citizen and Citizeness.

But society must have its leaders. The great ladies of the past had fled or perished. Their places had to be filled.

Not for soldiers and politicians only had the Revolution produced 'the career open to talent.' No longer need the stern decrees of fashion be dictated by ladies of noble birth and high degree.

The beautiful Thérèse Cabarrus, daughter of a once needy adventurer, wife of Tallien, mistress of Barras and of many others, was one whom all aspirants to elegance sought to imitate, and eager eyes noted every detail of her scanty clothing as she sat in her box at the opera or passed in her claret - coloured chariot. The lovely young wife of Récamier, the banker, was another. Her bedroom, furnished with mahogany, with bronze swans carrying wreaths of flowers above the bed, with classical lamps and marble statuary, was the last word in interior decoration. Josephine, widow of Beauharnais and bride of the young General now doing so well upon the Italian front, had recently yielded to the prayers of her ardent husband and joined him at Montebello. Before she left, her house was, as Barras described it, the best in Paris, because she belonged to the old society as well as to the new, and because, although she had been a revolutionary and a Jacobin, her first husband had been guillotined as an aristocrat. She was thus able to give to the penniless Corsican the social background which he lacked.

In this new world, ruled by charlatans and dominated by demireps, Talleyrand may have found much to shock his sense of decorum, but little to outrage his moral standards. It was an age of corruption. In France, as in England, men who went into politics expected, as a general rule, to be paid for their pains. That they received profitable posts or pecuniary rewards from their leaders did not necessarily mean that they sold their consciences, but merely that they demanded solid remuneration for solid services. Like many questionable practices the system worked well enough until it was carried to its logical conclusion, when it became a scandal. Talleyrand in France, like Henry Fox in England, acted on the same principles as his contemporaries, but because he took millions where they took thousands, he became an object of general obloquy.

It is impossible to defend a statesman who turns his public position to his private profit, and it can only be in slight mitigation of censure that we remember the lower standards of another age. A William Pitt, or even a Newcastle, is capable of rising above such standards and setting an example which raises the tone of succeeding generations.

During these years Talleyrand laid the foundations of a tremendous fortune. He received vast sums from many sources, principally from the Governments of other countries. When three Commissioners arrived from the United States in order to negotiate a settlement of certain questions relative to the seizure of ships during the war, it was made plain to them that it would be useless to open proceedings until they had made a very substantial present to the Minister for Foreign Affairs. The honest Americans were indignant, and, so far from parting with a penny, they immediately returned to their own country, where they published the facts to the world, and so put Talleyrand in an extremely inconvenient position.

Among the principal agents who served him in this affair, and in many similar ones, was the celebrated Casimir de Montrond who became at this time the firmest of his friends and remained so, with one brief interval of quarrelling, until his death. 'Le beau Montrond,' as he was called, was a dandy, a gambler, a swordsman, and a wit whose successes, both with the ladies and at the card table, had already acquired for him a large measure of notoriety. Talleyrand said that he liked him because he was not overburdened with scruples, to which Montrond replied that he liked Talleyrand because he had no scruples at all. Despite their cynicism the affection that united them was genuine, and it survived the storms of many tempestuous years.

3

The Minister whom Talleyrand succeeded in the department of Foreign Affairs in July 1797 was Charles Delacroix, who had long been suffering from a distressing malady which rendered it impossible for him to become a father. In the following September, however, he underwent a dangerous but successful operation, and some two months later he was restored to normal health. In April Madame Delacroix presented him with a son.

The paternity of this child, who was to become the celebrated painter, was generally ascribed to Talleyrand, and the theory was supported by a strong facial resemblance and by the fact that in the early days of his career the young artist was always in receipt of very valuable patronage and support from some mysterious and powerful source.

The most curious feature of the whole affair is to be found in a paragraph published in the *Moniteur* shortly before the birth of the child, giving, ostensibly in the interests of surgical science, a full account of the operation performed on Delacroix, and stating in so many words the disability from which he had previously suffered. Talleyrand in his ministerial position exercised considerable control over the *Moniteur*, which was an official publication and did not usually contain items of this nature. If, as seems not unlikely, Talleyrand was responsible for the announcement, we can only wonder what can have induced him to commit an act of such apparently wanton malice. To have succeeded the unfortunate Delacroix simultaneously in his ministerial appointment and in the favours of his wife would have seemed sufficient without proclaiming to the world in the solemn columns of the *Moniteur* that the late Minister for Foreign affairs could not be the true father of his accepted son.

The effect produced by the charms of Madame Delacroix, a mature beauty of thirty-nine, was soon effaced by a stronger influence which at this time entered into Talleyrand's life. Exactly how he first met the lady who was eventually to become his wife is uncertain. There is a story that she applied to him for assistance in connection with her passport and as the result of difficulties which were being made for her by the police. It is certain that when she was arrested on a charge of espionage, Talleyrand appealed to Barras for her release with the result that Barras had one of many stormy interviews with his fellow Directors and had to listen to a lengthy denunciation of Talleyrand's vices from Rewbell, the Director who most hated him and who was responsible for the Department of which he was the head.

Catherine-Noel Worlée had been born some thirty-five years earlier of French parents in the Danish Indian colony of Tranquebar. Her parents were government officials in a small way, and at the age of fifteen she married an English employee of the East India Company named Grand. This gentleman was appointed to a post in Calcutta where the remarkable beauty of his young wife soon attracted attention.

Most distinguished of those who were affected by her charms was Sir Philip Francis, the reputed author of the Junius letters, and now a member of the Supreme Council of Bengal. It is strange that he should have found time to spare from the fierce struggle with Warren Hastings in which he was engaged, for the seduction of the young wife of Mr. Grand. He had to aid him in the task, besides such assistance as wit and intellect of the first order can confer, a salary of £10,000 a year and a position second only to that of the Governor-General. It is little wonder then that he succeeded, but more surprising that one who had previously shown such discretion in maintaining anonymity should have marked the day of his success in his diary with the unambiguous motto: *Omnia vincit amor*.

Some ten days later, however, there occurs an entry in the same diary that tells a less fortunate tale. 'This night, the devil to pay in the house of G. F. Grand, Esq.' On that night the servants of Mr. Grand had descried a bamboo ladder hanging from the window of their lady's chamber, and on breaking into it, hoping to secure a robber, they had secured instead, and bound with ropes, a member of the Supreme Council of Bengal.

Mr. Grand brought an action, obtained large damages, pocketed his money, and returned his wife to her parents. Sir Philip, however, persuaded her to come back to him, and for a year lodged her under the same roof with Lady Francis, whom he persuaded that their relations were purely platonic—a feat in comparison with which the authorship of the letters of Junius sinks into insignificance.

Such a situation could not continue, and soon Madame Grand departed for Paris, where she spent the years before the Revolution in such variable and uncertain splendour as great beauty unaccompanied by brains is usually able to command. Tall, with the supple figure of a Creole, blue eyes, a slightly retroussé nose, which strangely enough resembled that of Talleyrand, and a wealth of very fair hair, so thick and long that it could, and upon a certain occasion did, serve as sufficient clothing for her whole body, these were the gifts that secured for Catherine Grand an assured position in the profession into which she had drifted.

Of her intelligence there were two opinions, of her

beauty there was only one. With regard to the former the general view was that she was more than ordinarily stupid and it became the fashion to attribute to Madame Grand, and subsequently to Madame de Talleyrand, every absurd remark that was made in Paris. But if she was neither witty, refined, nor highly educated—and it is difficult for a commonplace wife to shine in the presence of a husband of genius—she must at least have possessed a fund of common sense and an appreciation of her own interests which enabled her to bring a dangerous career to a comfortable conclusion.

Before the Revolution she had been the mistress at one time of de Lessart, who has already been mentioned as Minister for Foreign Affairs in 1791, and who became a victim of the September massacres. It is improbable that Talleyrand should not have met or heard of her at this time. In her anxiety to acquire some measure of respectability, so dear to the heart of a courtesan, she used to call on her lover's mother, who apparently was willing to receive her. A certain young Baron de Frénilly, who lived opposite to Madame de Lessart, noticed the beautiful visitor, who at first regarding him as a boy would pay no attention to him. But as he grew older he made his presence felt, and discovering that she had a charming carriage but no horses, whereas he had some fine white horses but lacked a carriage, he was able to persuade her to combine their advantages in order to drive down to a cottage which he owned in the suburbs on the side of a lake. She was, in those days, he writes, good natured, beautiful, and silly, and after she had become Princess de Talleyrand she was always the same. From 1797 she lived openly in Talleyrand's house and performed in public the duties of the wife of the Minister for Foreign Affairs.

4

But matters more important than the paternity of Delacroix or the protection of Madame Grand claimed the attention of the new Minister. As a man of acknowledged ability he had obtained a high position in a weak Government that was already doomed. He had to think of the future—immediate and distant. Reviewing in his own mind the lamentable condition in which France found herself as the result of the Revolution, he saw one, and only one, satisfactory feature—the success of the French army in the north of Italy. Within less than a week of taking office he wrote a letter to the young General commanding that army, to Napoleon Bonaparte, whom he had never seen, assuring him in terms of the most adroit and tactful flattery of his admiration and respect. Napoleon replied and the correspondence became regular. Napoleon was quick to realise that there was one man in Paris whose support was precious and whose advice was invaluable, and Talleyrand learnt that this soldier's genius was not purely military and that he would prove a force to be reckoned with in the changes that were at hand.

Talleyrand was not the only emigrant who had returned recently to France. Paris was full of former members of the nobility, some of whom had received permission to return, others who had never left but had gone into hiding or shrunk into obscurity from which they now emerged, and many who relied for their safety upon false names and forged papers. Madame de la Tour du Pin, whom we last saw working on a farm at Albany, had returned with her husband, and records in her memoirs the extreme impudence with which the Royalists were boasting in public of their future plans. 'People thought me ridiculous and pedantic when I told them, as I knew to be the case, that Monsieur de Talleyrand was well aware of all that was being plotted, and was laughing at it in his sleeve.'

The hopes of the Royalists had been raised by the result of the recent election of one third of the Assembly which had gone entirely in their favour, by the selection, as its President, of Pichegru, the former conqueror of Holland, who was already in the pay of the Bourbons, and by the appointment to the annually vacated place on the Directory of Barthélemy, who was a diplomatist of the old régime and a reactionary at heart. Carnot also, who was still the most respectable member of the Government, was believed to be weary of the existing system and prepared to welcome its overthrow; and if there had then been upon the spot a resolute leader with the courage to strike a blow for the Royalist cause, it is possible that it might have triumphed. But two men of courage and intelligence decided otherwise, and although they preferred to remain in the background when the blow was struck, it was mainly due to Talleyrand and to Napoleon that the plans of the Royalists were thwarted and the Restoration postponed for seventeen years.

In opposition to Carnot and Barthélemy within the Directory was the triumvirate of Barras, Rewbell, and La Revellière. Rewbell was a lawyer, a good speaker, and a bully. An austere moralist himself, he resented the lack of austerity in Talleyrand, whom he lost no opportunity of abusing, both behind his back and to his face.

La Revellière was a revolutionary of the feebler, doctrinaire, idealistic type. He bitterly hated the Christian religion and Carnot. In the place of the former he had attempted to introduce a new pseudo-philosophical fad manufactured in England called 'Theophilanthropy.' On one occasion he read a long paper explaining this novel system of worship to his colleagues. When he had concluded it and received the congratulations of the other

Ministers, Talleyrand remarked: 'For my part I have only one observation to make. Jesus Christ, in order to found His religion, was crucified and rose again—you should have tried to do as much.'

Of Barras, Rewbell, and La Revellière it has been said with truth that the three of them did not amount to a man. When therefore they found themselves faced with the necessity of taking firm action in a dangerous world, in a Paris where the sound of the last tumbrils had hardly ceased to echo in the streets, and where the threat of a new and a White Terror was gathering in the air, it is not surprising that this tremulous triumvirate looked anxiously round for a real man to do the work. After overtures had been made to Hoche, a sincere republican and one who had no taste for the intrigues of politics, it was finally decided, by Napoleon and Talleyrand rather than by the Directors, that Augereau was the right man for the job. He was a soldier of fortune who had served with unvarying courage in many countries. He had the appearance, manners, and vocabulary of a sergeant-major, the principles of a Jacobin, and a string of oaths without which he never mentioned the name of a hated aristocrat. He was to become in course of time the Duke of Castiglione.

Augereau was admirably suited to the work in hand. He had the professional soldier's contempt for politicians, and nothing could give him greater pleasure than to lay violent hands on a bevy of deputies. At three o'clock in the morning of 4th September—18 Fructidor—the discharge of a cannon warned the sleeping Parisians that the coup d'état, which both sides had been anxiously awaiting, was about to take place.

Everything passed off admirably. Carnot, the 'organiser of victory,' bolted through the back door and made good his escape to Switzerland. Barthélemy, too proud to fly, was arrested and, together with Pichegru and some fifty others, was sent across France in an iron cage exposed to the insults of the populace and then embarked for Cayenne, a sentence which was considered to entail such certain death that it was described at the time as the 'dry guillotine.' However Barthélemy and Pichegru both succeeded subsequently in escaping. All the elections which had resulted in Royalist victories were declared void, a large number of deputies and journalists were arrested and a great many newspapers were suppressed. Augereau reported to Napoleon —'General, my mission is accomplished. Paris is calm and astonished by the crisis which threatened to be terrible and which passed off like a fête.'

All that day Talleyrand remained at home playing whist, piquet, and hazard. Every quarter of an hour a messenger arrived with the latest intelligence. As the news came in he smiled but made no comment, continuing his game without interruption. He always arranged to spend the day of a coup d'état as comfortably as possible.

5

The result of the action taken on the 18 Fructidor was to strengthen the party in power and to postpone the fall of the Directory for two years. It is possible that Talleyrand expected to play a larger part in the new administration, although there seems to have been small ground for such expectation, seeing that he had only been in office for two months, and that it was barely a year since he had dared to return to Paris. If he nursed such hopes they were disappointed. The two vacant places in the Directory were filled by Merlin de Douai, a mediocre lawyer, and François de Neufchâteau, a mediocre poet. Talleyrand continued, while performing his ministerial functions, to prepare the

way for the downfall of the Government he was serving and
to secure his own position in that which he intended should
succeed it.

In October Napoleon concluded with Austria the Treaty
of Campo Formio, thus bringing his Italian campaign to a
triumphant conclusion. One article of that treaty, however,
might have been considered by political moralists to have
robbed the triumph of all its glory. Venice, alone among
the states of Northern Italy, had not been conquered by
Napoleon, but had rather been cajoled by the revolutionary
jargon of the time, and the usual claptrap about freedom,
into destroying her ancient Constitution and setting up a
supposedly democratic Government which was prepared to
accept the dictation of the French. Now by the recently
concluded treaty, in order that Napoleon might obtain
certain territorial advantages in other parts of Europe, the
old, invincible Republic, which had rejoiced in the pride of
her independence for over a thousand years, was handed
over, bound and fettered, to the House of Habsburg. And
so the chief result of the most successful campaign that the
soldiers of the Revolution had conducted was the destruction of a republic for the profit of an emperor.

Talleyrand had very strongly urged Napoleon not to
interfere with the independence of Venice. While he had
his own conscience sufficiently under control, he was wise
enough to realise that it is never good policy to outrage the
consciences of others. Those who believed that the Revolution had introduced a new era, and who had been wont to
denounce such manifestations of the old diplomacy as had
led to the partitioning of Poland, were naturally distressed
to find that the new diplomacy differed from the old only
in the increased amount of hypocritical verbiage with which
it sought to conceal its crimes. Talleyrand not only realised
this but also deprecated the excessive additions of territory

upon which Napoleon's ambition was already set. The one was thinking of the restoration of order and the maintenance of peace, while the restless brain of the other was scheming for the domination of the Mediterranean and dreaming of the conquest of the East.

But Talleyrand could accept a fait accompli, and the effusive congratulations that he despatched to Napoleon upon the signature of the treaty contained not the slightest allusion to the views which he had previously expressed with regard to the fate of Venice, nor any regret that they had been disregarded. Napoleon was now upon his way home, and Talleyrand was determined that no shadow of disagreement should mar their first meeting.

On the evening of 5th December Napoleon arrived in Paris. Within a few hours of his arrival he sent to inquire when it would be convenient for Talleyrand to receive him, and the interview was arranged for eleven o'clock on the following morning. As a small instalment of the debt of gratitude which he owed her, Talleyrand informed Madame de Staël of the expected visit, and she, who had already pictured herself as the Egeria of the young genius upon whom the eyes of France were fastened, was waiting in the anteroom on the following morning. Unfortunately for her, Bougainville, the explorer, was present also, and Napoleon showed more interest in the man of action than in the woman of letters. It was the first of many rebuffs which she was to experience from one whom she had been so ready to admire and serve.

Of this first meeting and conversation between the two men Talleyrand has left us only the briefest record, written many years later when the whole dazzling drama of Napoleon's career was closed. It is plain that the impression which each produced upon the other was favourable. 'At first sight,' writes Talleyrand, 'his face appeared to me charming. A score of victories go so well with youth, with fine eyes, with paleness, and with an appearance of exhaustion.' Among the first things that Napoleon said was: 'You are the nephew of the Archbishop of Rheims who is with Louis xviii' (not the Count de Lille, as it was customary to call him in Paris).—'I also have an uncle, who is an archdeacon in Corsica. He brought me up. In Corsica, you know, an archdeacon is the same as a bishop in France.' Very human are these ingenuous efforts of the young conqueror to show that he was also a gentleman. In a few years he will be talking of 'We nobles,' and yet a few years more and he will be referring to Louis xvi as 'my poor uncle.'

What more serious subjects they discussed we do not know. Napoleon said that it had been a pleasure for him in Italy to have a correspondent such as Talleyrand who was so different from the Directors. We may safely conclude that this led the General and the Minister into a frank discussion of the Government they were serving. They found themselves agreeing to despise their masters and speculating upon how long the regime was likely to endure. Talleyrand doubtless explained how the recent coup d'état, at which they had both connived, had strengthened the Administration and prolonged its existence, and possibly they discussed, even at this first interview, the future that lay before them and the parts they were to play in it.

The time was not yet ripe for a military dictator. Every general who returned to Paris was regarded with suspicion as a potential Cromwell, and the two new allies now deliberately planned their conduct with a view to removing such suspicion from people's minds. A few days later Talleyrand was entrusted with the task of introducing Napoleon to the Directorate at an official reception which had been planned with elaborate care. The ceremony took place amid scenes of wild enthusiasm, but it was noticed and favourably

commented on that the Minister for Foreign Affairs
referred to the General throughout his address as 'Citizen
Bonaparte.'

Later, when Talleyrand gave at his Ministry a magnificent
fête which surpassed, in elegance as well as in splendour,
any of the vulgar entertainments provided by the Directors,
it was expressly stated that the affair was in honour of
Madame Bonaparte, and Napoleon himself appeared at it,
as was his custom at this time, in civilian attire. The impression that he was attempting to convey and, to a large extent
succeeded in conveying, was that away from the battlefields
he was a quiet individual of a retiring character, only
desirous of being left in peace to pursue the study of science
and muse over the sublime poetry of Ossian. He showed
interest only in his candidature for the Institute, and when
his election was secured he let it be understood that the
highest ambition of his life was accomplished.

6

There now took place in the career of Napoleon an
event which came near to wrecking it, and which, the more
we consider it, becomes the harder to understand. The
youthful and ambitious adventurer, whose military prestige
already stood far higher than that of all his rivals, at a moment
when the Government was failing and the Constitution
threatened, when a thousand conspiracies were afoot and
none could prophesy the events of the next few weeks,
deliberately turned his back on Paris and France to plunge
into the most hazardous enterprise that he ever attempted,
across the sea which the English fleet commanded and
away into the deserts of Africa.

How far was Talleyrand responsible for this decision?
During the early days of his return, before he had succeeded

in obtaining employment under the Directory, he had delivered two carefully prepared lectures at the Institute of France.

The first of these was concerned with Anglo-American commercial relations, and the second, a natural sequel, dealt with the advantages that France might gain from the creation of new colonies. In the course of the second lecture ne mentioned, with emphatic approval, the plan that Choiseul had conceived years earlier for the conquest and colonisation of Egypt.

The lecture was delivered at the beginning of July 1797. In August Napoleon, writing from Italy and referring to the dismemberment of the Turkish Empire, impressed upon the Directory the importance to France of acquiring Egypt. Henceforward he and Talleyrand frequently mentioned the project in their correspondence. In January of the following year Talleyrand laid before the Directory a memorandum on the subject in which the despatch of an expedition was recommended, and in February he followed it up by a voluminous report which urgently and eloquently insisted upon the desirability of the enterprise. In April Napoleon was appointed Commander of the Army of the East, in May he left Paris, in June he conquered Malta, in July he landed at Alexandria.

Although he subsequently denied having had anything to do with it, the evidence is overwhelming that Talleyrand strongly favoured and pressed forward the expedition to Egypt from the first. And it is further proved that he had an understanding with Napoleon according to which he was to proceed at once to Constantinople as the Ambassador of France, and there await the arrival of the conqueror, who should have marched in triumph through Egypt, Palestine, Syria, and Asia Minor. The work of conquest completed, the new Emperor of the East would need a practised statesman at his elbow, and Talleyrand was the man he had selected for the post.

However wild and fantastic the dreams of Napoleon at this time may have been, they were hardly wilder or more fantastic than what he subsequently accomplished. To what extent the clear-sighted and cool-headed older man may have shared these dreams it is impossible to say. He had seen many unlikely things happen already, and was to see stranger ones before he died. Napoleon had made a deep impression upon him and had taken him more closely into his confidence than any other man. It is possible that he may for a moment have been infected by the other's enthusiasm. It is possible again that he may have intended to get rid of so explosive an element in French politics in order to free his hands for dealing with more malleable stuff. More probably he considered that the time was not yet come for the blow that he was preparing to strike, and that the interval might be well employed in adding fresh laurels to those that already graced the brow of the man he had selected as best fitted for the task. If while attempting to gather those laurels he should merely lose the ones he had previously collected, if the proud brow itself should strike the dust, there remained other men in France and other generals at the front to fill the gap, and other cards in the hand of the Minister for Foreign Affairs.

Talleyrand never went to Constantinople. It was the first evidence received by Napoleon that his new friend was not always to be relied upon. Perhaps he had never meant to go; perhaps, on the other hand, an event which took place upon the 1st of August altered his intention. On that day the whole of the French fleet which had transported the army of Bonaparte to Egypt was destroyed by Nelson in Aboukir Bay. The conquest of the East was hampered by the impossibility of receiving reinforcements, and the swift return to Paris of the popular hero was complicated by the fact that he was cut off from his base. Should his wildest dreams come true and all obstacles on the road to Constantinople fall before him like the walls of Jericho, Talleyrand would be kept informed, and would yet arrive in time at the appointed place.

But meanwhile the heart of his world was beating fast in Paris, events were rapidly culminating towards a crisis, the air was so thick with intrigues that it would be as impossible for an historian to dissect them as it would be for a scientist to recover and analyse the misty vapours that rose that season from the Seine. The whole rotten edifice of the Directory needed only one match to send it flaring to the sky. That match might be set to it at any hour of the day or night. Talleyrand remained in Paris.

7

As is usually the case when democratic institutions are failing, the general demand among all classes and in all parties was for one strong man who would sweep away the politicians, who would not pander to the ephemeral powers that were, but would give good government to the majority, who wanted it, and impose firm government upon the few, who did not. Talleyrand, ever sensitive to popular opinion, and gifted with a power of perception that could penetrate the future further than most, was aware of this widespread desire, and was determined to satisfy it.

Conscious of his own limitations, and never anxious to play a leading part or to court the limelight, he did not even aspire to be a Warwick or a Monk, but preferred to be one step further removed from the throne and to push another forward into the dangerous rôle of the king-maker. Barras was too discredited, the other Directors were too incompetent, and it was Sieyès whom Talleyrand finally selected as his instrument for the destruction of the Directory.

The easiest way to destroy a Government is from within. Talleyrand, having decided upon the destruction of the Directory, and having chosen Sieyès as his agent, proceeded to make Sieyès a Director. That cold, clever, cowardly man was glad to find that his abilities, which everybody but himself had seemed so long to underrate, were beginning at last to be appreciated. Mirabeau had once said in one of his finest flights of oratory that the silence and inactivity of Sieyès were nothing less than a public calamity. But silence and inactivity had saved his life, and when men asked Sieyès what he had done during the Terror, he who had previously incurred the enmity of Robespierre had some reason to be proud of his reply—'I lived.'

It was in the month of May that the annual retirement of one Director took place. The name was drawn by lot, but it needed no special powers of perception to discern behind the hand of chance the hand of Barras. The unpopularity in which all the Directors shared had seemed recently to concentrate upon Rewbell, and it was therefore no surprise when Rewbell's name emerged from the urn in May 1799, and any awkward questions which he might have asked as to the regularity of the proceeding were silenced by a generous parting gift from his grateful colleagues.

They had intended to replace him by a dummy, but to their annoyance the Assembly insisted upon nominating, and the Senate upon electing, Sieyès, a result to which, in the words of the best historian of the epoch: 'Talleyrand had contributed by some backstair manœuvre.' His enemy had been removed, his ally had been appointed, and now nothing remained but, with the assistance of that ally, to carry out his policy.

While Sieyès was returning from Berlin, where he had

been acting as French Ambassador, elections took place to refill the vacancies caused by the annual retirement of one-third of the Members of the Assembly. The result was a victory for the Jacobins, so that when the new Director arrived in Paris he found that it was for the moment the Red Terror rather than the White which was principally occupying the minds of his nervous colleagues. It appeared, indeed, not improbable that the violent extremists, who less than ever represented the will of the majority, might once more obtain control of Paris.

The Directory was terrified. Barras, playing, as ever, for his own hand only, was intriguing with the Assembly against the other Directors, and such force was brought to bear that the election of one of them was annulled and two others were compelled to resign. Of the three new Directors one was Roger Ducos, who was expected to prove a tool of Barras, but disappointed expectations by becoming instead a tool of Sieyès. Another was Gohier, of whom little is to be recorded except that he entertained hopes of becoming the lover of Josephine Bonaparte, who was an intimate friend of his wife. The last Director to be appointed to that office was General Moulins, a melancholy and quite undistinguished soldier. Neither he nor anybody else ever understood why he was selected for this important position. He stumbles into the pages of history, muttering gloomily, and wondering why he has been sent for. At the end of four months he escapes through a window and regains the obscurity from which he should never have emerged.

But the Jacobins were not content with their victory, nor prepared to leave even the reconstructed Directory in peace. The press, which had been muzzled since Fructidor, became once more vocal, and the scandals of the Directory provided sufficient material for some fifty new newspapers, which, together with a spate of pamphlets, suddenly sprang into being. One of the most popular objects of attack was the Minister for Foreign Affairs, whose public and private morals, whose notorious corruption, and whose suspected designs against the Republic furnished an easy target for every tyro in the profession of slinging ink. Talleyrand realised that the time had come to sink a little further into the background and, appearing to bow his head to the storm, he resigned his office at the end of July, having arranged that his successor should be Reinhard, a man upon whom he could rely, and who could not arrive in Paris for several weeks as he was Ambassador at Florence. In his absence Talleyrand continued to fill his place, and on his return Reinhard adopted the policy of his predecessor.

8

Meanwhile Sieyès was cautiously preparing his plans. 'Two things are needed,' he said to Fouché, whose appointment he had secured as Minister of Police—'a head and a sword.' So far as the head was concerned Sieyès was very well satisfied with his own. He had, in fact, the greatest contempt for all others. But whose was to be the sword? That of Bonaparte seemed indicated. He had been careful, when in Paris, to pander to Sieyès's insatiable appetite for flattery and had produced a favourable impression. But to Bonaparte there was one insuperable objection. He was in Egypt. Time was short. If Sieyès did not strike soon the Jacobins might strike first. Any morning might see the guillotine mounted again in the Place de la Révolution, and the first head to fall under it would be that of the ci-devant Abbé Sieyès.

In these circumstances the choice fell upon Joubert. He was young, the same age as Bonaparte, under whom he had served with great distinction in Italy; he was handsome and popular, a romantic figure, and he was in Paris. But before the great task could be entrusted to him he must win a great victory, so he was given the command of the Army of Italy, and sent off to inflict a spectacular defeat upon the enemies of France.

But the plan failed, for at the battle of Novi it was the enemies of France who proved victorious, and one of the first to fall was the gallant young General, upon whose brow Sieyès had thought to lay the wreath that was destined for another.

The work had to be resumed from the beginning. Once more the conspirators looked round for the sword that was to save them. For four months no news had been received from Bonaparte, and people in Paris imagined him still battling in the wilds of Syria with the army of Turkey in front of him and the fleet of England behind. Talleyrand, who had taken part in the plot to promote Joubert, as he took part in every plot that was spun, came forward now with the proposal that negotiations should be opened with Turkey in order to conclude a treaty whereby, in return for the restitution of Egypt, Bonaparte and his army should be allowed to return to France. The plan was adopted by the Government, and Talleyrand hoped that his friend's sword might thus be placed at the disposal of Sieyès in the spring of the following year if the coup d'état could be postponed so long. He did not know that Napoleon was already at sea, having sailed from Alexandria a week after the battle of Novi.

Time pressed. While the vessel that bore Napoleon and his fortunes was dodging across the Mediterranean and narrowly escaping encounter with an English ship, events were moving so rapidly in Paris that Sieyès was already at his wit's end to discover a saviour of society who would accept the job. There was Bernadotte, already well

advanced on the career that was to lead him to a throne;
but the future King of Sweden was at this time too pronounced a Jacobin for the kind of coup d'état that Sieyès
was planning and was, in fact, being urged by the Jacobins
to make a coup d'état on their behalf. Besides, Sieyès had
no confidence in him and said: 'He looks like an eagle but
is really a goose.' There was Macdonald—but he was a
soldier and nothing but a soldier, in the finest sense of the
word. Finally there was Moreau, a soldier too, and one
whose fame would be fairer if he had never been lured,
always against his will, into the labyrinth of politics. Sieyès
tried them all, and it was while he was in conversation with
Moreau, urging him to accept the task, that news arrived
of Bonaparte's landing at Fréjus. 'There's your man,'
exclaimed Moreau, and Sieyès, who had always feared that
Bonaparte might prove to be something more than his man,
was reluctantly compelled to agree.

9

Napoleon made straight for Paris. Private reasons as well
as public hastened his steps. News which had reached him
in Egypt of the failures of the Directory had been accompanied by reports of the infidelity of his wife. She,
anxious to meet him before her accusers, hurried out along
the road by which she thought ' e would come. But she was
mistaken and missed him, so that the little house in the Rue
Chantereine was empty when he arrived there on the morning of 16th October. He brought with him nothing but
the clothes he stood in, for the whole of his luggage—such
was the state of France—had been stolen by brigands on
the way.

When Josephine returned she was, after a violent scene,
forgiven, and did her best during the crowded days that

followed to make up by her zeal in her husband's service for any errors of which she may have been guilty during his absence. She was an excellent hostess and this small house became her admirably. It had been built for Julie Talma, the gay and wealthy wife of the great actor. There was a courtyard in front and a garden behind, an oval dining-room and a circular boudoir decorated with Pompeian paintings, the latest fashion of the day. It was as suitable a setting for Josephine, with her fading beauty and her tarnished fame, as it was a strange one for the thin young soldier in his plain attire and the scarred and bronzed veterans who thronged around him, telling stories of campaigns under distant suns and clanking their heavy sabres on the parquet floor. Not that Josephine had omitted to impart a military touch to her decorations. In her bedroom drums were made to serve as stools, the backs of the chairs were shaped like crossbows supported by sheaves of arrows, and the bed itself was in the shape of a tent.

Within this frame of fashionable elegance the plot was laid that was to change the history of France. Against this background of pretty women, which gave to all an air of frivolity and flirtation, came and went the soldiers, lawyers, politicians, and diplomatists who were playing a desperate game, upon the result of which their own heads as well as the fate of their country depended.

We have a portrait of Talleyrand from the pen of a contemporary as he appeared at the nightly reunions in the little salon of the Rue Chantereine—'nonchalantly lounging on a sofa . . . his face unchanging and impenetrable, his hair powdered, talking little, sometimes putting in one subtle and mordant phrase, lighting up the conversation with a sparkling flash and then sinking back into his attitude of distinguished weariness and indifference.'

There is another picture which should be set by the side

of this one if we would appreciate the reality of the drama that was being played. It has been drawn for us by Talleyrand himself in the pages of his memoirs.

He was living at this time in the Rue Taitbout. The house had a courtyard in front of it, and from the first floor two wings stretched out ending in small 'pavilions' that gave on to the street. It was one o'clock in the morning. By the light of one or two candles Talleyrand and Napoleon were eagerly discussing the details of their plot. Suddenly through the night there resounded the clatter of a detachment of cavalry passing down the street. Opposite the house they halted. Napoleon turned pale and Talleyrand blew out the candles. Had the blow fallen? Had they delayed too long? Were these the emissaries of their enemies come to arrest them? Would they share in a few hours the fate of all the other leaders of the Revolution? These were the thoughts that flashed through Talleyrand's quick brain as he stole on tiptoe down the corridor to the window that looked on to the street. For a long while his small green eyes peered into the gloom of that misty November night seeking to solve the enigma, while his ears were stretched for the sound of hammering at the door.

At last, with a sense of infinite relief, he found the explanation. The gambling-rooms in the Palais Royal closed late. Their banker lived in the Rue de Clichy, and so dangerous were the streets of Paris that nothing less than a troop of cavalry was considered sufficient to protect the bearer of the day's takings on his nightly journey. On this particular occasion the cab with the money in it had broken down opposite Talleyrand's house, and a quarter of an hour was needed to repair it.

'The General and I,' he concludes the story, 'laughed heartily at our panic, although it was only natural when one knew, as we did, the character of the Directory and the extremities of which they were capable.'

The delay which occurred between the arrival of Bonaparte in Paris on 16th October and the striking of the blow on 9th November was mainly due to the difficulty of establishing harmonious relations between the military and the civilian leaders of the conspiracy. Sieyès was a pedant, and Napoleon combined greatness with pettiness to an unusual degree. No greater proof of it can be adduced than the fact that at this moment, when the two men were engaged upon a scheme in which their whole future was at stake, they allowed precious days to pass while they wrangled like a pair of old women as to which ought to pay the first call upon the other.

Bonaparte seems at first to have thought that he might achieve his object as successfully with the help of Barras as with that of Sieyès, and it took him some days to realise that Barras, his former patron, was sunk beyond redemption and beyond hope of ever serving any useful purpose again.

At last an aide-de-camp was sent to announce that he would call upon Sieyès at a certain hour on the morrow. Sieyès, who thought he had been kept waiting too long, sent a messenger with the reply that the hour selected was not convenient. Bonaparte, receiving the message when surrounded by a crowd of his supporters, lost his temper, declared that he had never sent the aide-de-camp, who had acted without orders, that he paid calls on nobody, but that people ought to call on him, who was the glory of the nation.

Talleyrand was horrified at the news. He hurried round to the Rue Chantereine, where he talked seriously to Bonaparte. He did not hesitate to reproach him violently for the folly of his action, and to insist upon his repairing the blunder at once. His firmness proved completely successful, and his diplomacy did the rest. Bonaparte called on Sieyès and on Roger Ducos. The following day Sieyès and Roger Ducos called on Bonaparte. The two visits were announced simultaneously in the press. Although Bonaparte still grumbled that the drums had not been beaten on his arrival at the Luxembourg, that the large folding doors had not both been opened, and that he had been kept waiting, none the less the ice was broken, the first difficulty had been surmounted, and nothing now remained but to determine upon the details of the plot.

During the feverish fortnight of intrigue that followed, the difficulties of the conspirators were increased by the fact that the five Directors lived in one house, each occupying different apartments in the Palace of the Luxembourg. It seemed difficult to conspire with Sieyès under the nose of Barras without arousing the latter's suspicions, until they hit upon the happy plan of allowing Barras to believe that he was himself in the conspiracy. More indolent and pleasure loving than ever, Barras remained convinced until the last moment that he was in the intimate councils of the men who had decided upon his fall.

But there were the other Directors to be thought of, and great secrecy had to be preserved. The task of preparing the necessary literature, posters, pamphlets, and decrees had been entrusted to Roederer, who had a ready and an able pen. It had nearly landed him at Cayenne after Fructidor. His name was actually on the list of those to be deported and it was due to the intervention of Talleyrand that he was spared. On two occasions during these days it was necessary for Roederer to see Sieyès. He was conveyed there after dark by Talleyrand and was left below in the carriage while Talleyrand first mounted the stairs to make sure that the coast was clear and that the Director was alone.

It was typical of Talleyrand that in this, as in every

other channel of the vast labyrinth of intrigue, he fulfilled himself no definite function, but served only as the go-between, acquainted with everybody, knowing everything, and holding in his hands the end of every string.

10

Nothing could have been worse planned nor worse performed than the coup d'état that now took place. The most important quality of a coup d'état is speed. It should be over before those who are likely to oppose it are aware it has begun. No moment should be allowed for the forces of the other side to organise. Yet this was deliberately designed to occupy two days. It should be ruthless. Men who are smashing a system of government must not be afraid of breaking a law. But these conspirators were so scrupulous in their observation of forms that they seemed to be attempting to do nothing unconstitutional except destroy the Constitution. Above all, success must usually depend upon the calmness and decision of the leader. At the critical moment Napoleon lost his head.

At six o'clock in the morning of the 9th November (18 Brumaire) Roederer called on Talleyrand. He brought with him his son who, under the pretence of becoming a printer's apprentice, had been busy for days printing the notices which his father had composed, and with which at this early hour the walls of Paris were already plastered.

Talleyrand was still dressing. They had, he said, an hour to spare, and they had better employ it in writing out Barras's resignation. They were to make it as easy for him as possible. Talleyrand never drafted anything himself if there was somebody else to do it, and accordingly Roederer dictated to his son a brief but dignified statement which, after a few corrections, obtained Talleyrand's approval. He slipped it into his pocket, and the three of them drove off together to the town hall of the department, which was situated in the Place Vendôme.

Barras's resignation having been drawn up, the next step was to induce him to sign it. Admiral Bruix was the man whom Talleyrand had selected for this task, and before midday they proceeded together to the Luxembourg. Barras had had an anxious morning. He believed himself to be so deeply involved in the conspiracy that it seemed to him impossible that it could now be taking place without his co-operation. Gradually the truth was brought home to him. Of his four colleagues Sieyès and Roger Ducos had already disappeared while the insignificant Gohier and Moulins were loudly demanding his assistance. Josephine had been detailed to look after Gohier, and had sent him a note urging to him to visit her at eight o'clock that morning. It was hoped that he would then have been persuaded to form one of the escort of generals and prominent people who accompanied Napoleon on his ride to the Tuileries. But Gohier, either scenting danger or being too experienced a voluptuary to appreciate a rendezvous at such an early hour, refused the invitation, so that he and Moulins, two marionettes whose strings for the moment nobody was concerned to pull, were left impotently gesticulating in the Luxembourg, and appealing to Barras for assistance, who sent, for an answer, that he was still in his bath.

Thérèse Tallien came to see him in the course of the morning, cheerful, confident, and beautiful as ever; so did the financier, Ouvrard, who, although he did not mention the fact, had already promised pecuniary assistance to the contrivers of the coup d'état. The table was, as usual, laid for thirty, such was the scale on which the Director entertained, but no other guests arrived that morning, and Barras and Ouvrard were sitting down at one end of the long

table to a melancholy meal when Bruix and Talleyrand were
announced.

Barras had wits enough to appreciate the situation, and
when what was required of him had been explained he did
not take long to persuade. Perhaps he thought himself
fortunate to escape so lightly, he who had sent many others
to their death. He signed the resignation that had been
prepared for him and promised to give no further trouble.
In his memoirs he denies that he received at the same time
a substantial sum of money, and suggests that if there had
been any intention of offering it to him Talleyrand must
have retained it for himself. There is no reason to believe
him. He had taken bribes all his life and had seldom had
anything more valuable to sell than was his acquiescence
upon this occasion. He left Paris immediately for his
country seat. A troop of cavalry was sent with him to protect him on his journey and to make sure that he did not
return.

II

So far all had gone well. The Council, in which Sieyès
could command a majority, had met early the same morning,
having been summoned by a special message which had
failed to reach some sixty members of whose support the
conspirators were uncertain. Those who obeyed the sum-
mons had been informed that the Jacobins had set on foot a
dangerous plot to overthrow the Republic, and that therefore, in accordance with the powers entrusted to it by the
Constitution, the Council decreed that both Chambers should
meet on the following day at St. Cloud, where they would be
removed from the menace of force which the Jacobins might
exercise in the capital.

The Assembly met later in the day. They were taken by
surprise. The decree passed by the Council was com-

municated to them, and before they had had time to consider it the sitting was adjourned until the morrow by the President, Lucien Bonaparte.

On the following day the scene changed to St. Cloud. Talleyrand drove down there in the morning accompanied by the Roederers, father and son, and by des Renaudes, who had been Vicar-General when he was Bishop of Autun, and who remained his devoted secretary and friend all his life. They had arranged for a house to be placed at their disposal, and there a continual stream of messengers kept them informed of every incident that took place on that eventful day.

There they learnt how Bonaparte had appeared in the Council, how he had failed completely in his attempt to address them, and had done far more harm than good to his cause. Then came the news that he had entered the Assembly, where he had been greeted with cries of 'Down with the tyrant,' that some of the deputies had laid violent hands upon him, and that he had been rescued by his grenadiers. Next it was reported that the Assembly was outlawing him. That terrible cry of *'Hors la loi!'* had sent Robespierre, the dictator, to his doom. When this news reached him, Talleyrand turned at once to Montrond and told him to go and inform Bonaparte. Montrond found him with Sieyès and Roger Ducos. When he heard that he was being outlawed, Bonaparte, who had never shown emotion in battle, turned pale, whereas the timid Sieyès, the man of peace, remained calm and said firmly: 'If they seek to outlaw you they are outlaws themselves.' Stirred to action Bonaparte then met the cry of *'Hors la loi!'* with the only effective rejoinder—*'Aux armes!'*

But there was further hesitation and further delay. It was not until Lucien, who was fighting nobly for his brother within the Assembly, sent a message that something must be done immediately, that Napoleon was spurred, first to send in his soldiers to 'rescue' Lucien, although Lucien was in no danger, and then, fortified by the presence of Lucien who, as President of the Assembly, lent a shadow of legality to the deed, to allow Murat to charge into the Chamber at the head of a column, and to disperse the terrified deputies at the point of the bayonet. Through doors and windows and every available exit they vanished into the deepening shades of night.

When the information reached Talleyrand he turned to Roederer and said: 'We must dine,' and he took them, the two Roederers and Montrond, to dine with a certain Madame Simons who was living in a small house at Meudon. With his usual foresight he had arranged beforehand to spend the evening of the coup d'état as agreeably as possible, and their hostess was expecting them. She had been an actress and a favourite of Barras and had subsequently married a wealthy carriage-builder from Brussels. Talleyrand had been present at the wedding and had signed the register.

It was a pleasant little dinner that they enjoyed that evening while the republican legislators were wandering disconsolately in the forest of St. Cloud. But Montrond, who had seen Napoleon turn pale that day, kept repeating at every pause in the conversation: 'That was not correct, General Bonaparte, that was not correct.'

Chapter Five

THE CONSULATE

It was the opinion of the Duke de Broglie that the four years of the Consulate formed one of the two most glorious periods of French history, the reign of Henri IV being the other. They were certainly the happiest years of Napoleon's life. He used to sing at his work in those days, and sing very badly, according to his old schoolfellow and private secretary, Bourrienne. His work was the reconstruction of France and the pacification of Europe.

He was still young, only thirty years of age, ignorant, anxious to learn, and not ashamed to be taught. The wisest and the best liked of his tutors was Talleyrand. 'He was always pleased to see Monsieur de Talleyrand,' writes Bourrienne, and adds: 'I have frequently been present at this great statesman's conferences with Napoleon, and I can declare that I never saw him flatter his dreams of ambition; but, on the contrary, he always endeavoured to make him sensible of his true interests.'

Talleyrand did not share Napoleon's fondness for work. Naturally lazy he pretended to be lazier than he was and made a principle of never performing any task himself that could possibly be delegated to another. If a despatch was to be written, or a memorandum drawn up, he would hastily set down in an almost illegible handwriting all that he wished it to contain without paying any attention to form or order. One of his subordinates, and the principal ones had worked with him so long that they could interpret his mind as well as decipher his handwriting, would then reduce these rough notes to the correct diplomatic shape and return it to the chief, who would make numerous corrections, and it would then, perhaps, be discussed at length between the two before the document received its final form. There is a story how, upon one occasion, the head of one of the departments of the Ministry asked the Minister to write a letter in his own hand, as the recipient was a ruling prince of Germany—'Must I write it myself?' he pleaded. 'Yes, to an Elector.' 'But to write and compose at the same time is really too much. So I will write but you must dictate it.'

This love of idleness, partly natural and partly affected, he was prepared to defend as the wisest policy for a diplo-matist. He discouraged excessive zeal even in his sub-ordinates, and when he relinquished the Ministry for Foreign Affairs he said, presenting the permanent officials to his successor: 'You will find them loyal, intelligent, accurate, and punctual, but, thanks to my training, not at all zealous.' As M. de Champagny evinced some surprise, he continued, affecting a most serious manner: 'Yes, except for a few of the junior clerks who, I am afraid, close up their envelopes with a certain amount of precipitation, every one here main-tains the greatest calm; hurry and bustle are unknown.'

This deliberate manner of conducting business was really of service to Napoleon, who, working with lightning rapidity himself, was often glad to find that instructions which he had given with too little consideration had not been acted upon several days later, when he was already prepared to cancel them.

2

It is one of the ironies of history that the main reason for the popularity of Napoleon's usurpation of power was the

conviction in the minds of the people that he would bring
them the blessing they most desired, a permanent peace.
Talleyrand, a consistent lover of peace, contributed more
than any other statesman during these early years, when he
was working in complete harmony with his master, towards
the task of pacification both at home and abroad. It was he
who smoothed down relations between Napoleon and
Sieyès, which became after the coup d'état as acrimonious
as they had been before, and which narrowly escaped leading
to open conflict when Sieyès realised that, whatever ingenious and intricate shape he might devise for the Constitution, Napoleon was determined that there should be
only one voice in the government of the country.

It was Talleyrand also who brought Napoleon into touch
with emissaries of the Bourbon princes, who were still
uncertain as to whether the victorious General was to prove
a Cromwell or a Monk. Hyde de Neuville, who, at the risk
of his life, was at this time hiding in Paris, was enabled
through the agency of Talleyrand to obtain an interview
with Napoleon. So great was the secrecy which it was
considered necessary to observe, that Talleyrand arranged
that Hyde should await him at a corner of the Place Vendôme, where he picked him up in his carriage and drove him
to the Luxembourg. On the way he did not miss the
opportunity of impressing upon the Royalist his own
friendliness towards the Bourbons, and especially his
affection for the Count d'Artois. He did not, however,
encourage the supporters of Louis XVIII to hope for any
early developments in their favour. Questioned as to what
was about to happen he replied: 'Nobody knows the secret
of the future.' Questioned as to Bonaparte, he said: 'If he
lasts a year, he will go far.'

The interview, and another one that followed it, led to
nothing. Napoleon had not the slightest intention of play-

ing the part designed for him by the Bourbons, and had
only consented to receive their representatives in the hope
of effecting a speedy and peaceful settlement of the civil
strife that still persisted in the west of France. This he
subsequently accomplished by taking the necessary military
measures and by supporting them with a policy that combined firmness, conciliation, and duplicity.

Having thus disposed of his open enemies in the fields of
La Vendée, the First Consul had to turn his attention to the
more formidable antagonists who awaited him under
various disguises in the streets of the capital. Like the
Directory before him, he found himself between two fires,
and the clue to the history of the Consular period is the
alternating apprehension with which he regarded the dangers
that threatened him from the Royalists upon the one hand
and from the Jacobins upon the other. His sympathies were
with the former. Indeed there was little to which he objected
in the Royalists except their attachment to the Bourbons.
For the Revolutionaries upon the other hand—from the
loftiest idealist of 1789 to the most bloodstained Terrorist
of 1794—he had nothing but detestation and contempt.
These sentiments inclined him, at first, to the view that he
had most to fear from those whom he most disliked, whereas,
in reality, the Royalists constituted by far the greater menace,
appealing as they did to a larger number of people in the
country, and supported as they were by the wealth and sea
power of Great Britain.

The new Constitution consisted of three Consuls, it being
the duty of the Second and Third to do little more than
supply the First with information and advice. Napoleon
had appointed his two assistants with his customary discrimination and had not only secured two colleagues upon
whose loyalty he could rely, but had so selected them that
while the Second Consul, Cambacérès, seemed to provide a

pledge of his fidelity to the principles of the Revolution, the Third Consul, Lebrun, who was noted for leanings towards the Right, gave ground for hope to those who desired it that the Government would eventually proceed in that direction. But neither Cambacérès nor Lebrun was to play an important part in the events that followed. Among the Ministers there were only two, if we except Lucien Bonaparte, who was shortly afterwards dismissed, who had the character or the ability to become more than mere tools in the hands of their master. The divergent tendencies in French politics were more effectively represented by these two Ministers than they were by the two Consuls. Talleyrand, who became immediately Minister for Foreign Affairs, was still a *grand seigneur* in this world of *parvenus*, and had retained not only the fine manners of the old Court but also most of his associations and friendships with the proudest families of the aristocracy; whereas Fouché, the new Minister of Police, the regicide, the organiser of massacre on the largest scale, from whom the underworld of Paris could hold no secrets, remained as the representative of the Jacobins, and as one who was too deeply implicated in their crimes ever, as it then seemed, to hope for forgiveness from the Bourbons.

The two Ministers presented a remarkable contrast— Talleyrand, suave and courteous, as exquisite in dress as in conversation, restrained in both, and conquering by charm even his enemies; Fouché, brutal in manner, foul mouthed in company, ill dressed, ill washed, with an unprepossessing appearance which his reputation rendered sinister. Talleyrand, the ex-bishop, living openly with a beautiful mistress; Fouché, the ex-Terrorist, a tender father of a family and faithful husband of an ugly wife. For Talleyrand the word politics meant the settlement of dynastic or international problems discussed in a ball-room or across a dinner-table;

for Fouché the same word meant street corner assassination, planned by masked conspirators in dark cellars. Each had a shrewd appreciation of the other's qualities, and when it suited them they would work together, but they could never be friends. It was Talleyrand who had advised Sieyès to secure the assistance of Fouché, and the latter had played a somewhat equivocal rôle in the events of Brumaire, but had hastened to the assistance of the victors as soon as he was certain who they were. But now Fouché was alarmed at the turn events were taking and the natural antipathy between the two men was increased by the different policies that they pursued.

Napoleon was anxious to assist the return to France, and to secure the support, of the old nobility. Public policy and personal predilection urged him in the same direction. It was part of his design to reconcile the old France with the new, it was part of his vanity to delight in the inclusion amongst his courtiers of the greatest names that decorate the pages of French history. Here Talleyrand could prove of invaluable assistance, and at the costly and elegant entertainments that he provided Bonaparte met for the first time such members of the aristocracy as had remained in France or had ventured to return.

Talleyrand, who believed always in monarchical government, did nothing to discourage Napoleon from the goal towards which he was manifestly directed. He suggested that in view of the importance and the urgency of the affairs dealt with in his department and of the desirability of maintaining secrecy he should make his reports to the First Consul only and not be compelled, as were the other Ministers, to consult with all the three. Such a proposal, which enhanced Bonaparte's predominance, not unnaturally received his warm approval.

Later, when the First Consul's brother-in-law, Leclerc,

died of fever in the West Indies, Talleyrand persuaded the representatives of foreign Powers in Paris to appear at the Consular Court in mourning, an honour never accorded to any save royal personages. Napoleon was deeply touched, and the letters which Talleyrand addressed to him at this period, couched in terms almost of adoration, provide interesting evidence as to the amount of flattery which a great man will gladly swallow. For we may be certain that such a feast would not have been provided if the donor had not felt confident that it would be thankfully received.

3

In June of 1800 the victory of Marengo further tightened and strengthened the hold of Napoleon upon France. There is a story, for which little solid evidence can be produced, that while Napoleon was absent upon this campaign Talleyrand entered into a plot with Fouché, Sieyès, and others, for effecting a coup d'état if he met with defeat, and either re-establishing the Directory or setting up the Duke of Orleans as king. That Talleyrand and Fouché were at this time working together is improbable, but we need have little doubt that they both had some plan in readiness for the situation which would have arisen had Bonaparte's prestige been destroyed by defeat, or had he shared the fate of Desaix, the true victor of Marengo, who perished in the hour of victory.

The battle of Marengo was followed by negotiations for peace with Austria in which Talleyrand played the principal part, and which he brought to a successful conclusion in the following year. The Treaty of Lunéville was admittedly a great diplomatic success for France, greater even than was warranted by her martial triumphs. She gained the left bank of the Rhine and territories beyond it as her eastern

frontier. Belgium and Luxembourg were acknowledged to
be part of France. She was left in possession of Piedmont,
with the Cisalpine Republic and Liguria under her protection, and the King of Naples was compelled to maintain
a French garrison at Taranto.

Lately France had been opposed by nearly the whole of
Europe, now, with her dominions more widely extended
than at any period throughout her history, she saw all her
enemies, save only one, defeated. There is little wonder if
the heads of most Frenchmen were inflamed by success so
dazzling, but that of the Minister for Foreign Affairs
remained cool. To Ouvrard, the great financier, he observed:
'I am well aware what the First Consul ought to do in his
own interest and also in that of the peace of France and of
Europe. Two roads are open to him—the federal system which
leaves each ruler, after his defeat, still master in his own
territory on conditions favourable to the victor . . . but on
the other hand does he intend to unite and to incorporate?
If so he will enter on a course to which there is no end.'
We know which road Napoleon took and whither it
led him.

Among the less important conditions of the Treaty of
Lunéville was a clause which gave France the right to take
part in fixing the indemnities to be granted to the various
German princes whose territory had been forfeited. The
duty naturally fell to Talleyrand's department and proved
the source of enormous increase in his wealth as he did not
scruple to accept bribes and commissions from all who were
interested in the large sums of money that were at stake.

4

Meanwhile another treaty was in process of conclusion,
and one that affected Talleyrand in his private as well as in

his public capacity. Napoleon may not have believed in God, but he certainly believed in the desirability of religion, and, while his outlook was naturally Erastian, he was anxious from the first to restore normal relations with the Papacy. That his Minister for Foreign Affairs should be an excommunicated priest he regretted, and that he should be living in open sin with a notorious lady outraged his profound respect for convention. He was determined that his Court should be respectable, and when Thérèse Tallien appeared at the opera as Diana the Huntress in nothing but a tiger skin, he had it conveyed to her that mythological fancy dress was no longer fashionable. So that when he learnt that the wives of Ambassadors were reluctant to pay their respects to Madame Grand at the Ministry for Foreign Affairs he felt that the time had come for him to put an end to the scandal, and that the negotiations which were being conducted with the Vatican offered a suitable opportunity.

His first suggestion was that Talleyrand should resume the episcopal robes that he had doffed with so very little ceremony, or that he should exchange them for the more impressive apparel of a cardinal. But to this proposal Talleyrand replied with an uncompromising negative. He had never wanted to be a priest, he had been thankful to escape from the priesthood, he had never regretted that action, and he would not re-enter a profession for which he was honest enough to admit that he was utterly unfitted.

Thwarted in one direction Napoleon turned to another. If Talleyrand refused to be a cardinal he must at least dismiss his mistress, or if he refused to dismiss her he must make her his wife. To the objection that a married priest was impossible and a married bishop unthinkable he replied that the Court of Rome could do anything, and that, while they were negotiating a settlement upon which the fate of millions of the faithful depended, they could surely slip in a clause to make things comfortable for Madame Grand.

Even before Napoleon's intervention Talleyrand had independently been pressing the Vatican for permission to forgo his vows of celibacy, with the intention, it was rumoured, of marrying not Madame Grand but another lady to whom he was also attached at the time. The papal diplomatists were anxious to do everything in their power to placate him in order to secure the conclusion of the Concordat; some things, however, were beyond their power, and the Church's blessing on a bishop's marriage was one of them. In vain did Talleyrand ransack history for the production of precedents. A flaw was found by the experts of the Vatican in every case, even in that of Caesar Borgia, who was one of the reverend prelates cited by Talleyrand to support his argument. Permission was accorded for his secularisation but with regard to his marriage the Church was adamant.

It is therefore the more surprising that Talleyrand should, in this matter, have bowed to the authority of Napoleon or surrendered to the blandishments of Madame Grand. A misalliance is more shocking to a Frenchman than to an Englishman, and Talleyrand was very French in his appreciation of the importance of family, and in his insistence upon outward correctness of behaviour. Madame Grand was not only of low origin, but the folly of her conversation in society was a perpetual reminder of it. She was no longer young, he had already been living with her for four years and had not always been faithful, and yet in September 1802 he settled a fortune on her, and they were publicly married both according to the civil law and in church. The proud descendant of one of the oldest families of France conferred his name upon one who, to the knowledge of all, had been little better than a woman of the town; and an ex-bishop

was joined in holy matrimony to a married woman who had
not even obtained a legal divorce from her first husband.

It is not surprising that his contemporaries, as much
astonished as we can be by Talleyrand's action, and at a loss
to find the cause of it, were driven to the surmise that
Madame Grand must be in possession of some secret of
which Talleyrand could not afford to risk the discovery.
That so astute a man, who was never outwitted by the best
brains of the age, should have allowed himself to be black-
mailed by a silly woman is more than improbable. Far
easier is it to suppose that, naturally indolent and easy
going, accustomed to the presence of his still beautiful and
good-natured mistress, contemptuous of religion and of
public opinion, he found it difficult to resist pressure brought
to bear upon him from more than one quarter, and consented for the sake of peace and quietness to go through a
ceremony that had for him no significance.

5

One of the first diplomatic documents for which Talleyrand was responsible after his return to the Ministry for
Foreign Affairs in 1799 was a note to England conveying
the desire of the First Consul for the termination of hostilities between the two countries. The British Government
returned a haughty and foolish reply to the effect that the
best guarantee that France could give of her desire for peace
was the immediate recall of her legitimate monarch. For
the Ministers of George III to preach the doctrine of
legitimacy while the legitimate grandson of James II still
lived an exile in Rome, was to lay themselves open to the
charge of insincerity or of remarkably short memories. It
is such actions that have caused Englishmen to be suspected
by foreigners of cant and hypocrisy. Talleyrand was not

slow to remind the English Cabinet of the true nature of
their master's claim to the throne.

So the war dragged on, and, after the conclusion of peace
with Austria, Napoleon was about to concentrate all his
forces upon the destruction of England when two events
occurred which caused him to change his mind.

The most favourable feature of the situation, so far as
the struggle with England was concerned, was the recent
conclusion of an agreement between Russia, Prussia, and the
Scandinavian Powers which under the guise of armed
neutrality effectually closed the ports of northern Europe
to British shipping and practically rendered the states in
question the allies of Napoleon. But the unstable policy of
Russia depended upon the whims of a mad autocrat who
had been led by judicious flattery into a kind of hero worship
for the First Consul. On the night of 22nd March 1801 a
palace revolution put an end to the Czar Paul and to his
policy. Alexander, his successor, had, at present, no admiration for Napoleon, and was determined to improve his
relations with England. A few days later Nelson defeated
the Danish fleet at Copenhagen, and the English were once
more masters of the Baltic.

Napoleon was therefore compelled to revise his projects
and the altered conditions of Europe lent weight to Talleyrand's advocacy of the negotiation of peace with England.
There also an important event had taken place in the month
of March, namely the resignation of Pitt after nearly twenty
years of office. But while the Czar Paul still lived, while
Pitt was still Prime Minister, and before Nelson had sailed
for the North, Talleyrand had taken the first step towards
peace by despatching, in January, the faithful Montrond to
England. It was possible in those days, while a war was
proceeding, for an envoy of one belligerent to be hospitably
receiveid in the capital of another, and 'le beau Montrond,'

who spoke English well, was always a popular figure in London society—'Who the devil is this Montrond?' asked the Duke of York. 'They say,' somebody replied, 'that he is the most agreeable scoundrel and the greatest roué in France.' 'Really,' said the Duke, 'then we must immediately ask him to dinner.'

Montrond had no doubt kept Talleyrand well informed of every development in English politics, and he was aware that Addington, the new Prime Minister, and Hawkesbury, the new Foreign Secretary, would prove very much easier to deal with than Mr. Pitt. In fact the principal difficulty that Talleyrand and his diplomatic representatives encountered in concluding a satisfactory treaty for France came rather from the intransigence of Napoleon than from any obstinacy on the part of the English Government. The latter indeed were willing to relinquish nearly all the conquests of the last ten years. The Cape of Good Hope, Demerara, and Surinam went back to the Dutch; Spain recovered Minorca; Martinique and Guadeloupe were returned to France; and Malta was to be restored to the Order of St. John of Jerusalem. Ceylon and Trinidad were all that remained and, if it had not been for the insistence of Talleyrand, Napoleon would have allowed negotiations to break down rather than allow the English to retain possession of the island of Trinidad.

The preliminaries of peace were signed in London in October 1801 and both in London and Paris the news was received with acclamation. The salvos of cannon that conveyed the announcement to the people of Paris were the first intimation which Talleyrand received that the preliminaries had been signed, for the couriers had gone direct to the First Consul, who had not troubled to send a personal message to his Minister for Foreign Affairs. Talleyrand was annoyed, and had his revenge a few months later when

the final treaty was concluded at Amiens. On this occasion
he was the first to be informed and appeared before
Napoleon one morning with the customary bundle of papers
that contained the business of the day. It was only after
all the routine work had been disposed of that he finally
produced one remaining document and nonchalantly observed: 'Here is something that will please you. It is the
Treaty of Amiens, which has been signed.' 'Why didn't
you tell me at once?' demanded Napoleon in astonishment.
'Because I knew that if I did,' calmly replied Talleyrand,
'you would not have attended to any other business this
morning.'

6

Among the many English people who availed themselves
of the Peace of Amiens to pay a long-desired visit to Paris
came Charles Fox, bringing with him the lady he had
recently married. Resembling Talleyrand in his love of
pleasure and passion for gambling, he had also acted like
him in marrying his mistress, and indeed the career of Bet
Armistead had been even less conventional and more
unblushingly professional than that of Catherine Worlée.
So much was this the case that Lady Bessborough, who was
also in Paris at the time, was surprised that Madame de
Talleyrand should consent to receive Mrs. Fox and to pay
her, as was said, great attention.

Lady Bessborough herself was careful whom she visited,
although care for the conventions was not the distinguishing
mark of her career. 'I will not visit Madame Cabarrus,' she
writes to Granville Leveson Gower, referring to Madame
Tallien, 'though I hope to *see* her to-morrow. Your natural
sense of justice makes you place Madame Talleyrand in the
same line, but power and marriage make so great a difference
here that not visiting the latter would be reckoned a ridicule.'

In another letter she describes a dinner-party at the Ministry for Foreign Affairs. 'I never saw anything so magnificent—the apartments beautiful, all perfumed with frankincense (*cela sent l'Evêque*) and as soon as seventy-eight people (of which the company consisted) sat down, an immense glass at the end of the room slid away by degrees, and soft and beautiful music began to play in the midst of the jingle of glasses and vaisselle. The dinner was, I believe, excellent but from some awkwardness in the arrangement it was very difficult to get anything to eat. Madame Talleyrand is like the Duchess of Cumberland and perfectly justifies the reason he gave for marrying her: "*Qu'elle emporte le prix de la bêtise.*"'

To Lady Bessborough, most charming of correspondents, we owe also an account of a conversation between Fox and Talleyrand. She was an intimate friend of Fox and he no doubt repeated it to her soon after it had taken place. Talleyrand 'asked him if he approved of the peace. Mr. Fox said he liked peace better than war, but that he could not conceive a worse than what we had made. Talleyrand told him it was lucky for France that England gave way, for that Bonaparte had declared repeatedly that he must have given up the chief points in dispute had they been persisted in. . . . This is a secret and moreover very possibly not true as Talleyrand is, I believe, a great flourisher.'

Fox and Lady Bessborough were Whigs and would not have approved of any treaty concluded by Addington's Government, but the Peace of Amiens certainly was a very good one for France and a very bad one for England. Lord Cornwallis who signed it on behalf of the latter country was the same who, twenty-one years earlier, had been compelled to capitulate to the Americans at Yorktown. A man of ability and high character, he seemed destined to do his country harm and he was even less capable of negotiating

with Talleyrand than he had been of fighting against
Washington. In return for all that England gave up she
received no commercial advantages, her merchants continued
to be treated in France as alien enemies, nor had she any
guarantee that Napoleon would set a limit to his ambitious
schemes on the continent of Europe. Talleyrand, preferring
always permanent peace to temporary triumph, said that he
would rather have made a treaty far more favourable to
England if it had but borne the signature of Pitt or Fox
instead of that of Addington. He was right. Neither the
Treaty of Amiens nor the premiership of Addington was
destined to last for many months.

Nevertheless, as a Frenchman and a faithful Minister of
the First Consul, Talleyrand had every reason to be proud of
his work. In the short space of two years France had been
raised from humiliation to supremacy. Victory abroad had
produced peace, clemency at home had silenced discord.
If Napoleon had at this moment been capable of moderating
his thirst for dominion the history of the world would have
been altered. Talleyrand knew it and strove in vain to
influence his master. Napoleon was bent upon incorporating Piedmont in France, Talleyrand was anxious to restore
it to its legitimate ruler. He went so far as to warn the
British Ambassador of Napoleon's projects and the famous
scene at which Napoleon insulted Lord Whitworth before
the whole diplomatic corps was partly due, as he himself
admitted, to the irritation that he was feeling as the result
of Talleyrand's representations.

There is no reason to doubt Talleyrand's own assertions
with regard to the line that he adopted at this time. His
conviction as to the desirability of peace, and above all of
peace between France and England, never altered. He was
not afraid of Napoleon, his personality was not dominated
as were those of the other Ministers, he had a clear vision

of the policy that would be best for France, he saw plainly
whither Napoleon's ambition was driving him, and all
contemporary evidence agrees that his influence was exerted
against the resumption of war.

He failed, and it is easy to say that having failed he should
have resigned his office. But it would indeed have shown
an attachment to principle amounting to pedantry volun-
tarily to have quitted Napoleon's service in that splendid,
and still unclouded, dawn of his achievement. No useful
purpose would have been served by resignation. Less com-
petent hands and a more subservient brain would have been
set to grapple with the task, and the young autocrat would
have been deprived of the ablest councillor that he possessed, and the one best qualified to act as a brake upon his
headlong progress. In May 1803, fourteen months after
the signature of the Treaty of Amiens, war between England
and France broke out again.

In the summer of this year Napoleon undertook a tour
of northern France and Belgium. Talleyrand with whom, at
this period, he was in continual consultation accompanied
him, and it was during this journey that he laid the basis of a
lasting friendship with Madame de Rémusat. Although
Bonaparte bore still no higher title than that of First Consul
and although there was no place in the Constitution for his
wife, already he was beginning to put on all the trappings of
royalty and was glad to find in Madame de Rémusat a
member of the aristocracy who was content to act as lady-
in-waiting to Josephine.

Madame de Rémusat, like Madame de la Tour du Pin,
was a good woman who, starting with prejudices against
Talleyrand, found it impossible to resist his charm. 'The
elegance of his manners was such a contrast with the
rough ways of the soldiers by whom I was surrounded. He
maintained always amidst them the unmistakable appear-

ance of a *grand seigneur*. The contempt of his silence was impressive. . . . More artificial than anybody, he was able to build up a natural character out of a thousand affectations. He retained them in every situation as though they had become his real nature. His way of always treating serious subjects frivolously was of great assistance to him. . . .

'One of the first things that struck me when I talked with him a little was his complete lack of any illusion or of any enthusiasm regarding what was taking place around us.' All others, both the soldiers and the politicians, even her husband, who had accepted a post at Court, were duly impressed by the great events that every day produced, and she herself was deeply moved by them. 'The calm and the indifference of M. de Talleyrand disconcerted me. "Good heavens," I dared to say to him one day, "how can you bear to live and to act without receiving any emotion from what is happening, nor from your actions?" "Ah, how young you are, and how much a woman" (*Ah que vous êtes jeune et que vous êtes femme*), he replied, and then he began to make fun of me as of everything else. His raillery hurt me but made me smile and I was angry with myself for being amused by his jokes and for allowing my vanity at being able to appreciate his wit to lessen my dislike for the coldness of his heart. Indeed, I did not yet know him, and it was only later, when I lost that feeling of shyness which overcomes every one who meets him for the first time, that I was able to observe the curious mixture of which his character is composed.'

7

The gradual assumption of supreme power by the First Consul during the five years of the Consulate did not pass entirely without protest on the part of people who still believed in some of the principles of the Revolution. Benjamin Constant was one of those who had thought that under the new regime parliamentary privileges would be tolerated and that freedom of speech would be permitted in the Senate, the Tribunate, and the Legislature. He was soon undeceived. On the evening after the first declamation in which he had dared to make open allusion to the autocratic tendencies of Bonaparte, it so happened that his faithful friend, Madame de Staël, was giving a dinner-party with the object, no doubt, of collecting congratulations upon Benjamin Constant's eloquence. Unfortunately, however, it so happened that all her guests, and Talleyrand, who owed so much to her, among them, were prevented at the last moment from accepting the invitation. The age of oratory was over.

Republicanism thus driven underground is lost sight of, and it is difficult to say whether it remained as formidable as Napoleon affected to think it. Fouché, as Minister of Police, dealt with the Jacobins rather as professional rat destroyers are said to deal with their quarry, sacrificing a certain number from time to time in order to satisfy their clients, but leaving a sufficient stock to render their further services necessary. Fouché knew the Jacobins and did not fear them. When popular clamour or the First Consul's suspicions demanded a victim Fouché would select one, or several, of whom for some private reason he did not approve. When a serious attempt was made upon Bonaparte's life by the explosion of an infernal machine, Fouché knew that the plot had been hatched and carried out by Royalists but public outcry led by Bonaparte himself denounced the Jacobins and, since Fouché's own position was in danger and he could not for the moment lay his hands upon the real criminals, he drew up a list of a hundred and thirty Jacobins, who were sentenced to deportation. Talleyrand and the other enemies of Fouché made the most of the incident to secure his downfall, accusing him of complicity with his former allies, but their case was considerably weakened when he succeeded in producing the actual culprits, who proved, as he had asserted, to be Royalists.

He was less successful in the following year in clearing himself of suspicion of being involved in a more formidable but less developed conspiracy of which the background was the army and the figure-head no less a person than Bernadotte. Talleyrand had the satisfaction of persuading Napoleon to abolish the post of Minister of Police, but Fouché's disgrace was only partial and he remained on friendly terms with Napoleon, who appreciated the value of his knowledge, experience, and advice.

The successful suppression of both the pretended and the real conspiracy freed Napoleon from further anxiety with regard to the activities both of Jacobins and of moderate Republicans. Only then was he gradually and against his will compelled to realise that the danger which threatened him lay in another quarter. His tenure of the First Consulate had been extended for ten years and then for life; the stream of former emigrants returning to France continued to flow, and few were too proud to take service under the new master whose household took on daily a greater resemblance to a royal court. Two incidents, however, occurred about this time which opened his eyes to the insecurity of his position. Emboldened by the facility with which he appeared to be achieving all his objects, and with the foundation of his dynasty already in sight, he caused the suggestion to be officially conveyed to the Bourbons that, in return for a very substantial settlement of their proprietary claims in France, they should renounce their rights to the throne. The reply of Louis XVIII was firm, dignified, and must have made Napoleon feel that he had been foolish to make the proposal and need never repeat it.

At the beginning of the year 1804 the most formidable conspiracy which had yet threatened the Government and the life of Napoleon was discovered. Moreau, the victor of Hohenlinden, was involved; Pichegru, the conqueror of Holland, was deeply implicated; Georges Cadoudal, the Breton peasant, who was the very soul of the Royalist party, was the moving spirit.

Napoleon's eyes were opened. He realised at last that however glad the old nobility might be to return to their native country, however willingly they might do lip service to the risen star, he could never be, either for them or for the peasants of La Vendée, the natural and legitimate ruler of France; that between himself and the Bourbons there was a gulf fixed which diplomacy could never bridge; and that some terrible event, which should startle Europe, was required in order to paralyse conspiracy and stifle disaffection.

8

The execution of the Duke of Enghien is the blackest deed in the career of Napoleon. It was a political crime of the first order which it is impossible to defend. Nor can Talleyrand be acquitted of some share in the guilt; but whether, as alleged by his enemies, he was the principal criminal, must remain doubtful.

The Duke was not only the least blameworthy but the most admirable of the Bourbon princes. He alone, while prepared to fight for the rights of his family, had refused to have any dealings with the conspirators who sought to attain their ends by plots and assassination. Young, handsome, and chivalrous he resembled more a hero of romance than a prince of the nineteenth century. At the time of his arrest he was neither scheming against Napoleon nor giving a thought to politics but was living quietly at Ettenheim in the state of Baden, and paying court to a lady to whom he was passionately devoted. He was the son of the Duke of Bourbon, grandson of the Prince of Condé, and so heir to the most illustrious name in France.

On 10th March 1804 Napoleon held a council at which Talleyrand was present, where it was determined to send a small armed force into the territory of Baden for the purpose of kidnapping the Duke. During the night of 14th March this decision was carried out and on the afternoon of 20th March he arrived at the castle of Vincennes where two hours earlier his grave had been dug. After a short examination which cannot be called a trial, he was condemned, and was shot in the disused moat of the castle at half-past two the following morning. He behaved with the greatest courage and dignity throughout.

Chateaubriand claims, in his memoirs, to have seen a letter from Talleyrand to Napoleon, dated 8th March, suggesting and recommending the arrest of the Duke. Independent and strongly corroboratory evidence as to the existence of this same document is given by Méneval, Napoleon's private secretary, through whose hands it must have passed. He states that the letter referred to a conversation which had taken place between the writer and the First Consul the day before, that the gist of it was to urge that action should be taken against all the conspirators, however highly placed, and that the safety of the State demanded it because the people, while content with the existing Government, were still uncertain whether Bonaparte did not intend to play the rôle of Monk and recall the Bourbons to the throne. The letter went on to suggest the name of the officer to whom the arrest of the Duke should be entrusted.

In the year 1814, after the downfall of Napoleon and before the arrival of Louis xviii, Talleyrand had the opportunity, of which he availed himself, to destroy such documents in the archives of the Ministry for Foreign Affairs as might subsequently prove compromising. Both Chateaubriand and Méneval allege that by an oversight the letter in question escaped destruction. Yet we have no evidence save theirs that it ever existed or that it was ever seen by other eyes. They were both bitter enemies of Talleyrand.

At the time Napoleon accepted full and sole responsibility for the deed. He could not have done otherwise. A dictator cannot blame others for what is done in his name unless he punishes them. Nor can he admit to error. In after years, however, he frequently stated in private conversation that Talleyrand was the originator of the idea. Josephine, according to Hortense, had heard him say so, and Roederer gives evidence to the same effect. At St. Helena he repeated it, and on one occasion he reproached Talleyrand with it, in public, to his face. Napoleon, of course, could repeat the same thing many times without its being true, but there is a curious similarity in all the evidence. On each occasion Napoleon is represented as saying that he did not even know who the Duke of Enghien was, nor where he was living, until Talleyrand brought him the information.

On the morning after the execution Talleyrand was working at the Ministry with the Count d'Hauterive, head of the southern department and a devoted adherent of his chief. Like everybody else in Paris he was shocked and horrified at the news, and made so little effort to conceal his emotion that at last Talleyrand was obliged to comment on it. 'What's the matter with you?' he asked testily, 'with your eyes starting out of your head?' 'The matter with me?' replied Hauterive, 'Why you would feel the same if you had read the *Moniteur*. What a horrible event!' 'Come, come,' said Talleyrand, very calmly, 'are you mad? What

is there to make such a fuss about? A conspirator is captured near the frontier, he is brought to Paris and shot.
What is there so extraordinary about that?' This anecdote
bears the hall mark of truth. We can almost see the scene
and hear the tones of the shocked official and the irritated
Minister. The fact that the official was shocked was the
cause of the Minister's irritation for he realised that the
Government had committed a blunder, which in his eyes
was worse than a crime, that where they had meant to strike
terror they had roused horror, and that the voice of Hauterive
that morning was the voice of France.

9

Long afterwards, when Louis xviii had been for nine
years on the throne, Savary, who had been created by
Napoleon Duke of Rovigo, and who had been present at
the condemnation of the Duke, standing behind the judge,
found himself attacked in the press for the part that he had
played. His defence was to claim that he had merely acted
as a soldier obeying orders, and that the real guilt was to be
attributed to Talleyrand.

Although Talleyrand was in the country at the time he
immediately hastened to Paris indignantly to deny the
charge, and he addressed a lengthy letter to the King
demanding a full investigation by the House of Peers. This
was refused, but the King made it plain that he accepted
Talleyrand's statement of innocence and the Duke of
Rovigo was forbidden the Court.

In his memoirs Talleyrand asserts that his part in the
affair was limited to his presence at the council where the
decision was taken, and to his signature of the necessary
documents emanating from his department. These included
two despatched to the French representative in the state of

Baden explaining and excusing the violation of territory, and a letter of instructions to the officer who was charged with the arrest. He does not claim to have opposed the proposal when it was brought before the council. The only member who ventured to do so, curiously enough, was Cambacérès who was supposed to represent the revolutionary interest in the Consulate.

Talleyrand further defends himself on the ground that such an action was entirely out of keeping with his character and his record. This is true, for he was neither cruel nor violent. He also demands what interest he could have had in tendering such advice. While it is easy to suggest motives, such as a desire to strengthen his position with Napoleon by making him an accomplice in crime, it must at the same time be admitted that it was never his policy to close any avenue of retreat and that, as we have seen, he had constantly in mind the possibility of his own reconciliation with the Bourbons, which the proof of his responsibility for the execution must have endangered or rendered impossible.

The lack of sufficient motive is indeed the strongest argument in favour of suspending judgment, although it is impossible at this distance of time to unravel the tangled web of policy at the bottom of such an intricate and so profound a mind. That he did not protest against the crime, carried out his instructions in connection with it, and subsequently defended it, is proved. Neither the Duke of Baden nor the Emperor of Austria dared offer a protest, and when Alexander of Russia demanded an explanation Talleyrand politely and pointedly replied that, so far as he was aware, nobody had been punished for the murder of the late Czar Paul, but that the French Government had not felt it their duty to intervene in the matter.

There is a story, repeated by Balzac who was a child at the time, that on the night of the tragedy Talleyrand was playing hazard at the house of the Duchess of Luynes. In the early hours of the morning he looked at his watch, and gravely inquired whether the Duke of Bourbon had any other son beside the Duke of Enghien. The other guests replied that, as he was well aware, the Duke was an only son. 'Then,' observed Talleyrand, 'the house of Condé is no more.' Three days later he gave a large ball at the Ministry for Foreign Affairs.

Chapter Six

THE EMPIRE

THE execution of the Duke of Enghien was the last scene
in the brilliant drama of the Consular period, which had
started so hopefully, prospered so wonderfully, and was thus
brought to a conclusion in tragedy and crime. Two months
later Napoleon became Emperor of the French Republic,
for with a remarkable lack of French logic the latter name
was for the time retained, and Talleyrand became Grand
Chamberlain of the imperial Court.

So far he had served his master loyally and at the same
time he had served France. The reconciliation of the old
order with the new had been his principal object so far as
the interior was concerned; in foreign affairs he had not
only striven consistently for peace, but, well knowing upon
what conditions the hope of permanent peace depended, he
had endeavoured to moderate Napoleon's ambitions. He
had sought, in his own words, 'to establish monarchical institutions in France which should guarantee the authority
of the sovereign, to keep her within her just boundaries,
and so to handle the Powers of Europe as to make them forgive France her good fortune and her glory.' But this task
was gradually rendered impossible by the ever-expanding
ambitions of his master. Talleyrand said with truth that
the most difficult person with whom Napoleon's Foreign
Minister had to negotiate was Napoleon himself. And the
time was fast approaching when the interests of France and

those of Napoleon not only ceased to be identical but became diametrically opposed.

In vain had Talleyrand used every effort to prevent the renewal of war with England, in vain did he now attempt to restrain Napoleon from actions which were bound to provide England with the allies that she lacked. He had advocated, as will be remembered, the return of Piedmont to her legitimate sovereign, instead of which she had been incorporated with France. Venice had been sacrificed to Austria, and the remainder of northern Italy had been turned into a republic with Napoleon himself as President. Having transformed the First Consul into an Emperor it was not his intention to turn the President into a King. Talleyrand knew that there could be no peace in Europe so long as the same head wore the crowns of Italy and France. Despairing of persuading Napoleon to allow anyone save a relative to occupy the former throne, Talleyrand pressed forward the claim first of Joseph and then of Lucien, the most intelligent of Napoleon's brothers and the one who obtained least reward. But Joseph did not want to be king of Italy and Lucien had married beneath him, so in the following year the new Emperor of the French placed upon his own head the iron crown of the Lombard kings. Talleyrand was present at the ceremony in the cathedral of Milan and was accompanied throughout the tour by that same Madame Simons with whom he had dined on the night of 19 Brumaire.

It could not be expected that Europe would calmly contemplate this continued extension of Napoleon's power. Already the Emperor of Russia, who had not forgiven the execution of the Duke of Enghien, nor forgotten the reply to his protest, had formed an alliance with England; and now Austria, who saw French influence reaching to the borders of Venetia, was added to the coalition. Hopes of peace seemed slight but Talleyrand still struggled for it. In January of this year he had made overtures to England but had received the reply that England must first consult the other continental Powers, especially the Emperor of Russia. Meanwhile Napoleon was waiting at Boulogne for the favourable breeze that never blew. To him at the beginning of September Talleyrand brought the news that Austria had delivered an ultimatum. The Prussian Minister in Paris reported to his Government: 'Monsieur de Talleyrand is in despair; if he had been able, or if he still were able either to prevent the outbreak of war or promptly to arrest its course before victory or defeat had excited ambition or compelled honour to go on with it, he would consider such an action the most glorious event in his tenure of office.'

What Talleyrand dreaded Napoleon welcomed. He was tired and his army was tired of gazing in idle impotence at the white cliffs of England. War with Austria suited his plans perfectly, so turning his back upon the Channel he marched resolutely eastward across Europe.

2

When the Commander-in-Chief is also the Emperor and the Prime Minister he must be accompanied on his campaigns by the greater part of his Cabinet. Talleyrand who loved idleness and comfort found himself compelled to trail behind his master in the wake of the victorious forces. He hated the life and complained of it bitterly. He was a cripple, and to some extent an invalid. A young Scotsman, who was visiting Paris after the Peace of Amiens, described 'M. Talleyrand, the Minister of the Interior' as resembling 'nothing so much as a dead man. His feet are distorted in a shocking manner and I think he deserves well of his country for having by unremitting perseverance learned to walk upon them.'

Writing to a friend from Brunn, where he found himself compelled to spend some weeks, he says: 'This is a horrible place—there are four thousand wounded here at present. There are a great many deaths every day. The smell yesterday was detestable. To-day it is freezing, which is a good thing. Please be sure to send me some very dry Malaga wine—the least sweet possible.'

Yet it was not the luxury-loving Minister but the iron-willed soldier whose health gave the greater cause for alarm during this campaign. On 1st October 1805 an incident took place at Strassburg which Talleyrand has recounted in his memoirs as follows: 'I had dined with the Emperor and on leaving the table he had gone alone to see the Empress Josephine. A few minutes later he came back hurriedly to the salon and taking me by the arm led me into his room. M. de Rémusat . . . came in at the same time. We were hardly there before the Emperor fell to the ground; he had only time to tell me to shut the door. I tore off his cravat because he appeared to be stifling; he was not sick, but groaned and foamed at the mouth. M. de Rémusat gave him water and I poured eau-de-Cologne over him. He had a kind of convulsions which lasted a quarter of an hour; we put him in an arm-chair; he began to speak, dressed himself again, and swore us to secrecy. Half an hour later he was on the road to Carlsruhe.'

The campaign was a series of triumphs which began with the capitulation at Ulm of the Austrian, General Mack, who, completely out-manœuvred, surrendered with his entire army. No sooner did the news reach Talleyrand, who had remained at Strassburg, than he hastened to draw up a memorandum on the policy that France should follow as the result of this important event. He was quick to appreciate the danger that the short-sighted and ambitious soldiers, encouraged by this bloodless victory, would demand that it should be followed up by a vigorous offensive, which would either lose what had been gained or else would reduce Austria to such a plight that she must be compelled to accept temporarily whatever terms were dictated and to prepare patiently for revenge.

It is the moment of victory that tests a statesman, and the situation of Talleyrand at Strassburg after Ulm was curiously similar to that of Bismarck at Nikolsburg after Sadowa. On each occasion Austria had been defeated, on each occasion the royal Commander-in-Chief was being urged on by his own ambition and by the voices of all his staff and of every soldier in the field to further triumphs, on each occasion the solitary, mistrusted voice of the Minister for Foreign Affairs, who alone could see in the defeated foe of to-day the potential ally of to-morrow, was raised in passionate pleading for moderation. Bismarck succeeded where Talleyrand failed, but we know from Bismarck's own memoirs how near he came to failure and how the unexpected assistance of his old enemy, the Crown Prince, who came to his aid at a moment when he was contemplating suicide, turned the scales in his favour. Talleyrand did not take life or politics so seriously as Bismarck, but he saw the future as plainly, and once more he sought to dissuade Napoleon from the course that led to immediate triumph and ultimate destruction.

In this important memorandum of 17th October his main thesis is that Austria must be the future ally of France. In order that their friendship may be secure it is desirable that their territories should not be contiguous. Northern Italy is the danger zone. Let Austria renounce her interest and possessions in that part of Europe, and, in order that she may cast no longing, lingering look behind, set up between her and them the ancient republic of Venice, restored to independence, which will serve as a substantial barrier. But, because it is impossible to convert a vanquished and humiliated foe into a firm and faithful ally, Austria must be compensated in the east for all she forfeits in the west. Moldavia, Wallachia, Bessarabia, and part of Bulgaria will increase rather than diminish the power and prestige of the Habsburg Empire, which in the future will stand with its back towards Europe and its face to the East, thus acting as a bulwark to protect western civilisation from the aggression of Russia. The latter, faced by so powerful an antagonist on her western frontiers, and knowing that behind that antagonist there stands her still more formidable ally, will also be driven to look eastward for expansion, where she will find herself hampered by the oriental possessions and ambitions of Great Britain. So Russia and Great Britain, the two most dangerous enemies of France, would be set to grapple with one another in Asia, and Europe would be left in peace.

Napoleon was impressed by so lucid, far-sighted, and statesmanlike an exposition of policy, and summoned a special council at Munich to consider the adoption of Talleyrand's memorandum. But events were moving too quickly and the tide of success was carrying him too rapidly along. The desire to march a victor into Vienna and to dictate his orders from the palace of the Habsburgs was too strong for him, and all counsels of moderation were thrown to the winds. The capitulation of Ulm was followed by the victory of Austerlitz, and the Emperor of Russia joined the Emperor of Austria, both fugitives before the irresistible armies of France.

Such an astounding and unprecedented series of successes was enough to turn the strongest of heads, and all France participated for a period in the intoxication of her triumphant Emperor. But Talleyrand remained a cool spectator. Three days after Austerlitz he wrote once more to the Emperor using the same language, pressing the same policy that he had used and advocated after Ulm six weeks before. 'The Austrian monarchy is a combination of ill-assorted states, differing from one another in language, manners, religion, and constitution, and having only one thing in common—the identity of their ruler. Such a power is necessarily weak, but she is an adequate bulwark against the barbarians—and a necessary one. To-day, crushed and humiliated, she needs that her conqueror should extend a generous hand to her and should, by making her an ally, restore to her that confidence in herself, of which so many defeats and disasters might deprive her for ever. I implore Your Majesty to read again the memorandum which I had the honour to submit to you from Strassburg. To-day more than ever I dare to consider it as the best and wisest policy.'

Few men would have had the courage to recommend such a course at such a moment; none could have persuaded Napoleon to adopt it. Once again the stern moralist will have it that Talleyrand should have resigned his office rather than assist in carrying out a policy of which he did not approve. But Talleyrand was not guided by stern morals and had little respect for those who were. He knew what was politically right and had not hesitated to risk disfavour by urging it upon the Emperor with all the power at his command. His advice was disregarded, and with a shrug he resigned himself to obeying his instructions. At the same time he knew to what disaster those instructions would ultimately lead, and he had to prepare for his own salvation as well as for that of his country in the day when what he foresaw should come to pass.

By the Peace of Pressburg, which Talleyrand negotiated

with Austria in accordance with Napoleon's wishes, the Emperor Francis lost nearly three million subjects and one-sixth of his revenue, and agreed to pay an indemnity of forty million francs. Even so Napoleon was not content and accused Talleyrand of having concluded a treaty too favourable to Austria. From this moment we may take it that Talleyrand finally abandoned hope of ever inducing Napoleon to pursue a reasonable policy, conducive to the welfare of France and the peace of Europe.

Talleyrand's reward for the services that he had rendered was the principality of Benevento, a small enclave in the kingdom of Naples, which had hitherto been a papal state. He was therefore known as Prince of Benevento during the remainder of Napoleon's reign. The revenue which he drew from this source was inconsiderable in comparison with the fortune he had already accumulated. He never visited his new subjects, but by means of a deputy he ruled them wisely and for their own benefit. He lightened their burden of taxation and protected them from conscription into Napoleon's armies.

3

The year 1806 which opened with the Peace of Pressburg and the death of Pitt was crowded with events. In March Murat was promoted to the Grand Duchy of Berg and Joseph Bonaparte to the Kingdom of Naples. In June his brother Louis became King of Holland, and the same summer witnessed the end of the Holy Roman Empire, which had lasted for a thousand years. It was partially replaced by the Confederation of the Rhine. Two new kings were set up in Germany, the Kings of Saxony and of Wurtemberg, and there were endless rectifications of frontier and redistributions of territory. Talleyrand played a leading part in the complicated negotiations which were rendered necessary, and once more took full advantage of his public duties to increase his private fortune.

In the Ministry of All the Talents which had succeeded that of Pitt, the Foreign Office had passed into the hands of Fox who, having consistently denounced the war for the last thirteen years, felt himself called upon to suggest some method of ending it. The discovery in England of a plot to assassinate Napoleon provided him with a suitable opportunity of manifesting his good intentions and he forwarded to Talleyrand full details of the conspiracy.

In the official English note which conveyed this information Napoleon was referred to as the 'chef des Français,' a curious designation which was not likely to produce a good impression on the Emperor. Fox therefore sent at the same time a private letter to Talleyrand explaining that no offence was meant by the phrase, which was rendered necessary by the relations then existing between the two Courts, the British Government not having yet recognised the new Empire. In the same letter, which was as friendly as it was informal, he asked to be remembered by Talleyrand as an individual and sent his regards to Marshal Berthier.

If ever there was a real opportunity for making peace between England and Napoleon it had now occurred. Not only were Talleyrand and Fox equally sincere in their desire for it, but they were two men of outstanding political ability who were personally acquainted, and who understood one another.

Among the Englishmen who had been detained in France as prisoners at the renewal of the war, was Lord Yarmouth, whose portrait in later age has been drawn for us by the pen of Thackeray as the Marquess of Steyne and by that of Disraeli as the Marquess of Monmouth. He was an able man, more devoted to pleasure than to business, and an intimate friend of Montrond with whom he had much in

common, including, it was alleged, Lady Yarmouth, a
fact which did not interfere with their friendship.

Lord Yarmouth was selected by Talleyrand as a suitable
intermediary between himself and Fox. The British Government, however, gave Lord Yarmouth a colleague in the
person of Lord Lauderdale, whom Talleyrand in his
memoirs blames for the failure of the negotiations. But it
was not, in truth, the fault of Lauderdale or of any subordinate that the peace which was so eagerly desired by
both nations was not concluded. Napoleon had passed the
period when he was prepared to make a reasonable peace
with any country. He was attempting to dictate separate
treaties to Russia and Prussia as well as to England, and he
was seeking to conciliate Prussia with the promise of
Hanover which at the same time he undertook to restore
to England. Yarmouth indeed 'with all the arrogance of
an English aristocrat,' says the French historian Sorel,
refused to undertake the negotiation unless all the King's
German possessions were guaranteed, as he said that he
himself would vote against any cession of them in the House
of Lords. When Talleyrand satisfied him on this point he
asked about Sicily where the Bourbon King, who had been
driven from Naples, still ruled under the protection of the
British fleet. 'You have got it and we shan't ask you for it,'
was Talleyrand's reply which encouraged Yarmouth to proceed with the mission but which did not in fact represent
the intention of Napoleon.

Yarmouth soon showed that he was not so easy to deal
with as Talleyrand had hoped. He was a hard drinker, a
high gambler, devoted to women, and with no previous
experience of diplomacy save such as may be acquired in
the pursuit of the wives and mistresses of others, but, to
quote Sorel again, he soon began to give evidence of those
qualities of a 'sly and obstinate bulldog which are revealed

in all Englishmen as soon as the interests of England are at stake.' Montrond was set to spy upon him, but, unfortunately for Montrond, Yarmouth had the stronger head of the two and would drink the Frenchman under the table, acquiring the while a great deal more information than he gave.

Fox soon learnt, what many leaders of opposition have learnt since, that it is easier to criticise the actions of Ministers than to improve upon them. He began also to understand that Napoleon was not the lover of peace and liberty that some of the Whigs had believed him to be. Fox himself was prepared as a last resource to give way on the question of Sicily. 'It is not Sicily,' he exclaimed in despair, 'but the shuffling, insincere way in which they act that shows me they are playing a false game.' In September of the same year Fox died, and with him perished the last hope of peace between England and Napoleon.

4

Meanwhile the weak and vacillating diplomacy of Prussia was preparing the way for her downfall. Yarmouth did not omit to inform the Prussian representative that Napoleon had been willing to hand over Hanover to England; and the execution of Palm, a harmless bookseller, for the crime of having sold a pamphlet deploring the condition of Germany, had inflamed public opinion against France. Napoleon demanded nothing better. In vain Talleyrand once more attempted to prevent the war which was declared in September, and in the following month he found himself on the road again, behind the army that was marching on Berlin.

We possess a picture of him as he appeared during this autumn to the Queen Hortense. In the memoirs that she wrote many years afterwards she says: 'It was during this journey that I came to know Monsieur de Talleyrand better. I had often wondered how people could judge of his intelligence and say he was so witty when he offered so little proof of it. I had seen him for years limping into the salon at Malmaison, with his cold and nonchalant air, leaning on the nearest chair and hardly bowing. He had seldom spoken to me. At Mainz on the other hand he sought me out and was polite. I was surprised and even flattered, for the attentions of a man who pays so few have always more effect, and I am sure that his great reputation for cleverness is due more to his saying so little and saying it so well than to anything remarkable that he does. . . . The charm of his wit makes up for his lack of strength of soul and character. . . . His great attraction is largely due to the vanity of others. I was caught by it myself. The day that he deigns to speak to you he seems charming, and if he inquires after your health you are prepared to love him.'

Hortense had certainly little reason to be fond of Talleyrand for he was no friend to her family, and she records that an old negress who in the West Indies years before had prophesied her mother's wonderful fortune had particularly warned her against a priest. The fact that he was the father of the Count de Flahaut, the one man whom Hortense did love, does not appear to have prejudiced her in his favour.

While Talleyrand and Hortense were making friends at Mainz the military power of Prussia, about which there had hung for nearly half a century the prestige conferred upon it by Frederick the Great, was being crushed to atoms on the fields of Jena and Auerstadt. Presently Talleyrand had to join his master in Berlin. His arrival there, such was his reputation, was awaited with a last glimmering of hope

by the statesmen of the defeated nation. Haugwitz wrote
to the former Prussian representative in Paris: 'Provided
that Monsieur de Talleyrand arrives, I do not despair of
your being able to arouse some sounder political ideas than
this terrible principle of the destruction of Prussia as a
guarantee for the future peace of France. That enlightened
Minister will easily understand that when Prussia is rendered powerless to restrain Russia or to threaten Austria . . .
those two Powers will be in a stronger position to disturb
the peace of France.'

Talleyrand arrived in Berlin at the end of October, but
he could no longer exercise the slightest influence over
Napoleon. The events which he was now compelled to
witness, and even to assist in as an unwilling agent,
finally convinced him that the time had come for him to
quit the office of Minister for Foreign Affairs. In the first
place Napoleon's treatment of Prussia was as impolitic as it
was merciless. His fatal error, both as statesman and as
diplomatist, was that he never determined upon his ultimate
objective before entering upon a war, but allowed his projected terms of peace to vary with every change in the
fortunes of the campaign. In November the King accepted
the proposals which had been made to him at the end of
October, but as matters had gone worse for Prussia during
the interval Napoleon increased his demands. Finally
Frederick William was compelled to submit to the loss of
half his territory and the reduction of his population to a
little over five million. The beautiful and spirited Queen
Louisa was persuaded to follow Napoleon to Tilsit in order
to endeavour by charm and pathos to soften the heart of the
conqueror and obtain more favourable conditions for her
unfortunate country.

Her efforts were in vain, but while they lasted she was
able to perceive who was her only friend among those who

surrounded the Emperor, and to express her gratitude. Talleyrand thus recounts the incident:

'I was indignant at all that I saw and heard, but I was obliged to hide my indignation. Therefore I shall all my life be grateful to the Queen of Prussia—a Queen of another age—for having appreciated it. If when I look back upon my life much that I find there is necessarily painful, I can at least remember as a great consolation what she was then good enough to say and almost to confide to me. "Monsieur the Prince of Benevento," she said, the last time that I had the honour to conduct her to her carriage, "there are only two people here who are sorry that I came—you and I. You are not angry, are you, that I should go away with this belief?" Tears of emotion and pride that came into my eyes were my answer.'

Talleyrand knew, what Napoleon persisted in ignoring, that a nation crushed and humiliated as Prussia had been, could never form a reliable pillar in the framework of a reconstructed Europe. She might be compelled, as she was by the terms dictated to her, to declare war upon England, but the sympathies of her whole population must in future remain with the enemies of France, and as soon as the opportunity arose those sympathies would be translated into action.

Fortified by the support of such doubtful allies Napoleon proceeded to intensify the bitterness of the war with England. From Berlin he launched the decrees which declared the British Isles to be in a state of blockade, and prohibited all commerce or correspondence with them. Talleyrand was compelled in his official position to sign the document that explained and defended this policy, but he could not approve of it.

Finally, it was at Berlin that Napoleon confided to Talleyrand his determination to destroy the Bourbon dynasty in

Spain. 'I then swore to myself,' writes Talleyrand in his memoirs, 'that I would cease to be his Minister as soon as we returned to France.'

5

Many months, however, still separated Talleyrand from his home in the Rue d'Anjou. From Berlin he was obliged to travel in great discomfort over broken roads to Warsaw, where Napoleon was spending the early days of the year 1807. Here Talleyrand's time was divided between tendering his master such tactful assistance as he required in the early stages of his liaison with the Countess Walewska, and submitting to him memoranda dealing with the thorny question of the future of Poland.

As a young man Talleyrand had deplored the series of treaties which had brought about the partitioning of that country amongst the greater Powers. He now welcomed the opportunity that seemed to present itself of reversing that policy. He believed that a strong and independent Poland would contribute towards the stability of peace in Europe, his one and constant aim. He often said to Madame de Rémusat that the solution of the problem lay in Poland. As Austria should form the southern, so, in his opinion, should Poland form the northern barrier against Russian aggression.

If Napoleon had been willing to listen to his advice with regard to this question he would have had reason to be grateful to him in the days to come. As it was Napoleon, who never had in his mind any picture of Europe save as of one vast estate with himself as master and the various territories farmed out to his subordinate allies and relatives, had from first to last no Polish policy at all. The Poles were prepared to welcome him as a liberator and because he liked to be welcomed and had grown up in the period when it was fashionable to speak loudly about liberty, he gave them considerable if vague encouragement. The Emperor of Russia, whose intimate friend in youth had been Adam Czartoryski, a Polish prince, had also once dreamt of restoring the independence of Poland. That dream was already growing dim, but he was determined that if he could not restore Polish independence himself nobody else should be allowed to do so.

Napoleon played with the idea now, and continued to play with it until the end. Had he abandoned it completely he might have secured the permanent friendship of Alexander; if he had adhered to it firmly and insisted upon the creation of a free Polish state under an independent monarch he would have forfeited the possibility of an alliance with Russia, but he would have secured as an ally not a prince but a whole people, whose support would have proved as valuable as the enmity of the people of Spain was to prove disastrous.

This latter was the policy which Talleyrand urged now and again at Vienna in 1815 and once more from London in 1830. It was the policy which Europe eventually was forced to work out for herself after many wars and more than a century of travail. It was characteristic of Talleyrand that he saw no harm in accepting large sums of money from the Polish nobility for advocating this policy in which he believed, and it is equally characteristic and more important to remember that having failed to secure the adoption of the policy he felt obliged to return to those who had paid it him the money that he had received.

By the agreements concluded between Napoleon and Alexander at Tilsit, on a raft on the River Niemen, some of the Polish provinces were formed into the Grand Duchy of Warsaw under the sovereignty of the King of Saxony. But far more important were the arrangements entered into for the furtherance of the continental war against England.

The terms of the treaty were conveyed with singular rapidity to the British Foreign Office and Canning, realising the danger that faced Great Britain with nearly the whole continent of Europe allied against her, and the possibility of the fleets of the northern nations falling into the hands of France, took the high-handed measure of sending a squadron into the Baltic which bombarded Copenhagen and captured the whole of the Danish fleet.

There has been much speculation as to the source from which this valuable information reached the British Government and it has been alleged that Talleyrand was the traitor. The theory rests upon one statement contained in some doubtful memoirs attributed to Fouché, and the fact that when this statement was brought to the notice of Canning he is reported to have smiled and said nothing.

Talleyrand had nothing to gain from so gross an act of treachery commensurate with the danger involved in sending the information. Any message sent by him from Russia ran the risk of discovery en route and it was not his manner to adopt such crude and uncompromising tactics. The solution of the mystery appears to have perished with Canning, but the most probable explanation is that some member of the Emperor Alexander's staff was responsible, for both at this time and throughout the Franco-Russian alliance a considerable majority of the Russian aristocracy were strongly pro-English.

It is one of the gravest defects of autocracy as a system of government that it allows no room for legitimate opposition. The individual who sincerely believes that his country is suffering, and will continue to suffer as the result of bad policy, has to choose between becoming either a passive spectator of his country's ruin or taking steps to prevent it which his enemies will denounce as disloyalty. When open opposition is rebellion, secret opposition becomes treason; yet there are circumstances in which such treason may become the duty of a patriot.

From the year 1807 Talleyrand did all in his power to thwart Napoleon's ambitions and to hasten his downfall. It is the turning-point in the history of the Empire. He was convinced that for the good of France and for the good of Europe the power of Napoleon had to be destroyed. Therefore he is not to be blamed because he sought to attain that end, but because, while so seeking, he continued to receive benefits from the man whom he was scheming to destroy. The only grounds upon which such conduct can be defended are, in the first place, that if he had shown less duplicity he would have destroyed his own position and lost the power to achieve his purpose; and secondly, that he did, in fact, show so little duplicity that his hostile manœuvres became common knowledge in which the Emperor himself shared.

6

At the beginning of the year 1808 Napoleon had reached the summit of his triumphant career. The continent of Europe lay at his feet, the Emperors of Austria and Russia were his humble allies, three of his brothers sat upon thrones and it seemed that no limit was set to his power of achievement, save only the continued resistance of England. Yet already he had determined upon and had taken the first step towards that policy which was to prove his undoing.

On the return from Tilsit Talleyrand was relieved of the Ministry for Foreign Affairs and promoted to the office of Vice-Grand Elector. He asserts that this change was in accordance with his own wishes, and Napoleon's statement at St. Helena to the effect that he was dismissed as the result of complaints concerning his rapacious demands on the

Kings of Bavaria and Wurtemberg need hardly be taken seriously, for his new position was both superior and better paid than his old one and carried with it equal opportunities of increasing his income by doubtful methods. He continued to play an important part in the direction of foreign affairs, but was relieved of the routine of office. His position was the third highest in the land. Outside the royal family only the Arch Chancellor, who was Cambacérès, the former Second Consul, and the Arch Treasurer, who was Lebrun, the former Third Consul, took precedence of him. It would therefore be absurd to suppose that he had been elevated to so lofty a position as a reproof for rapacity.

It may, however, be true, as some people at the time believed, that Napoleon was displeased at the great importance which he found was attached to Talleyrand's opinion and advice in all the capitals of Europe that he had recently visited. As he grew more self-confident and more autocratic he resented the presence of a Minister with views of his own, and hated it to be thought that he was dependent on the assistance of any individual. The new arrangement perfectly suited Napoleon, whereby he secured a docile Minister—Champagny was the man selected—while the services of Talleyrand remained available when required. It also suited Talleyrand to be more highly rewarded for less work, and he hoped that Champagny, with whom he was on the best of terms, would become as faithful an instrument of his own as Reinhard had proved in the last days of the Directory. Here he was mistaken, for Champagny became a faithful and docile servant of Napoleon.

7

In October 1807 there was concluded at Fontainebleau a secret convention between France and Spain, the ostensible object of which was the partition of Portugal. The excuse for it was the refusal of the Portuguese Government to enforce the blockade of Great Britain, but Napoleon's real intention was to secure the peaceful occupation of Spain by French troops with a view to establishing French domination over the whole peninsula. In this way the French army was enabled to enter Spain and to march from Bayonne to Lisbon without encountering any opposition save what was offered by the climate and the natural conditions of the country which, indeed, proved formidable enough. At their approach the Regent of Portugal sailed with his Government and his fleet to Brazil, much to the annoyance of Napoleon. The troops, together with considerable reinforcements, proceeded peacefully to take possession of the most important strategic positions in Spain.

Gradually that futile couple, King Charles IV of Spain and Queen Maria Luisa—whose futility still postures before us in the canvasses of Goya—realised that their country was in the hands of their treacherous ally and turned to Godoy, the man whom they both loved and who was the principal cause of their misfortunes, for advice. He suggested that they should follow the example of their neighbour of Portugal and fly the country. On the way to the coast they were met by a revolution. The infuriated populace, believing that their country had been sold by Godoy, demanded his head and were only appeased by the abdication of the King in favour of his son, Ferdinand, and by the promise that the favourite should be brought to trial.

The King revoked his abdication as soon as he thought that it was safe to do so, and thus created a confused situation which admirably suited Napoleon's plans. He announced his intention of visiting Madrid and promised Ferdinand the hand of some Bonaparte princess. Meanwhile he continued to negotiate with the King and Queen and arranged for them, together with Godoy, to meet him at Bayonne, with a view to settling all their differences. To persuade Ferdinand also to cross the frontier proved only slightly more difficult, although the Spanish people, more perspicacious than their Prince, sought in vain to detain him and actually removed the horses from his carriage.

On his arrival at Bayonne Ferdinand was informed that he must immediately abdicate, and when he refused to do so he was threatened with a trial for high treason. He agreed, in terror, to sign a document restoring the throne to his father and subsequently learnt that his father had already made over all his rights to Napoleon. The miserable old couple were allowed to depart first to Compiègne and then to Italy, where they spent the remainder of their days in universal contempt, but Ferdinand, together with his younger brother and his uncle, was sent to gilded captivity at Talleyrand's château of Valençay.

Such is briefly the story of Napoleon's conduct towards the ruling House of Spain, which led him into the Peninsular War. It seemed at first sight the least serious military operation that he had undertaken, but it was to prove the most disastrous. He thought that he could win a kingdom by tricking a king, and he did not realise that he had to fight against an united nation.

8

Talleyrand always asserted that he had been strongly opposed to the Spanish policy from the beginning, and that Napoleon acted throughout either without consulting him or refusing to take his advice when given. Napoleon, on the other hand, frequently stated that Talleyrand supported the policy when it was first adopted, and only denounced it later when the difficulties became apparent.

As is often the case when the choice lies between two directly contradictory statements the whole truth will probably be found to rest with neither, but to consist of a judicious combination of both.

In support of Talleyrand's assertion it may be argued in the first place that the Treaty of Fontainebleau did not bear his signature. Yet he was present with the Court at Fontainebleau when it was negotiated and signed, and his official position gave him the privilege of affixing his signature to treaties. If it were true, as Napoleon told Caulaincourt five years later, that Talleyrand actually negotiated this treaty, he would naturally have signed it, for what object could there be in obtaining the signature of a third party to an extremely secret document and omitting that of the person who was better acquainted with its contents?

Further, it is an established fact that Talleyrand had consistently opposed the policy of the firm hand in Portugal, which had led to the proposed partition. He realised that it must mean ruin for Portugal to enforce the blockade against England, and he had done his utmost to save Portugal from the consequences of the Emperor's wrath at her failure to do so. Izquierdo, the agent of Godoy, who had been plotting in France for the last year and to whose efforts the Treaty of Fontainebleau was mainly due, had never been on good terms with Talleyrand. Duroc was his friend and it was with him that he negotiated. Lima, on the other hand, the representative of Portugal, relied entirely on Talleyrand's support, and regarded his withdrawal from the Ministry for Foreign Affairs as a national disaster for Portugal. When congratulating Champagny, the new Minister, he said frankly: 'I should betray my conscience and my duty if I told Your Excellency that the retirement of H.S.H. the Prince of Benevento left me without regret.'

At the time of the Treaty of Fontainebleau, for which Talleyrand must be held guiltless, Napoleon could not have foreseen the course of events that was to bring him to Bayonne. It was never his way to look far ahead but rather to turn every circumstance to his advantage and to allow nothing but the adversity of fortune to limit the scope of his ambition. That Talleyrand should have advocated the policy of setting up a Bonapartist monarchy in Spain is almost unthinkable. It was in direct contradiction to all the advice that he had given Napoleon from the earliest days. He had always been in favour of limiting rather than extending France's liabilities. Why should he who had urged moderation after Ulm, after Austerlitz, and after Jena suddenly have become the supporter of the wildest and the most fatal of all Napoleon's schemes of expansion?

The theory that he did support this policy depends upon the testimony of Pasquier, Méneval, and Chateaubriand, who were all his enemies, and whose evidence is not supported by a single document. Chateaubriand says that Talleyrand destroyed the relevant papers in 1814, but it seems hardly probable that he would have had the effrontery to denounce, as he did denounce, the whole Spanish policy a few months after its adoption if at the time the documentary proof existed that he himself had been the instigator.

The facts afford a stronger argument still for lending credence to his oft reiterated statement that he was not responsible. If he had really been behind the policy it is at least surprising that he should not have accompanied Napoleon to Bayonne. Here were negotiations of extreme delicacy to be conducted; here it was necessary to induce a king and his eldest son to sign away their claims on the kingdom which they had inherited, and of which the inhabitants were devotedly loyal to their family. In return for this sacrifice they were to receive nothing but exile and captivity, although they had been the most faithful of Napoleon's allies, and their subjects had fought for him by land and sea. Here indeed was a task that should test the skill of the ablest diplomatist of the age. If that very diplomatist was also the moving spirit in the policy which was here being brought to its culmination surely his would have been the hand employed to complete the work it had begun?

He admits that he was consulted on the plan, but insists that he strongly opposed it, and the memoirs of Madame de Rémusat who saw him continually during that winter at Fontainebleau entirely bear out the truth of his statement. Those, on the other hand, who refuse to accept it, can point to a letter which he addressed to Napoleon afterwards warmly congratulating him upon the success of the action that was taken at Bayonne. Here, however, it should be remembered that in the days of an autocracy every states-man must be a courtier too, just as under a democracy every statesman must be something of a demagogue. The letter which the Vice-Grand Elector addressed to the Emperor upon this occasion was the letter of a courtier and it is perfectly legitimate for the courtier to offer his con-gratulations upon the apparent success of a measure which he had strongly deprecated as a statesman.

Again, if Talleyrand had been at Napoleon's elbow throughout the transaction the latter would hardly have rewarded him when it was so satisfactorily concluded by imposing on him the duty of acting as gaoler to the Spanish Princes. The office is never a grateful one, and there can be little doubt that Napoleon, as was generally believed at the time, selected Valençay as their prison in order that Talleyrand might be fully inculpated in the violence that was being offered to them.

For six years the Princes remained there, living in the

greatest luxury, no expense nor effort being spared to render their captivity as pleasant as possible. Hunting and the offices of religion filled their days, music and dancing occupied their evenings. Nor were the allurements of flirtation absent. The Duke of San Carlos, one of their principal attendants, fell a victim to the full blown and ample charms of Madame de Talleyrand, and was perhaps the last successor of the long-forgotten Mr. Grand of Tranquebar.

Napoleon, having learnt of the liaison and wishing to wound Talleyrand, said one day to him brutally before a crowd of courtiers: 'Why didn't you tell me that the Duke of San Carlos was your wife's lover?' Talleyrand replied coolly that he had thought the less said about that matter the better for the Emperor's honour as well as for his own.

Talleyrand admits in his memoirs that he suggested to Napoleon, as an alternative to the Bayonne policy, the occupation by French troops of Catalonia during the remainder of the war with England. The suggestion was in reply to Napoleon's argument that his Pyrenean frontier was in danger, and that at any moment when he was at war on the Rhine or in Italy he was open to a dangerous attack by Spain in the rear.

To some people the forcible seizure of a Spanish province will seem little better from the moral point of view than the forcible seizure of the Spanish Princes. But Talleyrand was a man of the world, and he knew which crimes the world will condone and which it can never forgive. He told Napoleon that he had lost more than he had gained by this policy, and when he was bidden to explain himself he did so by an analogy:

'If a gentleman commits follies,' he said, 'if he keeps mistresses, if he treats his wife badly, even if he is guilty of serious injustices towards his friends, he will be blamed, no doubt, but if he is rich, powerful, and intelligent, society will still treat him with indulgence. But if that man cheats at cards he will be immediately banished from decent society and never forgiven.'

So began the rupture between Talleyrand and Napoleon that was never healed. Napoleon was incapable of appreciating the difference between the coup d'état of Brumaire and the coup d'état of Bayonne, and could not forgive Talleyrand who had assisted him in the one for deserting him in the other. Talleyrand, on the other hand, was aware that while it might prove possible to prop up the façade of the Empire for several years, the fate of the Emperor was sealed. At Bayonne Napoleon had committed the unforgivable crime. He had cheated at cards.

Chapter Seven

TREASON

'ERFURT! Never has any name produced such an impression
on me as that of this outlandish place. I cannot think of it
without fear and hope: the fate of Europe and the world,
the future of political power and perhaps of European
civilisation depends on it.' So Talleyrand wrote on the eve
of the second meeting between Napoleon and Alexander.

At Tilsit much had been left unsettled. It had been
understood that the two Emperors should meet again, and
during the fourteen months that had elapsed negotiations
had been proceeding with regard to the time and place of
their meeting. The scene at Tilsit had been dramatic. The
sudden alteration from bitter enmity to warm friendship,
the raft on the river, the weeping Queen of Prussia, the two
young Emperors deciding the fate of the world. Erfurt in
comparison was a cold-blooded business. Both Emperors
had had time to reflect and to recover from the powerful
fascination which at their first meeting they had exercised
over one another.

The event of the year had been Napoleon's intervention
in Spain which had had for him the doubly disastrous effect
of proving to Europe that while his ambition was insatiable
his power was not invincible. It united kings and peoples
against him. No dynasty could feel secure after the manner
in which the Spanish Bourbons had been treated; no nation
could despair of liberty when they saw how the Spanish

people were refusing to accept an alien domination. The
Russians seriously feared that Napoleon meant to treat
Alexander at Erfurt as he had treated the Bourbons at
Bayonne, and the Dowager Empress besought her son with
tears not to walk into the trap.

Although Talleyrand was no longer Minister for Foreign
Affairs, Napoleon decided that his assistance would be useful at Erfurt. He foresaw the diplomatic difficulties that
would arise and realised the necessity of having somebody
at hand who would be capable of negotiating with the Czar.
Before Talleyrand set out he was shown, by Napoleon's
instructions, all the despatches which had passed between
Paris and the French Ambassador at St. Petersburg, in
order that he might be thoroughly acquainted with the
situation.

Napoleon's main object, now as ever, was the destruction
of Great Britain. To accomplish this purpose he had first
to make the blockade a reality, which could only be done
when Spain and Portugal had been reduced to submission.
But Napoleon feared that while he was thus engaged in the
Peninsula Austria might seize the opportunity to recover
her losses. Too late the wisdom of the advice given by
Talleyrand after Ulm and after Austerlitz was apparent.
Instead of a contented country, anxious to keep the peace
and concerned with the safety of her eastern frontier,
Napoleon had created an enemy, who had suffered too much
ever to forgive, and who, he knew, was only awaiting the
moment when he should find himself in difficulties in order
to sweep to her revenge.

For this reason he was anxious to obtain from Alexander
at Erfurt an assurance that if Austria decided to give trouble,
he could rely upon the armed force of Russia to come to his
assistance. Talleyrand was determined that that assurance
should never be given. He was a European as well as a

Frenchman and he was convinced that it was no more for the good of France than it was for the good of Europe that the whole continent should be subjected to the will of a single individual even though that individual might be the Emperor of the French. Born in the middle of the eighteenth century he was free from that narrow nationalist spirit which was beginning to grow up, and the idea of conquest made no appeal to his practical, peace-loving intelligence. He was intimately acquainted with the map of Europe which he wished to preserve and not to destroy. Of that map the Austrian Empire formed an integral part. Its destruction would mean the substitution of chaos for order.

Further, he had as little desire to destroy England as to destroy Austria. His well-balanced brain, fortified by thirty years of political experience, appreciated the fact that just as the conservative influence of Austria was essential to the maintenance of the structure of Europe, so the liberalising, anti-autocratic spirit of England was necessary in order to maintain the mental equilibrium of the Continent, and prevent the violence of reaction, provoked by the violence of revolution, from going too far in the opposite direction. 'Get this into your head,' he once exclaimed to Madame de Rémusat, 'if the English Constitution is destroyed, the civilisation of the world will be shaken to its foundations.'

Doubtful as he already was of Talleyrand's loyalty it is the more surprising that Napoleon should have employed him at so critical a juncture. So much had success affected his brain that he no longer believed that any individual was capable of harming him. It was about this time that he said scornfully: 'I don't employ the Prince of Benevento when I want a thing done, but only when I want to have the appearance of wanting to do it.' He was to learn that even he could not make a compliant tool of Talleyrand. Metternich, who

was now Austrian Ambassador in Paris, knew better. 'Men
like M. de Talleyrand,' he wrote to his Government, 'are
like sharp-edged instruments with which it is dangerous to
play; but for great evils great remedies are necessary, and he
who has to treat them ought not to be afraid to use the
instrument that cuts the best.'

Napoleon was not so wise. Talleyrand, he thought, was
just the man he needed at the moment. He wanted to impress
the Germans by the splendour of his Court; he wanted as
many kings and princes as possible to be standing round the
steps of his throne. When it was suggested that Eugène de
Beauharnais, who was now the son-in-law of the King of
Bavaria, should be entrusted with the task of collecting the
ruling princes of Germany, he said: 'No, Eugène isn't
clever enough. He can do exactly as I tell him but he is
useless at insinuating. Talleyrand would do it better. What's
more,' he added, laughing, 'he'll tell them, as a sneer at me,
how much they will please me by coming, and then it will
be for me to show them that I didn't care the least whether
they came or not, and that their coming has been rather a
nuisance than otherwise.'

He proceeded to give Talleyrand his instructions,
which were, briefly, to conclude a treaty that would give
him a free hand to deal with Spain in the knowledge
that Russia would prevent any possible action on the part
of Austria. Otherwise he was to be committed to nothing.
There might be vague talk and vague promises about the
partition of Turkey, and Russia might be humoured in her
immediate desire to acquire the provinces of Wallachia and
Moldavia (the modern Roumania) and to have her acquisi-
tion recognised, but the main sense of the treaty should be
to unite the allies in their hostility to England.

Talleyrand prepared a draft treaty on the lines indicated
but studiously omitted all reference to Austria. 'But how

can you have forgotten that?' exclaimed Napoleon, after reading it. 'That is the essential article. Are you still pro-Austrian?' 'A little, Sire,' replied Talleyrand, 'but I think it would be more correct to say that I am never pro-Russian and always pro-French.'

In this humour and with the deliberate intention of thwarting the will of his master, Talleyrand set forth for Erfurt.

2

If a Court painter had been commissioned to produce a picture portraying the apotheosis of Napoleon's power he would probably have selected Erfurt as the background. Never before had so many ruling princes been gathered together in one town in order to do homage to one man. All the arrangements which had been carefully planned beforehand to enhance Napoleon's prestige worked admirably. The princes vied to surpass one another in adulation of their master and Talleyrand said of them afterwards that he had not seen at Erfurt a single hand that dared courageously to stroke the lion's mane.

Alexander arrived on 28th September. Napoleon went out to meet him on the road and then returned to his own apartments to await the Czar's ceremonious visit. Talleyrand was present at the interview, and afterwards accompanied the Czar to his carriage. Several times as they descended the staircase Alexander said to him: 'We will meet again,' and when later in the evening he returned to his own lodgings he found awaiting him a note from the Princess of Tour and Taxis informing him of her arrival. He called on her immediately and had not been in her room for a quarter of an hour before the Emperor of Russia was announced. The evening was a success. The Emperor, charming and informal, asked for a cup of tea, and before they separated suggested that the Princess should entertain them every evening in the same manner after the duties and the pleasures of the conference were over. It would give them, he said, an opportunity of talking comfortably and would make a good end to the day. Thus the drawing-room of the Princess of Tour and Taxis, who was a sister of the Queen of Prussia, became the regular rendezvous of a little group of people who, meeting there of an evening, regaled one another with conversation, with anecdotes and witticisms usually of an anti-French complexion, while the Emperor of Russia either made love to the Princess Stéphanie of Baden, a relative of Josephine, or else conferred with Talleyrand as to the best means by which he could defeat the aims of Napoleon.

At one of the earliest of these interviews Talleyrand used these words: 'Sire, it is in your power to save Europe, and you will only do so by refusing to give way to Napoleon. The French people are civilised, their sovereign is not. The sovereign of Russia is civilised and his people are not: the sovereign of Russia should therefore be the ally of the French people.' He went on to explain and develop this statement. He insisted that the French people had one dominant desire—to have done with war and to be allowed to enjoy the fruits of conquest. Unless the Czar, for there was nobody else in a position to do so, constituted himself the mediator between Napoleon and his people, they would continue to be dragged as victims in the wake of his triumphal chariot to their ultimate destruction. Very skilfully, with consummate art and with the greatest care he contrived that the same views should reach Alexander's ears from many different sources until eventually the Czar was convinced that they represented the opinion of 'all sensible people in France.'

An element of humour is lent to the situation by the

fact that, while Talleyrand was so successfully deceiving Napoleon, Napoleon was less successfully attempting to deceive him. Believing that his best chance of persuading Alexander to do what he wished lay in dealing with him direct and avoiding interference by either Russian or French advisers, Napoleon drafted with his own hand a treaty which from his own point of view was an improvement on that submitted to him by Talleyrand, and in handing it to Alexander impressed upon him the importance of keeping its terms secret and of not communicating them even to the Russian Minister for Foreign Affairs. A few hours later, in the Princess's drawing-room, which had been closed to all other visitors that evening, Alexander produced from his pocket the draft treaty and handed it to Talleyrand, who thus obtained from his master's rival the very information that that master had so carefully attempted to conceal from him. If he had ever had any qualms about the deceit that he was practising they must have been considerably modified by this revelation of the deceit that was being practised against him. A master who will not trust his own servants is the more likely to be deceived by them.

Henceforward it became the custom for Alexander to inform Talleyrand every evening of the course which negotiations had followed during the day. The proposals which Napoleon had put forward, the arguments with which Alexander had met them were all duly recounted and Talleyrand would then proceed to give his advice and furnish Alexander with fresh arguments for the morrow. The Emperor of Russia would occasionally strengthen his memory by making notes of the suggestions put forward, and came near to taking down his instructions at the dictation of the French diplomatist.

This was treachery, but it was treachery upon a magnificent scale. Of the two Emperors, upon whose words the fate

of Europe depended, Talleyrand had made one his dupe
and the other his informant. He was playing a great game
for a vast stake, and although he never lost sight of his
private interests his main objective was neither personal nor
petty. Had he thought only of his own welfare he would
have acted differently, for he was putting all in jeopardy,
his position, his wealth, perhaps his life by opposing the
will of one who had hitherto destroyed all opposition raised
against him. But Talleyrand did care for the preservation
of Europe, was quite clear in his own mind as to how that
object was to be achieved, and in order to achieve it he risked
everything. As it proved he had six years to wait for his
reward and he was no longer young. If we compare his
conduct towards Napoleon with that of the majority of his
supporters, including the Marshals, who all deserted him
when it was manifest to the world that he was a broken
man, and who for the most part owed everything to him,
we shall find it less easy to condemn the politician who
turned against him at the height of his power because he
could no longer approve of his policy.

Not only did Talleyrand himself feel no shame but he
was actually proud of the part he played on this occasion.
He describes it at length in his memoirs and used to boast
of it in after life. 'It was the last service that I was able to
render to Europe so long as Napoleon continued to reign,
and a service which, in my opinion, I rendered to him as
well.'

The latter part of this statement he would probably have
justified by arguing that if Napoleon had taken to heart
the lesson of Erfurt he would have appreciated the need for
moderating his policy. He had failed to obtain from Alexander the support that he sought against Austria and that he
knew was necessary for the safe prosecution of his designs on
Spain. Having failed he should have altered his policy,

instead of which he continued to act exactly as if he had succeeded.

Shortly before leaving Erfurt Napoleon opened his mind to Talleyrand upon a subject that had long been occupying it. It was late at night and Napoleon had already retired but seemed unwilling to allow Talleyrand to leave him. 'His agitation was remarkable; he asked me questions without waiting for the answer; he was trying to tell me something; he said what he didn't mean; at last he got out the great word—divorce.' He then explained the necessity he felt under of getting an heir and mentioned that Alexander had a sister of a suitable age. Talleyrand promised to speak to Alexander on the subject and despite the lateness of the hour he went straight off to the usual rendezvous at the house of the Princess where he found the Emperor, who had stayed that night later than usual. He arranged an audience for the following morning, and learnt at the same time to his great satisfaction that Alexander was going that same morning to write a reassuring letter to the Emperor of Austria.

Talleyrand did not like the idea of the Russian marriage. True to his Austrian proclivities he preferred a Habsburg bride, and he was therefore relieved when on the morrow Alexander explained that while he was not opposed to the match, his sisters were entirely under the control of their mother, whose consent it would be necessary to obtain. Talleyrand arranged that Alexander should raise the subject at his interview with Napoleon the same morning, and having suggested the words that he should use hurried back to Napoleon to prepare him for what was coming. Napoleon was so pleased that the suggestion should emanate from Alexander that he was quite willing that it should be left entirely vague.

Shortly afterwards the two Emperors separated, to all

outward appearances well pleased with themselves and with
one another, but it was Talleyrand whose will had triumphed
and who emerged the real victor from the diplomatic battle-
field of Erfurt.

3

When the two Emperors parted at Erfurt, the one getting into the carriage that was to convey him to Paris and
the other returning to the north, Talleyrand whispered to
Alexander what a pity it was that they could not both take
the wrong carriages. Henceforth Alexander had two representatives in Paris, his Ambassador, who was little but a
figurehead, knowing nothing of what was taking place
behind the scenes and providing by his ostentation of
wealth a continual source of amusement to the Parisians,
and Nesselrode, who was to play a considerable part in the
diplomatic history of the century, and who was now secretly
accredited to Talleyrand, and served as a channel for the
conveyance of information to St. Petersburg.

Alexander was naturally grateful to Talleyrand for the
assistance that he had rendered him at Erfurt, and Talleyrand saw to it that this gratitude should take a practical
form. As he was without legitimate children, the heir to
all that he had accumulated and the future head of his
family was his brother's son, Edmond, who had now attained the marriageable age of twenty-one. Talleyrand, in
whom the pride of family was strong, was determined that
this young gentleman should form a suitable alliance, if
only to make amends for the extremely unsuitable one that
he had formed himself. Difficulties stood in the way. So
far as birth was concerned there was no family in France
save royalty that could confer honour on the house of
Talleyrand, but the heiresses of great names who were not
in emigration were carefully superintended by the Emperor

and reserved as rich rewards for his own nobility, it being a part of his policy thus to graft the new aristocracy upon a remnant of the old. From his point of view nothing was to be gained, and something indeed was to be feared, from a union between two families that both had origins earlier than the Revolution. Having forfeited already a large portion of the Emperor's favour, and confidently expecting by his future conduct to forfeit more, Talleyrand had no reason to suppose that in this matter an exception would be made on his behalf. He had, on the contrary, good grounds for thinking that Napoleon would be glad to repay an old grudge by preventing any desirable match that might be suggested. In the year 1803, before the Bonapartes had put on the imperial purple, the First Consul had thought that a Mademoiselle de Talleyrand-Périgord would be a suitable bride for his son-in-law, Eugène de Beauharnais, and when the young lady in question was somewhat hastily affianced and married to a member of the Noailles family, it was rumoured that her uncle the Minister for Foreign Affairs had had something to say in the matter. When therefore in the year 1808 the Prince of Benevento was looking to marry his nephew, it appeared plain that he would be well advised to cast his eyes beyond the broad territories under the sway of the Emperor Napoleon.

The Duchess of Courland was the widow of the last reigning Duke of that province, which had subsequently become incorporated with Russia. Although not old herself she was the mother of four daughters, three of whom had already been given in marriage to bearers of the greatest names in Europe. The youngest, Dorothea, was fifteen years of age, and it was for her hand that Talleyrand approached the Emperor. Alexander had no objection— the Duchess of Courland, who, it was subsequently alleged, cherished the project of supplanting Josephine on the throne of France,

welcomed the match, and the young lady herself, who had
dreamed of becoming the bride of that romantic figure,
Prince Adam Czartoryski, banished the dream and with a
sigh accepted Count Edmond de Périgord, explaining to him
at the time that she did so solely in order to meet the wishes
of her mother, to which he replied with equal frankness that
he was actuated by no other motive than the desire to give
pleasure to his uncle.

4

During the late autumn months that followed the conferences of Erfurt, Talleyrand took little pains to conceal
from his countrymen the lines along which his mind was
moving. Having deliberately thwarted his master's plans
and being determined to go on doing so, a lesser man, seeing that that master was a despot, would have been careful
to dissemble his opinions and conceal his movements. But
Talleyrand did the opposite. He went out of his way to
make it plain to Paris that he disapproved of the policy that
the Emperor was pursuing, and he allowed it to be believed
that he was engaged in conspiring with the Emperor's
enemies for his overthrow.

He had been ordered by Napoleon, who had left for
Spain shortly after his return from Erfurt, to entertain on a
large scale in his absence, in order to give his supporters the
opportunity of meeting and to provide a means of keeping
in touch with their opinions. Talleyrand carried out these
instructions in the large new house that he had purchased
in the Rue de Varennes, but he allowed himself both at his
own banquets and also in the smaller, more intimate but
not more private salons that he frequented, to let drop those
biting epigrams and wounding sarcasms of which he was a
master and which always find their way to the ears where
they will be least welcome.

The most sensational event in this campaign of intrigue took place at a reception given in Talleyrand's house in the month of December. For years the rivalry and mutual dislike between Talleyrand and Fouché had been as fixed and as familiar a feature in the political firmament as the hostility between Bonapartes and Bourbons. When, therefore, the name of the Minister of Police was announced at a reception given by the Prince of Benevento the other guests could hardly believe their ears and turned to watch with curiosity the encounter of two such adversaries. The sensation seekers were not disappointed. The host limped eagerly forward to extend the warmest of welcomes to the new arrival, and linking arms with him proceeded to pace up and down through the series of lofty apartments engaged in long and eager conversation, while the rest of Paris gazed and pointed, whispered and wondered.

The next morning the news that this conversation had taken place was on its way to every capital in Europe. Not least swiftly did it travel to Valladolid whence Napoleon was now directing operations in the Peninsula. Had he remained there longer the fortunes of that war would have been changed, but he considered it of greater importance to return to Paris. It was said that he had received reports to the effect that the Austrian Government were taking steps to prepare for a renewal of hostilities, but Napoleon believed that an alliance between Talleyrand and Fouché was more formidable than the mobilisation of Austria.

5

The question arises, and is not easy to answer, why Talleyrand, who could control his tongue when he wished and might have met Fouché a dozen times without anyone being the wiser, should have ghne about speaking his

mind so freely, and should have made a public exhibition
of his latest friendship. He knew well that his words and
deeds would be reported and that Napoleon could put only
the worst interpretation upon them. The explanation can
only be that it was his policy at the time to form the nucleus
of an open opposition which should by its very publicity
be able to rally to itself all the discontented elements in the
country and which might thus become strong enough,
without overthrowing Napoleon, to exercise so powerful an
influence as to compel him to alter his policy in the direction in which all moderate men desired.

It is true that there was an embryonic plot on hand to
substitute Murat for Napoleon and that Talleyrand was
probably acquainted with it. But the fact that he was aware
of or even involved in a conspiracy never meant with him
that that was the only or even the main line that he was
pursuing at the time. The things that he said and the
actions that he took during this period were not those of a
man who is secretly conspiring for a coup d'état but rather
of one who is openly advocating a change of policy and
hoping to carry it by weight of opinion.

The shrewdest foreign observer in Paris during these
days was Metternich, the Austrian Ambassador. In September of this year (1808) he reported to his Government
as follows: 'It is necessary to be at Paris, and to be there for
some time, to be able to judge of the real position of M. de
Talleyrand. In M. de Talleyrand one cannot but separate
the moral man from the political man. He would not have
been, he could not be, what he is if he were moral. He is,
on the other hand, pre-eminently a politician, and, as a
politician, a man of systems. . . .

'Two parties exist in France as much opposed to one
another as the interests of Europe are to the individual
ideas of the Emperor. At the head of one of these parties

is the Emperor with all the military men. He only desires
to extend his influence by force. . . . Napoleon sees nothing
in France but himself, nothing in Europe or in the whole
world but his family. . . . The other party is composed of
the great mass of the nation, an inert and unpliable mass. . . .
At the head of this mass are the eminent persons of the State,
M. de Talleyrand, the Minister of Police, and all those who
have fortunes to preserve.'

Metternich never ceases to insist in his communications
with his Government on the existence of this powerful opposition. It was not confined to people of doubtful reputa-
tions but included such stalwart heroes of the Napoleonic
legend as Lannes and Berthier. Even Caulaincourt, the
loyalest of the loyal, shared Talleyrand's opinions and was,
for this reason, on the best of terms with him, although his
strict sense of honour would not allow him to do anything
to further his own views except to express them boldly to
his master. That indeed was the dilemma of those who
differed from Napoleon—they had either to continue carrying out a policy that they condemned or else to pursue the
devious ways and dubious methods of Talleyrand and Fouché.

In December Metternich reports: 'Two men in France
hold at this moment the first rank in opinion and influence—
M. de Talleyrand and M. Fouché. Formerly opposed in
views and interests, they have been drawn together by circumstances; I do not hesitate to say that at the present
time their object and their means of attaining it are the
same. . . . M. de Talleyrand has, since the campaign of
1805, opposed with all his influence the destructive plans of
Napoleon. . . . We positively owe to him some more or less
favourable aspects in the Pressburg negotiation; he also
opposed as long as he could the campaign against Prussia.'
He goes on to trace how Napoleon got rid of Talleyrand
on account of his independent views and how Talleyrand

and Fouché are now working for a general peace and not for the overthrow of Napoleon but for the consolidation of his position by a new marriage and the establishment of a dynasty.

How far Metternich was correct in his interpretation of their plans it is impossible to say. No man will ever know all that took place behind the masks of Talleyrand and Fouché. It is true that they were both, especially Fouché, zealous advocates of the divorce from the first, and it is true that they both had more to hope for from a reformed Napoleonic regime than from any experiment with the Bourbons. Caroline Murat, who was probably Metternich's mistress at this time, seems to have been his informant. He quotes her as being in the confidence of Talleyrand and Fouché. But she may not have told Metternich all that they said, and they certainly did not say to her all that they meant.

6

Returning post-haste from Spain, Napoleon reached the Tuileries on 23rd January. A few days later he called a special meeting of the privy council at which the Grand Dignitaries of the Empire, including Talleyrand, and one or two Ministers, including Fouché, were present. According to one account Fouché had previously been summoned to a private audience when he had been bitterly reproached for the part that he had played. In any case he was merely a spectator of the scene which now ensued.

Napoleon began with a few remarks of a general nature to the effect that his Grand Dignitaries and his Ministers had no right even to think for themselves, far less to give their thoughts expression. To doubt was for them the beginning of treason, to differ from him was the crime itself. With that he turned upon Talleyrand who, in a characteristically graceful and negligent attitude, was half leaning against a small table by the fire. For one solid half-hour, without interruption a steady flow of invective poured from the Emperor's lips. There was hardly a crime omitted from the indictment, hardly a word of abuse that was not applied. Talleyrand was called a thief, a coward, and a traitor. He was told that he had never worthily performed a single duty, that he had deceived everyone with whom he had ever dealt, that he did not believe in God, and would sell his own father. He was accused of responsibility for the execution of the Duke of Enghien and for the Peninsular War. Maddened by the impassivity of his victim, the Corsican lost all control and proceeded to taunt him with his lameness and to throw in his face the infidelity of his wife. Finally, shaking his fist and seeming to be upon the point of striking him he informed his Vice-Grand Elector in the language of the camp, that he was nothing but so much dung in a silk stocking.

The witnesses were horrified. The Emperor had behaved in a manner for which a non-commissioned officer addressing a recruit would have been reproved. Even Méneval, his private secretary and staunchest admirer, admits that he forgot his imperial dignity. All testimonies, however, agree that the one man in the room who seemed the least moved by the outburst was the object of the attack. Talleyrand never changed his attitude. No spark of colour appeared in his pale cheeks. No flicker of an eyelid betrayed the fact that he was conscious of being addressed.

The meeting broke up at the end of the tirade; the Emperor was unfit for further business. As Talleyrand limped slowly down the broad corridor he turned to one of those who had been watching his ordeal and said calmly: 'What a pity that such a great man should be so ill-bred!'

That evening he told the whole story to Madame de

Laval as he reclined on a sofa in her drawing-room. She was an old and a dear friend, by birth one of the last of the great family of Montmorency. Her dark eyes, for which she was celebrated, flashed with anger as she listened to the catalogue of the insults that had been heaped on him. 'You listened to that,' she exclaimed at last in indignation, 'and you didn't snatch up a chair, the tongs, the poker, or anything and fall upon him?' 'Ah,' replied Talleyrand, 'I did think of doing so, but I was too lazy.'

If Talleyrand had acted as his hot-blooded friend suggested he might have incurred serious penalties, and would in any case have been debarred from playing any further part in the history of the Empire, and from preparing that more complete and satisfactory revenge for which henceforward his heart must have longed. Witnesses of the scene and those to whom it was reported, naturally concluded that it could only mean the end of Talleyrand, so far as Napoleon was concerned. Talleyrand was determined that it should mean nothing of the kind.

The next day was Sunday, and it was Napoleon's custom on Sundays to hold a reception at which he liked as many Ministers as possible to be present. The Minister of Finance, the Duke of Gaeta, was busy that day and, wishing to waste as little time as possible at Court, went very early to the reception in order to obtain a good place from which he could slip early away. He reached the Palace before the attendants had illuminated the apartments. When they did so he was astonished to discover that he was not the first arrival, for as the candles threw their light over the room he was able to discern, standing by the fireplace, the impassive figure of the Vice-Grand Elector whom he had thought never to behold at Napoleon's Court again. Curiosity got the better of Gaudin's desire to finish his work and he waited after the Emperor had passed him in order to see what reception Talleyrand would obtain. Napoleon spoke to the men on the right and on the left of him, ignoring his presence.

On the following Sunday he was once more in his place. Again on this occasion it was his neighbour who was spoken to and of whom a question was asked. The neighbour hesitating for the answer Talleyrand immediately supplied it, giving the information that Napoleon had asked for as naturally as though they were on the best of terms. The ice was broken. If the Emperor had not spoken to him he had at least spoken to the Emperor and there was no reason why their relations in future should not be as normal as those between any master and servant after an angry scene. Napoleon probably regretted his loss of self-control and was probably grateful to Talleyrand for easing the situation. Possibly, also, he was blind enough to believe that such insults, so offered, could be forgotten or forgiven. He deprived Talleyrand of his position as Grand Chamberlain but he continued to hold the empty honour of Vice-Grand Elector.

Chapter Eight

THE BEGINNING OF THE END

I

Dᴜʀɪɴɢ the next five years Talleyrand remained at the Court of Napoleon in a position with which it is difficult to find any parallel. He was out of favour. He had forfeited for ever the confidence of the Emperor, who was continually during that period receiving fresh proofs of his treachery. Yet he continued to be Vice-Grand Elector and to fulfil the functions that that office imposed on him.

Napoleon, when questioned afterwards as to his reasons for not taking stronger measures to deal with Talleyrand before it was too late, replied that in the first place he underestimated his power to injure him, and in the second place he had still at this time some affection for the man. There was probably truth in both explanations. His secret service was extremely efficient, he employed agents within the circle of Talleyrand's intimate friends, and he therefore could feel confident that he was being kept informed of every step taken by his enemies, and so long as he continued to win victories he had little to fear from them. At the same time his overmastering consciousness of his own genius and his exaggerated estimate of his own superiority over all his contemporaries made it appear to him to be little less than *lèse-majesté* towards himself to think it possible that any of those whom he had employed were capable of doing him serious injury.

Napoleon always grudged praise of other men's abilities,

and on one occasion when he was discussing Talleyrand with Count Molé went so far as to say that his great reputation was more largely due to luck than to merit. 'I swear to you,' he added, 'that I could not truthfully say that he has ever been of much assistance to me . . . and I don't even think that he is, as you say, a very clever man. You have only to look at his life. He was by birth and position one of the principal personages of the nobility and the clergy, and he did everything in his power to contribute to their downfall. When he came back from America he completed his degradation by publicly attaching himself to a stupid old courtesan. I wanted, in spite of himself, to get him out of that mess at the time of the Concordat by asking the Pope to grant him a cardinal's hat and I nearly got it for him. Well, he wouldn't let me, and in spite of me and to the scandal of Europe he married his shameful mistress from whom he could not even hope to obtain children. He is certainly, as everybody knows, the man who has stolen more money than anyone in the world, and he hasn't got a penny. I am obliged to support him from my privy purse and to pay his debts even now.' 'At least,' said Molé, 'the Emperor will grant me that his conversation is full of elegance and charm.' 'Oh,' replied the Emperor, 'that is his triumph, and he knows it.'

To argue that a man is not clever because he makes a foolish marriage or a bad speculation is as unreasonable as it would be to maintain that he cannot have possessed great gifts who only succeeded after twenty years of endeavour in becoming the lonely exile of St. Helena. Yet in this way, and with this manner of reasoning Napoleon persuaded himself that Talleyrand was a man of second-rate ability from whom he had nothing to fear, and this conviction was strengthened by the firm belief that he could never make his peace with the Bourbons and therefore had nothing to gain from the establishment of a new regime.

It does also appear that Napoleon had a genuine liking for Talleyrand. As has already been said he was able when they first met during the Directory to fascinate the young soldier who had not before encountered anyone of equal charm and distinction. This fascination died slowly for Talleyrand was the type of man that Napoleon preferred, and Metternich, who belonged to the same school, was equally successful with him.

2

Early in 1809 war broke out again between France and Austria, and in April Napoleon left Paris for the scene of operations. Had Russia been prepared to render the assistance that he demanded Napoleon would have had nothing to fear from Austria, but Alexander, pursuing the policy that Talleyrand had instilled into him at Erfurt, performed the part of little more than an interested spectator, moving troops occasionally from one part of the frontier to another, but being careful not to strike a single effective blow on behalf of his ally.

Whenever Napoleon was away from Paris intrigue and conspiracy once more raised their heads with the indefatigable persistence with which trodden grass rises behind the feet that have passed over it. Fouché, as we have seen, had not shared in the disgrace of Talleyrand and the remainder of this year was to mark the zenith of his career under the Empire. Napoleon was more inclined to trust Fouché than Talleyrand for the good reason that he found it more difficult to believe that Fouché could ever make his peace with the Bourbons. Talleyrand had at least left France before the Terror whereas Fouché had been a remorseless agent of the Terror in the provinces, and had himself voted for the death of the King. For the Liberal and the Constitutional there might be forgiveness but surely the descendant of St.

Louis could never make peace with the Jacobin and the
regicide?

Napoleon carried his campaign to a successful conclusion
and once more dictated peace from the palace of the Habsburgs but there were two events which robbed his victory
of half its glory and which stirred up hope in the hearts of
thousands who were weary of his rule.

During the attack on the town of Ratisbon Napoleon was
wounded. The wound was slight but the effect was immense. In every corner of Europe men began to ask themselves: 'If he were wounded again, if he were killed—what
then?' A year before there had been a plot to assassinate the
Bourbon claimant, and when a courtier congratulating him
upon his escape expressed his horror at the thought of how
terrible the results would have been if the design had succeeded, Louis xviii replied calmly that nothing would have
been changed except that the King of France would have
been called Charles x. But Napoleon could not even pretend
to think that the result of his death would be merely to
change the name of the Emperor of the French to Joseph,
and a single incident, such as this of his receiving a wound,
served to show up the fragility of the whole imperial
structure.

More important, however, than any wound was the result
of the battle of Aspern where after two days of the hardest
fighting and the greatest slaughter the enemy were left
in possession of the field. Napoleon could send home mis-
leading bulletins, and it is true that the battle hardly affected
the result of the campaign, but swifter than the messengers
who carried his despatches word sped through Europe
that the great man was no more invincible than he was
immortal.

3

Meanwhile in Paris on the top of these disturbing rumours it was reported that the English were despatching an expeditionary force to the Low Countries. It seemed that the very frontiers of France were in danger while the Emperor with his army was at the other side of Europe, and it took a month for a message to be sent to him and the answer received. So utterly without initiative were the creatures with whom Napoleon had filled the highest offices of state that there was scarcely one amongst them, who, in these critical circumstances, was prepared to assume the slightest responsibility. To distract attention from their own impotence they attempted to minimise the danger; Fouché alone, who was now Acting Minister of the Interior as well as Minister of Police, both realised how serious was the situation and determined to meet it.

Fouché had begun life in the Church, and the ex-Oratorian could appreciate the power of religion at its proper value. Ever since Talleyrand had left the Ministry for Foreign Affairs relations between Napoleon and the Vatican had been growing more strained, and in the summer of this same year the Emperor, invoking the authority of Charlemagne, whom he described as 'our august predecessor,' annexed Rome to the Empire, and imprisoned the Pope with such humiliating circumstances as to make it necessary for His Holiness to rely upon his valet to serve him as a private secretary. The news of these events, together with the news of Napoleon's wound at Ratisbon and defeat at Aspern, was received by the devoutly Catholic population of Belgium almost simultaneously with the report that the English fleet was in the Channel with an army aboard, the largest that had ever left the shores of England, and that their immediate destination was the mouth of the Scheldt.

Fouché decided to take action. His colleagues, including the Minister of War, preferred to await instructions. Of the Grand Dignitaries Talleyrand alone supported him and the support of Talleyrand no longer gave confidence to the timorous that their action would meet with the approval of their master. Fouché, whose official position should have confined his attention to matters of police and internal administration, decided to mobilise the National Guard, not only without the approval, but in direct opposition to the wishes of the Minister of War. He sent out the necessary instructions to the provinces, he saw to it that those instructions were carried out and he rallied to the defence of the frontier an army of 60,000 men. At the head of this army that he had created Fouché proceeded, with an audacity that still further astonished his colleagues, to place Bernadotte, who was never from start to finish of his remarkable career a loyal servant of Napoleon, and who happened to be in France at this moment only because he had been sent home from the Austrian campaign in disgrace.

The results of Fouché's independent action appeared to be highly successful. The English expedition came to nothing, defeated, it is true, not by Fouché's new army but by the climate of the Isle of Walcheren and by the lack of co-operation between naval and military authorities. Stranger still, the Emperor, instead of chastising Fouché, rewarded him with the Duchy of Otranto and severely reprimanded those who had hesitated to support him. With the political blindness that was falling upon him Napoleon failed to realise that the most important lesson provided by the events of the year 1809 was that one man, and even such a man as Fouché, could, in his absence, take control of the Government of France and call a new army into existence.

4

In his memoirs Talleyrand excuses himself for not having taken advantage of the disfavour into which he had fallen to retire at least temporarily from the stage and to devote himself to the pleasures of a quiet life which nobody was better fitted to appreciate. He explains how 'at the period of which I speak the calm pleasures of home life had ceased to exist for the majority of people. Napoleon did not allow one to become attached to them; he thought that those who belonged to him must cease to belong to themselves. Carried away by the rapidity of events, by ambition, by the interest of each day, placed in that atmosphere of war and political change which brooded over the whole of Europe, people found it impossible to pay due regard to their private affairs; public life occupied so great a part of their minds that private life was never given a single thought. One came to one's house like a visitor owing to the necessity of resting somewhere, but nobody was prepared to stay permanently at home.'

During these years Talleyrand's rôle was a small one but he was always busy behind the scenes. Banished henceforth from Napoleon's intimacy he continued to fulfil the functions that were connected with his office, and thus in November he was deputed to greet the King of Saxony on his visit to France and to conduct him from the frontier to the capital.

The question that was principally occupying people's minds at the end of this year was that of Napoleon's divorce, and in December his marriage with Josephine was finally annulled. Talleyrand and Fouché who had combined in working towards this end were divided when it came to deciding upon her successor. Talleyrand, as was to be expected, favoured an Austrian princess, while Fouché, true to his Jacobin antecedents, regarded with suspicion anything that came out of Austria, the country that has been described as the Faubourg St. Germain of Europe.

In January 1810 a solemn council was held at which the Grand Dignitaries and Ministers were asked to give their views on the question. Cambacérès and Lebrun, who were the first to speak, advocated the one a Russian and the other a Saxon alliance. Murat and Fouché supported the former. When Talleyrand's turn came he spoke at length in favour of an Austrian marriage. His secret motive was that he feared lest, failing such an arrangement, Napoleon should destroy Austria altogether. The preservation of Austria was still one of the essential points of his consistent European policy. The main reason, however, that he gave for advocating the match was that it would serve as a means of expiating the crimes of the Revolution, especially the execution of the Queen, who was also an Austrian archduchess, and thus reconciling France with Europe. The course that was thus recommended was the one adopted and the marriage took place in the following April.

For once Fouché had been found on the losing side and he proceeded to make other and graver errors. The success which had attended his independent policy during Napoleon's absence seems to have turned his head. Having successfully made, or threatened to make, war on his own initiative, he now sought to try his hand at the more difficult business of making peace. When it was discovered that he had secretly and without any authority opened negotiations with England Napoleon's patience was exhausted. He was not only relieved of his office but compelled to leave the country, his disgrace being thus rendered more complete than that which had befallen Talleyrand in the previous year.

5

Among those who were attracted to Paris by the festivities in honour of the Emperor's marriage was a Polish lady, the Countess Potocka, who had already come into contact with many of the principal members of the Imperial Court in her native capital of Warsaw four years before. She had then formed a deep romantic attachment to the Count de Flahaut which may have proved a more potent reason than the desire to witness an historic ceremony for the eagerness with which she sought and obtained her husband's consent to her visit to France in the year 1810. To her pen we owe a vivid account of French society at the time and particularly of the circle by whom Talleyrand was surrounded.

She made the greater part of the journey in a carriage with Talleyrand's old friend, Narbonne, and was as delighted with his astonishing powers of conversation as she was amused by his elaborate efforts at seduction. She belonged already to a different age (she died in 1867), in which conversation had ceased to be an art and love-making was taken seriously.

Her natural sponsor in Paris was her aunt, the Countess Tyszkiewicz, a lady of some forty-five summers who had long been and who remained a member of what her niece irreverently termed Monsieur de Talleyrand's elderly seraglio.

The most prominent star in that constellation was, for the time being, the Duchess of Courland, the mother of the young Countess Edmond de Périgord. To her Talleyrand was sincerely, even passionately, devoted, and his letters to her which remain are the most fervent that he is known to have written. She was no longer young but it was generally admitted that she retained a great deal of her beauty. She was enormously rich and her dresses and jewels were objects of universal admiration. The Countess Potocka recounts of her that often she would arrive long after midnight in the salon where the little coterie were collected, having come for the express purpose of showing them her ball dress or a new jewel, 'just as a girl of twenty might have done.'

The judgments of the Polish Countess on Parisian affairs and personalities are not flattering. Her relations with Monsieur de Flahaut were more romantic than pleasant, his freedom being considerably hampered by the fact that he was carrying on a more serious liaison with the Queen of Holland, that he was also slightly entangled with the Queen of Naples, and that he was not entirely neglecting certain lesser luminaries such as the celebrated Mademoiselle Mars. Knowledge or suspicion of these happenings may have thrown a shadow over the Countess's stay in Paris and may account for the unprepossessing picture that she draws of the society in which she moved.

On her first visit to Talleyrand's house she and the other guests were informed that he had been detained at Court, an explanation which they found satisfactory, 'but what did seem strange to us was that when we entered the drawing-room we found only the Princess's "lady-in-waiting" there to receive us and we were told that "Her Highness, tempted by a ray of sunshine, had gone out for a turn in the Bois." ' When the Princess returned after having kept her guests waiting for an hour she offered no apologies, believing, the Countess suggests, that ordinary politeness was beneath her dignity. Her appearance, she adds, was absurd, for she looked fully sixty years of age but, being persuaded by flatterers that she was still beautiful, she wore the clothes and the adornments of youth.

'Whether M. de Talleyrand was of the party or not the atmosphere in his house was always deadly dull. I have seldom received the same impression elsewhere. And yet the majority of those who regularly went there were intelligent people. But the Princess, in addition to her natural inanity, was so pretentious and set such store by etiquette that she became insupportable, so that people who were independent and had no business affairs with the Prince, went there only when they were sure to find him alone.

'About once a week M. de Talleyrand's society met at my aunt's house when I found it hardly more amusing. She invited distinguished compatriots and foreigners who were passing through. Her house was very fashionable.

'I cannot express what a disagreeable surprise it was for me when I found that the only form of amusement there was gambling for huge sums. The bank was taken by unknown people to whom nobody spoke. They spread out their wealth on the table in order to tempt the players. People seemed afraid to touch them and treated them like pariahs. . . . There was something humiliating and satanic about it all. Desire of gain was the presiding genius. The strained faces of the players, the gloomy impassivity of the bankers, the silence which reigned in this room—where the fate of an entire family was often risked in a single night—it all seemed to me hateful. I could not conceal my surprise, perhaps even my naïve indignation, but my aunt replied coldly that one could see that I had come from far away, that similar amusements took place everywhere, and that the Prince, who worked so hard, took part in distractions at her house which his position rendered impossible at his own.'

The Countess Potocka was not amused by the society into which her aunt introduced her. Her sympathies were with the Emperor whose very loyal aide-de-camp was the Count de Flahaut. Her aunt's friends were all of the Faubourg St. Germain, who were in opposition to the existing regime. 'They belittled everything, bewailed everything, and did not amuse themselves at all.' She made an exception, however, in favour of the house of Madame de Laval, Talleyrand's dark-eyed friend and the only one, according to some accounts, who exercised any influence over him. 'This intelligent woman had made the best of things. She gloried, so to speak, in being poor, never spoke of what she had lost and did not seem to resent the fact that other people had grown rich—her attitude seemed to be that it was only right that their large fortunes should console them for not having been born a Montmorency.

'A select circle, which included the younger people of all parties, who indeed vied with one another for admittance, met often in the Viscountess's little drawing-room; to go there was a certificate of being good company and of having good taste. The household staff consisted of one footman and a negress who was half slave and half confidante; she used to come in to make the tea. At these very unpretentious receptions I met all the most distinguished people in Paris. Monsieur de Talleyrand and the Duchess of Courland were among the most regular attendants. Madame de Talleyrand never came. She knew her place. It was there only that I heard people converse without restraint; politics and party spirit were excluded. With exquisite tact Madame de Laval controlled the subject of conversation; as soon as she saw the actors playing their parts she was silent and seemed absorbed in her thick wool knitting, unless some question of particular interest roused her to take part. Then the others in their turn were silent; she spoke with such grace, originality, and point that everybody fell under her charm. She had been extremely pretty; her dark eyes, so soft and intelligent, still shone with surprising lustre.'

It is plain that the Polish Countess produced a favourable impression on Napoleon both at Warsaw and in Paris, and the culminating point of her success was an invitation to

Saint Cloud where she dined at the Emperor's table. On the very next day 'M. de Talleyrand, who had not thought of calling on me before and had only left a card, came in person to hear the details of my dinner of the previous evening. He questioned me very skilfully on what I had seen and heard; I only told him what he probably knew already; contrary to his habit he was extremely agreeable, he talked to me of Poland and was full of praises and finally he fixed a day for me to have luncheon with him in his library. I went to this invitation with some eagerness and, as I make a point of always speaking the truth, I must confess that I never passed a more charming morning. M. de Talleyrand did me the honours of his collection; it was natural that so wealthy a connoisseur should have collected the most beautiful and the rarest editions, but the charming manner in which he showed me his books was beyond comparison; he never told one anything that one could know already, nor anything that other people had already said or written; he talked very little about himself and a great deal about the distinguished people with whom he had come in contact. In a word he was as well educated as it is possible for a great nobleman to be if he devotes a lot of time to pleasure. To complete this flattering portrait, which is not that of a flatterer, I will say that M. de Talleyrand possessed a marvellous art of making one forget his past when he talked about the present.'

Once again that invincible charm of his had succeeded in temporarily winning over a woman who thoroughly disliked and disapproved of him.

6

The books of which he was so proud and which he showed to Madame Potocka in the early part of 1810 were not to remain much longer in his possession. Napoleon's disastrous commercial policy was causing economic distress in all parts of Europe where the blockade was effective. Many important banking houses were ruined, amongst others the Belgian firm of Simons with which Talleyrand was connected, no doubt through the medium of his fair hostess of the night of 19 Brumaire. He lost a very large sum in this catastrophe and found himself unable to meet his creditors. Once more, as in 1792, he sold his library but although the present collection was very much more valuable than the former one, the proceeds of the sale were quite inadequate to meet his needs.

In this predicament he appealed to the Emperor of Russia for help. It is deplorable that delicacy, if no stronger motive, should not have prevented him from asking for financial assistance from a foreign ruler with whom he, although a high official in his own country, was in secret communication. Alexander was more sensitive, and replied to his application with a courteous but decisive refusal. He pointed out, in carefully guarded language, in what a false position both lender and borrower would be placed by such a transaction. The difficulty was eventually surmounted, thanks to Napoleon, who purchased for a large sum Talleyrand's house in the Rue de Varennes in order to oblige him. Perhaps even stronger motives should have prevented Talleyrand from receiving a favour from Napoleon at this time than those which ought to have deterred him from applying for one to Alexander, but his conduct with regard to money from the beginning to the end of his career is indefensible. He had only one principle so far as money was concerned which he himself enunciated in youth and clung to in age: 'Il ne faut jamais être pauvre diable.'

7

The scene of Talleyrand's activities between the years 1809 and 1814 was laid in the private houses of his friends, and it is therefore to those whose chronicles are principally concerned with private life that we must turn for the material of his biography during this period.

The Countess Kielmannsegge was, like the Countess Potocka, a foreigner, being born of a princely Saxon house; like her she was possessed of considerable personal attractions, like her she was in her early thirties, and like her she found herself on her arrival in Paris received as an intimate in the circle which Talleyrand frequented. Her link with it was the Duchess of Courland, with whom she was on terms of the closest friendship and whose assistance she sought in order to procure the release of her husband, who had recently been arrested in Hanover for participation in a conspiracy against the Napoleonic regime. She was on no good terms with the Count, and was living apart from him, but felt it her duty, as she expressed it herself, to save the father of her children. Under the powerful patronage of the Duchess she found no difficulty in obtaining access to Napoleon of whom she became immediately and remained until the day of her death an enthusiastic, almost an ecstatic worshipper. She soon, therefore, lost all sympathy with the aristocratic, discontented society in which she found herself and in which she remained with the sole purpose of acting as spy and informer. This task she was enabled to carry out the more satisfactorily after she had entered into somewhat intimate relations with Savary, Duke of Rovigo, who had taken Fouché's place as Minister of Police.

She has described her first impression of Talleyrand as follows: 'When he approached me with his limping gait, his heavy body, his flashing eyes, his snake-like mouth and jaw, his paralysing smile, and his affected flatteries, I thought: "Nature gave you the choice between snake and tiger, and you chose to be an anaconda." This first impression remained with me. Before I knew him better I avoided being alone with him owing to a certain feeling of discomfort. . . . When I did come to know him I found him easy in company both from disposition and from laziness, weak from habit and inclination, powerful in intellect and eloquence, clever and tireless in ensnaring those who easily gave in, who could be of use to him and whose minds allowed themselves to be enslaved.'

She spent the greater part of the summer and early autumn of 1811 at St. Germains, where the Duchess of Courland had taken a small château that had formerly been a hunting-box of Henri iv's. According to her own account she found herself in a world of ceaseless intrigue and conspiracy. The Duchess's letters to the Czar were composed by Talleyrand and the fair copy was written out by Madame de Laval. Nesselrode was constantly in the circle. Her dislike of Talleyrand grew into hatred. 'When he rode so clumsily on his small chestnut under the tall oaks of the forest or through the fields of roses, swinging his cane the while, faster or slower in accordance with the speed of his thoughts, when he showed off his deceptive paradoxes in the salon where Henri iv once lived, then I could not help thinking: "Would to God that you were under the earth, for you will have no peace until you have crushed underfoot all the friendliness of heart, all the nobility of mind that exists in the world." '

One day news was brought of a scene that Napoleon had made at Court in which he had reduced the young Countess Edmond to tears by his abuse of her husband's family. She had had, however, the spirit to reply: 'My husband and my uncle have at all times served your Majesty with zeal. It rests with you to make further use of them. And surely their earlier services have at least deserved that your Majesty should not ridicule them.' Talleyrand's comment on the scene was brief: 'It seems a poor way,' he said, 'of proving his power.'

In the same month of August another incident took place which seemed to threaten more serious consequences. One evening as the Countess Kielmannsegge was leaving the château she met a gendarme at the doorway who inquired if M. de Talleyrand were within. He was the bearer of a letter from the Minister of Police.

The grounds of the complaint that the letter contained appear to have been that Talleyrand's wife, who had been forbidden both by the Emperor and by Talleyrand to meet again her Spanish friend, the Duke of San Carlos, had contrived to do so; what harm, save to themselves, a meeting between these elderly lovers could have done, or why Talleyrand should have been blamed for it, is difficult to follow. That such an interdict should have been imposed reveals the extent and the pettiness of Napoleon's tyranny.

The threat of sharing his wife's exile if he could not control her movements was the gist of the message he received. Exile from Paris was, for him, almost a death sentence and never so deadly as in these eventful years. It is on this occasion that the Countess pays Talleyrand her only compliment. 'The whole behaviour of Prince Talleyrand and the general moderation of the sentiments that he expressed compelled admiration. He wrote his answer, destroyed and changed it several times—accordingly as his feelings grew stronger—and showed us each of the drafts. I saw the man, that strange man, just as he might have been without wickedness. He gave his answer to the gendarme at one in the morning. At five he was in the carriage in order to be at the Duke of Rovigo's levée.' He returned the same evening, the whole matter having been satisfactorily terminated.

The Countess, whose romantic temperament was apt to

see things in terms of melodrama, has left us a graphic
description of how once, listening at the door, she overheard the three conspirators, Talleyrand, the Duchess, and
Madame de Laval perfecting their plans. 'And that is how
we shall destroy him,' were Talleyrand's last words. 'We
shall destroy him, we shall destroy him'—repeated the two
ladies, clapping their hands and throwing their arms round
each other's necks. The Countess walked boldly into their
midst, which so much alarmed them that the Duchess subsequently attempted to swear her to secrecy. She refused,
however, to give any promise and warned them never again
to betray themselves in her presence.

Talleyrand enjoyed during these years the companion-
ship of a young girl who had grown up from childhood in
his household. Her name was Charlotte; she was now about
thirteen or fourteen years of age; her parents were unknown.
It was generally believed that Talleyrand was her father and
his tender love for her confirmed the theory. As to who was
her mother there were many rumours, but such as have come
down to us do not bear investigation. Many believed that
she was of royal birth, but romantic imaginations are always
inclined to fill up blanks with the names of royalty. He was
deeply interested in her education, he enjoyed riding with
her in the country, and a few years later he married her to
one of his nephews. She lived until 1873, and when she died
her death certificate recorded that she was the child of
unknown parents.

8

In February 1812 Talleyrand was appointed one of the
Commission of Inquiry into the conduct of General Dupont
in the matter of the capitulation of Baylen. He was much
impressed by the defence and was in favour of taking a
lenient view of what had at worst been only an error of

weakness. Napoleon insisted, despite the recommendation of the Commission, on condemning Dupont to imprisonment for life, a sentence which he was serving two years later when Talleyrand procured his release and his promotion to the post of Minister of War under the Restoration.

Later in the year there seemed to be a further prospect of practical employment for the Vice-Grand Elector. Although Napoleon would not commit himself to a definite policy with regard to Poland it was most important for him to be able to rely, during the Russian campaign, on the enthusiastic support of the Poles. The position of his Ambassador at Warsaw would therefore be one of great responsibility and would demand the exercise of first-rate diplomatic and political ability. Despite the grave misgiving with which he already regarded Talleyrand, Napoleon appears to have decided to entrust him with this mission for which he obviously possessed the necessary qualifications. But whether, as Countess Kielmannsegge asserts, some of Talleyrand's ladies talked too imprudently about the appointment before it was confirmed, or whether Savary's version is correct that the Emperor wrongly suspected Talleyrand of speculating in exchanges when he was only obtaining the necessary Polish currency to enable him to take up the post, whatever the reason may have been, the offer was withdrawn and Napoleon sent instead to Warsaw the Abbé de Pradt, whose hopeless incompetence proved more disastrous than treachery and whose mistakes contributed largely towards the approaching calamity.

9

With the departure of the Emperor for the Russian front treason once more grew busy, and very soon began to thrive and fatten upon the reports which reached Paris of unsuccessful military operations. Among the many who were dabbling in this dangerous pastime was a lady of singular charm and beauty who had had already a somewhat tempestuous career.

Aimée de Coigny, married in early youth to the youthful Duke de Fleury, had during the forty-two years that she had lived inspired many passions, one of which had bequeathed to her a lasting monument in the pages of French literature, for it was her beauty which in prison had moved André Chénier to write the verses addressed to *La Jeune Captive* a few days before his head fell under the guillotine. Another inhabitant of the same prison was Talleyrand's friend Montrond, who was not one to waste time in writing verses, but, making more practical use of his opportunities, succeeded both in winning the heart of his lovely fellow captive and, by judicious bribery of the gaolers, in postponing the day of her and his execution until after the fall of Robespierre and the end of the Terror. Aimée, in gratitude, married her deliverer, having previously divorced her first husband. But neither she nor Montrond was made for matrimony and more than one liaison intervened before we find her in the year 1812 living with the Marquis Bruno de Boisgelin.

Aimée de Coigny had always adopted with enthusiasm the political views of her ruling lover and she had thus already held nearly every shade of opinion from red republicanism to white reaction. Boisgelin had formerly been an emigrant and he was now an eager advocate of Bourbon restoration. Neither of them were in their first youth and politics therefore occupied a larger portion of their time than would have been expected in the case of a younger couple. Aimée de Coigny was on terms of friendship with Talleyrand. They belonged to the same world, they had both adapted too easily the new conditions to their own convenience, and they had both forfeited the respect but not the admiration of their contemporaries. She had difficulty in bringing Boisgelin round to her own opinion. 'I found him full of the prejudices which the emigrants harboured against the Bishop of Autun, regarding his conduct from a narrow point of view, reproaching him for his changes of form and even of fortune without thinking that the situation in which he found himself had changed much more often than he, and that having always played an active part in events he had used his influence to modify them and to guide them so far as possible towards an order of things where there was some hope of improvement.' Under the influence of his mistress Boisgelin soon came to realise that the Bourbons had no hope in France unless they could secure the support of a powerful section among those who had hitherto been loyal to Napoleon, that it was of the first importance to obtain a leader for such a section, and that Talleyrand was the man clearly designated for that position.

The presence of Boisgelin in the Rue St. Florentin would have aroused suspicion but nothing could be more natural than the visits of Aimée de Coigny. 'The weather was fine' (in the summer of 1812) 'and nearly every morning I went out for a walk which ended at the house of M. de Talleyrand. I often found him in his library surrounded by people who either liked or were engaged in literature. Nobody can talk like M. de Talleyrand in a library; he takes up a book and puts it down again, contradicts it, leaves it and returns to it, questions it as though it were a living being, and this procedure both enriches his conversation with the profundity and the experience of the ages and gives to the works in question a grace which their authors often lacked.' It is curious that Aimée de Coigny and Anna Potocka, who possibly never met, and certainly never read one another's reminiscences, should have both been struck by the same quality in Talleyrand and should have both recorded it.

Aimée de Coigny became henceforth a regular attendant at all the houses where the discontented faction were accustomed to meet. She describes them as being dominated by 'the enchanting grace of Madame de Laval, the soft conversational murmur of the Bellegarde ladies, my own efforts to please and to amuse myself and the inexpressible charm which M. de Talleyrand can exercise when he does not conceal it in a disdainful silence. It was at these meetings that I got into the habit of M. de Talleyrand and acquired the necessary familiarity to be able to talk to him about anything without embarrassment.'

As the winter of 1812 wore on, as the news from the seat of war grew worse, when the astonishing coup d'état of the half insane General Mallet almost succeeded, and when the celebrated 29th bulletin revealed to the Parisians the extent of the disaster, it seemed that Talleyrand was right in describing the Moscow campaign as the beginning of the end, and that the end itself could not be far distant. And then on the 19th of December Paris awoke to the surprising information that the Emperor had returned overnight. 'I ceased my frequent visits to M. de Talleyrand for fear of compromising him, and I moderated the language with which I was trying to stir up discontent.' So wrote Aimée de Coigny. Once more and for the last time treason hung its head, criticism sank to a whisper, and conspiracy crept underground.

10

Never had Napoleon been in such dire need of wise counsel as during the winter months that followed the retreat from Moscow. Talleyrand, who had not been afraid to urge peace upon him in the hour of victory was equally

insistent upon the necessity of concluding it now before
defeat should result in complete destruction. 'Negotiate
while you still have something to negotiate with,' was the
tenor of his advice. Napoleon saw the wisdom of it and
invited him to return to the Ministry for Foreign Affairs.
He refused, replying coldly: 'I am not acquainted with your
affairs.' For four years he had been banished from the
Emperor's confidence; how could he now at a moment's
notice pick up again the tangled skein of foreign policy?
'You are trying to betray me,' exclaimed the Emperor.
'No,' replied the Prince, 'but I will not assume office because
I believe that your views are contrary to what I believe to
be for the glory and the happiness of my country.' This is
Aimée de Coigny's account of what happened and it is
probably coloured in Talleyrand's favour. Savary tells us
that Talleyrand would not accept the post because Napoleon
insisted that he should at the same time resign the office of
Vice-Grand Elector. As this would have been the opposite
to promotion Napoleon can hardly have been surprised at
Talleyrand's attitude. What is certainly true is that the
offer was made and was refused.

Early in 1813 Napoleon appears to have received unques-
tionable proof that Talleyrand was in communication with
his enemies. He was strongly tempted to take violent
measures but he still hesitated. Talleyrand was after all one
of the Grand Dignitaries of the Empire. From the nights
when they had conspired together against the Directory,
throughout the glorious days of the Consulate, right on
until the culminating triumph of Tilsit, Talleyrand had
always been at his elbow with wise counsel that he had not
always followed. To strike down such a man, now when
the storm was threatening, would be like striking down one
of the pillars of his own house. Rotten it might be but the
moment seemed hardly well chosen for internal reconstruc-

tion. So he contented himself with repetitions of the scene of January 1809, calling Talleyrand a traitor to his face and threatening to shoot or hang him. After one of these scenes Talleyrand's comment to the assembled courtiers was: 'The Emperor is charming this morning.'

In April Napoleon returned to Germany to fight the campaign that was to end at Leipzig, and Aimée de Coigny resumed her visits to the Rue St. Florentin. Talleyrand appears to have encouraged her in the belief that it was she who gradually persuaded him to favour the return of Louis XVIII. At first he spoke to her of a regency for the King of Rome, and then of a national monarchy under the Duke of Orleans. Finally, when she insisted on speaking of the legitimate heir he explained to her the difficulties of his own position. 'I could put up well enough with the Count d'Artois because there is something between him and me which would explain much of my conduct'—(referring doubtless to their midnight interview in July 1789)—'but his brother does not know me at all. I confess that I have no wish to expose myself to forgiveness instead of gratitude, or to have to defend myself.' Aimée then told him of a precious letter which she and Boisgelin had been long working at and which was to be conveyed to Louis XVIII in England explaining to him the situation in France and insisting particularly upon the importance of Talleyrand's adherence to his cause. Talleyrand told her to bring the letter to him on the following day.

She ran home, fell into the arms of Boisgelin who was awaiting her and cried: 'He is ours, he wants to read your letter to the King.' 'Nothing could equal Bruno's transport of joy. We set ourselves to copying out the letter, taking particular trouble over the paragraph that concerned M. de Talleyrand.'

On the morrow she took the letter to Talleyrand who read

it aloud and commented upon it very favourably. He told her that she and her friend could count upon him, and encouraged her to carry on the correspondence with England. Then he burnt the letter. 'He twisted up the paper, lit it from a candle, threw it in flames into the fireplace and crossed the shovel and the tongs above it so as to prevent the ashes from flying up the chimney. "It is only from a statesman," I said, "that one learns how to destroy a secret very secretly." '

11

During the summer and autumn of 1813 the fortunes of Napoleon continued to fall. After the disaster of Leipzig in October he was almost surrounded by the enemy but succeeded in hacking his way through at Hanau and returned to France with his adversaries pressing on his heels.

Madame de la Tour du Pin was passing through Paris in November and was anxious for some authentic news to take back to her husband who was now holding the post of Prefect at Amiens. She called on Talleyrand. 'He received me, as ever, with that graceful and pleasant familiarity which he has always shown towards me. He has received much abuse and has probably deserved more but in spite of everything he possessed charm such as I have never met with in any other man.' He advised her not to leave Paris that day, which had been her intention, as the Emperor was arriving on the morrow and he promised to visit her after he had seen him.

On the following afternoon she heard the cannon which announced the Emperor's return. At ten o'clock her carriage was waiting at the door, but it was not until eleven that Talleyrand arrived. She was breathless for news.

'What madness to travel in this cold weather,' he said, and
asked her in whose apartment it was that she was staying.
It belonged, she explained, to Lally Tollendal, the same
who had read his tragedy aloud at Juniper Hall just twenty
years before. Talleyrand picked up a candle and began to examine the pictures on the wall : ' "Ah, ha, Charles II, James II
—that's right," he commented, and put the candle back on
the table. "Heavens," I cried, "what have Charles II and
James II got to do with it? You have seen the Emperor.
How is he? What are his plans? What does he say after his
defeat?" "Oh, don't bother me with your Emperor, he's
finished." "How finished?" I said." "What do you mean?" "I
mean," he said, "that he is a man who is ready to hide under
a bed." . . . I knew of M. de Talleyrand's hatred and rancour
against Napoleon, but never had I heard him express it
with such bitterness. I asked him a thousand questions to
which he only replied with the words: "He has lost all his
equipment—he is finished—that's all." Then he drew out
of his pocket a printed paper in English and throwing a
couple of logs on the fire, said: "Let's burn a little more of
poor old Lally's wood. Here, as you know English, read
me this paragraph." At the same time he showed me a fairly
long article marked in pencil in the margin.' It was an
account of a dinner-party given by the Prince Regent in
honour of the Duchess of Angoulême—the daughter of
Louis XVI. 'When I had read it I stopped and looked at him
in amazement. He took back the paper, folded it slowly,
put it into his huge pocket and said with that exquisite sly
smile that only he possessed: "Oh, how stupid you are!
Now be off, but don't catch cold." He rang and told the
footman to call my carriage. Then he left me, saying as he
was putting on his coat: "Give my love to Gouvernet" (her
husband's former title). "I send him that for his breakfast.
You will get there in time."' She understood the message

and delivered it when she arrived at Amiens in the early morning, but even then neither she nor her husband found it easy to believe that they were shortly to witness the end of the Empire and the return of the Bourbons.

Chapter Nine

THE RESTORATION

I

ALL that winter and on into the early spring of 1814 the tide of battle swayed between Paris and the frontier. For the first time Napoleon was fighting on French soil, and for the first time he was fighting with his back to the wall. Military experts have held the view that this was, from a purely technical standpoint, the most brilliant of his campaigns, and that never had his genius shown itself to better advantage. But whatever may be thought of his generalship during these months, it cannot be denied that the faults in statesmanship and diplomacy which had characterised his career were never more gross or glaring. In the days of victory these qualities had been inconvenient to his adversaries, in the days of defeat they proved fatal to himself.

Three armies, those of Russia, Austria and Prussia were marching on Paris, while Wellington was carrying all before him in the south. More than once during these days of anguish Napoleon exclaimed: 'If only Talleyrand were here—he would get me out of it.' But, in truth, no Minister could have saved him, except one who could have compelled him to pursue a consistent policy, and not to change his terms of peace daily, and almost hourly, with every alteration in the varying fortunes of the war.

In November the Allies actually offered him the natural frontiers of France—the Rhine, the Alps, and the Pyrenees.

That they should have made so generous an offer strengthened his opinion of his own position. He refused it. A fortnight later he would gladly have accepted, but it was too late. Again, in February, he was offered terms which would have left France the frontiers of 1791, terms which his Minister for Foreign Affairs, the faithful but clear-sighted Caulaincourt, was anxious to accept, but having recently scored one or two striking military successes he was now unwilling to listen to any terms, and even refused the Allies' offer of an armistice. Such conduct strengthened the bonds —always in danger of dissolving—which held the Allies together and gave life to the belief which was beginning to develop in many of their minds that a satisfactory peace with Napoleon was impossible.

Meanwhile behind the battle front Paris waited—a city of rumour, of conspiracy, of hope. Napoleon's popularity had vanished. Gradually the conviction grew that his rule was over, but great differences of opinion existed as to what alternative was either possible or desirable. It had taken Talleyrand some time to reconcile himself to the restoration of the old dynasty. The minds of his countrymen were moving slowly in the same direction. Meanwhile it seemed to him of some importance that the Bourbons should be made aware of his willingness to welcome their return before that return actually took place.

It was, however, one thing to talk treason in the safety of a Royalist salon, it was quite another to enter into active correspondence with the exiled princes, discovery of which might cost the culprit his life. The inhabitants of Paris were so cut off from the world that it was only from one smuggled copy of an English newspaper that they learnt of the departure of the Count d'Artois for the Continent and of the Duke of Angoulême for the south of France. Meanwhile they received exaggerated reports of Napoleon's victories, no word of his defeats and the disturbing intelligence that the Allies had opened negotiations with him at Châtillon.

A brave and a loyal messenger was needed who would carry through the line defended by Napoleon's army to the allied statesmen, and if possible to the Bourbon Princes themselves, news of the increased support which their cause was beginning to obtain in the capital. Such a man was available in the person of the Baron de Vitrolles, one of those faithful and fearless supporters of the old order, whose belief in the righteousness of their cause was as sincere as their religion, and whose services were as valuable in moments of crisis as they were embarrassing after the victory was won. The Baron had already fought for the cause, but this was his first introduction into the great world of high politics and he has left us in his memoirs the impression that it produced on him. He was naturally alarmed at the prospect of negotiating with statesmen whose names were already famous throughout Europe, but the more he saw of them the less he thought of them, and it appeared to him that both Talleyrand and Fouché were rather lacking in intelligence as neither of them seemed to have a clear idea of exactly what it was he wanted. Politics are indeed a simple science to honest souls like the Baron de Vitrolles, who believe that all solutions of the problem save their own are wrong, and who are prepared to die for their cause.

So the Baron de Vitrolles set out upon his dangerous quest, and after thrilling adventures and hair-breadth escapes reached first the Allies and finally the Count d'Artois. But he carried with him no written word from Talleyrand, nor any visible sign such as a ring or seal, whereby he could show proof of his approval. Such caution is hardly to be wondered at. The envoy was likely to fall into the hands of the enemy, and actually did so, although

he made good his escape. If definite proof of Talleyrand's
active treachery had then reached Napoleon it might well
have cost him his life. As it was, however, Vitrolles had
some difficulty in persuading the Allies of Talleyrand's
adherence to the cause of the Bourbons. After he had
stated his case at a formal meeting where Metternich,
Castlereagh, Nesselrode, and Hardenberg were present, one
of the first questions asked him was concerning the attitude
of Talleyrand. 'You can consider Monsieur de Talleyrand
entirely attached to the cause'—and then the honest man
added, 'at least in his heart,' whereat the grave statesmen
burst into laughter—until somewhat embarrassed he corrected himself and said: 'In his mind, if you prefer it.'

Again, when he came to discuss with the Count d'Artois
the difficult question as to who could be entrusted with the
task of carrying on the government during the interval that
was bound to elapse between the disappearance of Napoleon
and the arrival of the Bourbons, 'the name of M. de Talleyrand was the first, and indeed the only one, that suggested
itself. . . . The Prince liked to bring the conversation back
to M. de Talleyrand, whom he still called the Bishop of
Autun. They were contemporaries and, despite the repug-
nance which the renegade priest and the married bishop
inspired, he was still interested in him.'

2

While Vitrolles was discussing the future with his beloved
Prince at Nancy, the Allies were advancing rapidly on Paris;
and the position of Napoleon and of those who supported
him was growing desperate. On 28th March, at a meeting
of the Council of Regency, the question was discussed
whether the Empress and her son should seek safety or
should remain in the threatened capital. In private Talleyrand

had expressed the view that they should go, but on this official occasion he argued strongly in the opposite sense. There is little doubt that the advice which he gave to the Council was right. The flight of the Empress and of the acting Government entailed almost of necessity the capitulation of Paris. It was, as Talleyrand observed to Savary after the meeting, throwing away the game with good cards in the hand. His advice, however, was rejected, and on the following morning the Empress left for Blois.

When he was asked afterwards why he had given advice which, if it had been taken, would have proved injurious to the cause which he already secretly supported, he replied that his credit at that time stood so low that he knew that he had only to advise one course in order to be sure that the opposite would be adopted. This was an ingenious explanation of his conduct, but it is permissible to believe that in giving it he was doing himself, as not infrequently, less than justice. He may have doubted whether his advice would be followed, he certainly wished no good to the Napoleonic regime, but when required to deliver an opinion on a question of policy, he probably preferred to give the opinion which he really held, and which also was the wisest counsel in the circumstances. All through the previous year whenever Napoleon had asked for his opinion he had given it honestly, advising the Emperor to make the best peace he could, although with little expectation and less desire that such advice would be followed. Although conscience troubled him little there exists such a thing as professional pride, and it must have afforded him some consolation to feel that the advice which he had given was always sound and that those who refused to follow it were the architects of their own misfortunes.

On the following day it was Talleyrand's duty, as a

member of the Council of Regency, to follow the Empress. The battle was raging now at the very gates of Paris, where the Marshals Marmont and Mortier offered a last gallant defence. From the heights of Montmartre the Emperor's brothers, Joseph and Jerome, watched the contest, and when they saw that all was lost rode away to join their sister-in-law in the south. Similar action seemed indicated on the part of the Vice-Grand Elector of the Empire, who had, however, no intention of taking it. The Emperor of the French who had long distrusted and openly abused him was in retreat, the Emperor of Russia with whom he had been on terms of constant friendship was at the gate. This was no time for him to leave the city in which shortly the fate of France and of Europe was to be decided.

It might have been expected that he would have chosen this moment boldly to declare himself, and in the light of subsequent events, it would have been safe to do so. But in the beleaguered city news was scarce. The shadow of Napoleon that hung over it, though fading hourly, was still terrible. His whereabouts were uncertain. At any moment he might return and take stern vengeance on those who had betrayed him. It would be a pity, thought Talleyrand, to lose all—perhaps life itself—on the eve of success through taking action twenty-four hours too soon.

Therefore, with the help of the faithful Madame de Rémusat, a little stratagem was contrived. Her husband, as an officer in the National Guard, was in command at one of the gates of Paris and it so happened that it was at this very gate that the Prince de Benevento presented himself in his travelling carriage en route to join the Empress at Blois. With great courtesy M. de Rémusat expressed to the Prince his inability to allow him to proceed. The Prince, like a sensible man, forbore to argue with an officer who was doubtless obeying orders, and returned immediately to his own house. He could say that he had endeavoured to do his duty, but had been prevented by force.

Late that night he called on Marmont, who was about to sign the capitulation of Paris. What was said at this interview we do not know. When subsequently the defection of Marmont and the withdrawal of his forces dealt the last blow to the last hopes of the Imperialists there were many among Napoleon's supporters who attributed the Marshal's action to his midnight interview with the Prince of Benevento.

3

On the following morning, contrary to his custom, Talleyrand rose early; but he had hardly completed his elaborate toilet when Nesselrode, his old acquaintance, arrived at the Rue St. Florentin. Later the same morning the allied sovereigns made their formal entry into the conquered capital. While they solemnly proceeded through the streets at the head of their forces, being received mostly with silent acquiescence but meeting occasionally with a cheer, Talleyrand and Nesselrode were busily engaged with the drafting of a proclamation to the people of Paris. This document which Alexander subsequently signed, having amended it in a sense still more conciliatory to French national sentiment, expressed the determination of the Allies to make no terms with Napoleon Bonaparte or with any member of his family, and added that they would respect the integrity of France as it had existed under its legitimate kings, and would recognise and guarantee whatever Constitution the Senate, summoned for this purpose, should decide was the best for the French people.

Later in the day the Emperor Alexander arrived at Talleyrand's house, where it was arranged that he should stay while in Paris. This decision is said to have been due

to a rumour that the Élysée, which had been previously
suggested, was undermined; but this was not the reason that
Alexander gave on his arrival. 'Monsieur de Talleyrand,'
he said, 'I have determined to stay in your house because
you have my confidence and that of my allies. We do not
wish to settle anything before we have heard you. You
know France, its needs and desires. Say what we ought to
do and we will do it.'

There is a curious parallel between the position of the
Emperor Alexander at this time and that occupied a century
later by President Wilson. Both represented enormously
powerful nations called upon for the first time to play
decisive parts in the settlement of Europe. Both had been
nurtured in liberal principles and were actuated by generous
sentiments. Vague aspirations played a larger part in their
mental equipment than practical experience. They believed
that every nation should be given the government that it
desired, and they hoped, the one by means of a Holy Alliance
and the other by a League of Nations, to secure the future
peace of the world. Both these men of brilliant attainments
seemed for a short period to dominate the world; both of
them, a few years after their moment of triumph, ended
their careers prematurely in an atmosphere of tragedy and
failure.

Alexander was genuinely anxious to ascertain the wishes
of the French people. He had no predilections in favour of
the Bourbons. He had seriously considered the possibility
of replacing Napoleon by some other successful commander
such as Bernadotte. The alternative of a regency for the
little King of Rome had not been discarded, and it was one
that might secure the support of the Emperor of Austria
if he had any ambition to see his grandson on the throne of
France. Of the great Powers England alone definitely
desired the restoration of the former dynasty, and even

England would have accepted another arrangement if her allies had insisted. All therefore depended upon the decision of Alexander, and at this critical moment Alexander looked to Talleyrand for guidance, and there is no doubt that the decision at which he arrived and to which, in spite of other influences, he adhered, was mainly due to the advice which Talleyrand pressed upon him. For this reason it is difficult to exaggerate the debt of gratitude which the Bourbons owed to the ci-devant Bishop of Autun.

In normal times a statesman may have doubts and hesitations, but when the crucial moment arrives he must know his own mind and be prepared to force his opinion upon others. For six long years Talleyrand had lived in doubt and hesitation, but now at this great crisis of his own life and of the history of France his mind was made up and Alexander found in him the determined counsellor ever welcome to the weak and vacillating spirit. The new order in France and in Europe must be based, he argued, upon a principle and that principle must be legitimacy. To the doubts expressed by the Emperor and by Metternich as to whether the people would accept the return of their former princes —they had seen, they said, no evidence of any enthusiasm for the Bourbons during their progress through France— Talleyrand replied that the Legislative Councils appointed by Napoleon would themselves invite the Bourbons to return once they were convinced that such was the determination of the Allies. When others are uncertain it is easy for the man with definite views to get his way. Alexander and the others allowed themselves to be persuaded. The decision was taken, and when Caulaincourt, formally ambassador to Russia, close friend and firm admirer of Alexander, arrived to plead the cause of Napoleon it was already too late.

That night the allied sovereigns dined with Talleyrand

and afterwards he accompanied them to the opera. On their appearance the whole house burst into frantic cheers. The French are certainly not less proud or patriotic than other nations, and that they should have spontaneously applauded the masters of foreign troops upon their native soil, standing in the place so often occupied by their own Emperor, proves how profound their discontent had been. Not without reason could Talleyrand maintain that he never conspired, except when he had the French nation as fellow-conspirators.

4

On 1st April 1814 Talleyrand found himself in a position more powerful and more responsible than any that he had occupied before or was ever to occupy again. The Bonapartes had departed, the Bourbons had not arrived, and there was only one Frenchman to whom the Allies looked for guidance, counsel, and decision. Attention should therefore be given by those who wish to form a true estimate of his value as a statesman to the actions that he took and the policy that he pursued at this crisis of his career.

On the morning of this day he despatched his first message to the Count d'Artois by an emissary of the latter who had been waiting in Paris. This message contained an expression of his sincere hope that the Count and those who followed him would adopt the national colours of France, the tricolour, which her soldiers for twenty years had covered with glory. Unfortunately to the embittered souls of the emigrants these colours represented not the record of victory but the emblem of revolution, and this first effort to reconcile the return of the old order with the continuance of the new was indignantly rejected.

A meeting of the Senate, or rather the remains of the Senate, for a majority of the members were not to be found, was summoned to take place the same afternoon. The Vice-Grand Elector—the only dignitary of the Empire who was present—naturally presided, and recommended the senators to proceed with the construction of a Provisional Government. Without further loss of time a Government of five was set up, with Talleyrand at the head of it. The other members—Dalberg, Jaucourt, Beurnonville, and Montesquiou—were contemptuously described by Chateaubriand as Talleyrand's whist four, and they certainly played but a small part in the events that immediately followed.

Talleyrand's next step was to introduce the members of the Senate to the Emperor Alexander, a ceremony which took place on the following day. He did not fail to point out to the Emperor that many of these reverend senators who bowed so low before him had themselves voted for the execution of their last king, and he impressed upon him the importance of having obtained the support of the regicides for the restoration of their victim's brother.

The respect paid to the Senate, the suggestion with regard to the tricolour seemed to men like the Baron de Vitrolles signs of deplorable weakness if not of latent treachery. They believed that the battle was already won, that nothing remained but for the rightful heir to remount the throne of his ancestors, and that, so far from any concessions being necessary, the population might consider themselves fortunate if their former misdeeds were overlooked. They did not realise the fact that was plain to Talleyrand, that while the civil population was indifferent the army was suspicious if not hostile, and that some gesture was necessary in order to reassure so powerful a body that had long been encouraged to consider itself the most important section of the community.

The Baron de Vitrolles himself was once more in Paris, and was given a dramatic opportunity of appreciating how far less secure were his master's prospects than he supposed. He was to be the bearer of despatches from the Provisional Government to the Count d'Artois, and at ten o'clock on the morning of 4th April, he presented himself at the Rue St. Florentin in order to receive his instructions. He found Talleyrand still in bed in that bedroom on the entresol whence all the affairs of the Provisional Government were conducted. Sitting by his bedside Vitrolles proceeded to draw up the complete programme of the Prince's entry into Paris. He was then anxious to set forth, but Talleyrand asked him to delay his departure until later in the day as he would have a private letter to give him.

Vitrolles found Talleyrand easy to deal with. 'There was this advantage with him, that no question surprised him, and that the most unexpected ones pleased him the best. . . . The whole policy of the Provisional Government was the *laisser-aller* and the *laisser-faire* of Monsieur de Talleyrand; his genius hovered above all the intrigues and lurked behind all the business. . . . I overcame my awe of this famous statesman; his reputation was more imposing than his personality—he was easy to get on with; phantoms disappear when one is close to them. It was in the simplest conversation that Monsieur de Talleyrand let fall the remarks to which he attached the greatest importance, they always had an object; he sowed them carelessly, like the seed that nature scatters, and, as in nature, the majority perished without produce.

'It was thus he told me, with apparent indifference, of his last dealings with the Count d'Artois, in 1789. He spoke in a way which made me notice his words but with a smile that robbed them of all pretension. "Ask Monsieur le Comte," he said, "if he remembers our meeting at Marly." '

He then recounted the facts and the circumstances of that interview on the eve of the first emigration, which was, as

Vitrolles himself realised, 'the complete justification in a
few words of his conduct during the Revolution.' The story
as told by Talleyrand was confirmed in every particular by
d'Artois.

All that day Vitrolles waited. He was prepared to start in
the afternoon, but was put off until the evening. At eight
o'clock he was sitting with Talleyrand, who was about to
put the private letter into his hands, when he heard the
door open behind him and the sound of spurred heels on
the parquet floor. It was an aide-de-camp from Prince
Schwarzenberg—the commander-in-chief of the allied
forces—with the news that the Marshals Ney and Macdonald,
accompanied by the Duke of Vicenza (Caulaincourt), were
at the outposts asking for an interview with the Emperor
of Russia and bearing proposals from Napoleon.

'Prince Talleyrand immediately put back into his largest
pocket the letter destined for the Count d'Artois; and
taking my arm led me into the recess of the window.

' "This is an incident," he said, laying stress upon the
word to convey that it was serious; "we must see how this
turns out; you cannot leave at this moment. The Emperor
Alexander is capable of the unexpected; one is not the son
of Paul I for nothing." '

The honest Vitrolles having awaited the arrival of the
envoys until midnight went home to bed and slept soundly,
but Talleyrand stayed up all that night, and when Vitrolles
returned at seven o'clock next morning he learnt that the
Prince had just retired and that his departure had to be
deferred until later. While Vitrolles had slept the last card
had been played on behalf of Napoleon and it was due to the
vigilance of Talleyrand that it was played in vain.

Ever since the arrival of the Allies Caulaincourt had
worked tirelessly in the interests of his master. He had had
several interviews with Alexander, with his brother the

Grand Duke Constantine, with Schwarzenberg, and with others. He had haunted the Rue St. Florentin, had threatened to plead his cause before the Senate, had argued and remonstrated with Talleyrand, and had nearly thrown the Abbé de Pradt out of the window. What he had finally to offer was Napoleon's abdication on condition that his son should be recognised and a regency established.

Alexander had great affection and respect for Caulaincourt, who urged his case with eloquence and sincerity. This was the only solution, he believed, which could be imposed upon France without further bloodshed, for the army, he maintained, was faithful to Napoleon; it was also the solution desired by the majority of the population in whose internal affairs Alexander had expressed his unwillingness to intervene. Caulaincourt did not know that even while he was speaking the army of Marmont, that lay between Paris and Fontainebleau, was being transferred to Versailles, in accordance with an undertaking that Marmont had given to the Allies, but contrary to an order that he had given that same night to delay any action pending the result of these negotiations.

Alexander hesitated. He was impressed by Caulaincourt's arguments. He remembered his old admiration for Napoleon and had no desire to appear ungenerous in the moment of victory. When he was on the point of yielding he came to Talleyrand for advice. He found in Talleyrand no reflection of his own uncertainty. With overwhelming arguments and with irresistible logic the impression which the emissaries of Napoleon had produced on him was effaced. Whatever regency was set up, Talleyrand pointed out, Napoleon would in reality be the power behind it, within a year he would be once more openly in control, the army would be once more in the field, and all that had been accomplished would be undone. The opinion of Talleyrand

at this juncture proved decisive. The doubts of Alexander
were dispelled and Caulaincourt returned to Fontainebleau
empty-handed.

5

So Vitrolles set out for Nancy at last with Talleyrand's
letter in his pocket, and with the conviction in his heart
that Talleyrand shared his views with regard to restoring
the old monarchy on the old basis. Talleyrand had allowed
him to depart under this impression, but it was in fact no
part of his plan that Louis xviii should simply succeed by
right of inheritance to the same throne that Louis xvi had
lost. Before the King there was to come the Constitution—
and so Lebrun, former Arch Treasurer and former Third
Consul, had already been instructed to prepare a draft.
What he produced was practically the Constitution of 1791,
which Talleyrand handed over to the Senate for improvement and revision, insisting only upon the substitution of
two Chambers for one. At the same time he reminded them
that the new King would probably prove as good a judge of
a Constitution as any of them, that he had in the old days of
the constituent Assembly been noted for his liberal sentiments, and that his long sojourn in England had provided
him with the opportunity for further study of free institutions.

On 6th April the new Constitution was passed unanim-
ously, and Talleyrand christened it the Charter, by which
name it was henceforward to be known. The second article
read as follows: 'The French people freely call to the
throne of France Louis-Stanilas-Xavier of France, brother
of the last King—and after him the other members of the
House of Bourbon in the old order.'

When Vitrolles read the terms of the Charter, which
reached him under cover of a letter, signed by Talleyrand
and other members of the Government, he considered it a

calamity. He was already on his return journey to Paris together with the Count d'Artois, but he now hurried on in advance in order if possible to undo the work that had been accomplished in his absence.

Talleyrand received him with his usual urbanity and lightheartedly assented to the suggestion that the Senate should be requested to register the letters patent which appointed the Count d'Artois Lieutenant-General of the country. Vitrolles breathed again, believing he had gained a great point for the principle of absolute monarchy. A few minutes later, however, Talleyrand, who had in the meanwhile been talking to another visitor, returned to Vitrolles with the remark: 'Oh, by the way, His Highness's letters patent cannot be recognised by the Senate'—and he went on to explain that the King must first accept and take the oath to the Constitution. What then, objected Vitrolles, was to be the Prince's position? The King would not arrive for a fortnight and meanwhile it was unthinkable that his brother should occupy any subordinate post. Talleyrand eventually solved the problem by the suggestion that he should himself resign from being president of the Provisional Government and that the Prince should take his place. With this Vitrolles had to content himself, and returned once more to his master.

10th April was Easter Day. A solemn Te Deum was celebrated in the former Place de la Révolution according to the rites of the Orthodox Church. Talleyrand could watch it from his windows. That day the Emperor of Russia dined with him, together with the Duchess of Courland and her daughter, Dorothea de Périgord. On the 12th the Count d'Artois made his entry into Paris, and Talleyrand was one of those who greeted him on the outskirts of the city. On the 14th the Count was compelled to receive with none too good a grace the post of Lieutenant-General of

the Kingdom from the hands of the Senate. Talleyrand was
their spokesman, and the Prince in replying to him said
that, while he felt certain that his brother would accept the
principle of the Constitution, there were, no doubt, certain
alterations that could be necessary.

The King himself, who had been detained in England by
an unusually severe attack of gout, landed at Calais on 24th
April, and was met by Talleyrand at Compiègne. Louis
was fifty-eight and an old man for his age. Enormously
fat, his unwieldy bulk did not rob his appearance of dignity,
which was due to a profound self-confidence and complete
absence of doubt as to the sanctity of his claims and the
inviolability of his position. Thus he was able throughout
his life to meet all the vicissitudes of fortune with unruffled
serenity. A sound intelligence fortified by wide reading,
especially of the classics, enabled him to find the appropriate
words upon most occasions: 'I am pleased to see you,' he
greeted Talleyrand. 'Our houses date from the same epoch.
My ancestors were the cleverer; had yours been, you would
say to me to-day : "Take a chair, draw it up, let us talk of
our affairs." To-day it is I who say to you: "Be seated, let
us converse." '

With these friendly and flattering words, which were
much appreciated and recorded with pride by the hearer,
Louis concealed his distrust and his determination that
Talleyrand should have as little as possible to do with the
internal affairs of the kingdom.

At Saint Ouen, on the eve of the royal entry into the
capital, it was Talleyrand who presented the members of the
Senate to the returned monarch. The concluding words of
his address were as follows: 'The nation and the Senate,
full of confidence in the enlightened and magnanimous
sentiments of Your Majesty, share your desire that France
should be free in order that her King may be powerful.'

The King's reply left little doubt as to the attitude he intended to adopt. He was not opposed to constitutional government. He was, in fact, far more broadminded on the subject that the majority of his supporters. But he was determined that the Constitution should be granted as an act of grace from the Throne, and should not be insisted upon as a right of the people and a condition of his accession. This was Talleyrand's last official act as a member of the Provisional Government.

What should be the verdict of history on the important and decisive part that he had played during the eventful days between the end of March and the beginning of May? In the first place he had had a policy when all the other principal actors were without one; in the second place he had so contrived that his policy prevailed; and in the third place it must be generally admitted—Napoleon admitted it himself—that no other policy could at that juncture have been better calculated to promote the restoration of order and peace.

The suggestion that the national colours should be adopted, the insistence upon the importance of the Senate, the haste with which a Constitution was produced—the work of months compressed into two days—the substitution of two Chambers for one, the bestowal of the name 'the Charter,' the reluctance to receive the King's brother as Lieutenant-General before the acceptance of the Charter— all point to Talleyrand's desire to reconcile the restored monarchy with the Empire and the Revolution, and to achieve this purpose if possible by a Constitution on the English model. Moderation, reconciliation, and constitutional monarchy, these, as ever, were the principles to which Talleyrand was attached and for which he was prepared to work when circumstances permitted. He was not one who would die for his principles, nor even suffer serious inconvenience on their account, but he held to them with singular tenacity and was faithful to them—in his fashion.

Guizot has said that the Restoration was a victory for the English constitution over the model of 1791. We have seen how it was the English constitution which Talleyrand preferred in 1789, twenty-five years before, and it was the same to which he was to adhere in 1830, sixteen years afterwards.

6

In the new Government set up by the restored monarchy Talleyrand was appointed to the post of Minister for Foreign Affairs. Once more he took charge of the department which he had administered under the Directory, the Consulate, and the Empire.

His first task was one which no diplomatist could envy. France was still in a state of war with the Allies. He had therefore to conclude first an armistice and then a peace with the victorious Powers whose troops were distributed in various parts of the kingdom and whose sovereigns were firmly established in the capital. Talleyrand has been unjustly criticised by his compatriots for the nature of the treaty which, in these circumstances, he concluded. An unprejudiced observer is, however, more likely to be surprised by the generosity than by the severity of the terms which he succeeded in extracting from the Allies. They were in a position to dictate whatever conditions they desired. If Napoleon, who was still the greatest captain of the age and whose name still kindled enthusiasm in the army, was unable to put a force into the field or to strike another blow, what hope had Talleyrand, without an army or a following, of offering any effective resistance to the demands presented to him? In such a situation only two courses were open, either to obtain by negotiation the best terms possible and to accept them with a good grace or else to refuse to treat and sullenly to make plain that whatever settlement was arrived at was dictated by force. Talleyrand adopted the former alternative and abundantly justified his conduct by the argument that it was of the first importance at that moment for the future Government of France to obtain the confidence and the good will of Europe.

When it is remembered that for twenty years the great Powers had, with brief intervals, been at war with France, and that she had inflicted immense damage on the interests of England and Russia, and had subjected Austria and Prussia to the deepest humiliation, it can hardly be contended that the terms of the treaty were harsh which left France, now completely defeated, with more extended territory than she possessed before the war began, which allowed her to retain the invaluable works of art which her victorious troops had rifled from the galleries of Europe, and which exacted no indemnity for all the losses suffered by other nations. That France had to surrender her conquests in the Low Countries and in Holland, that she had to withdraw from Germany, Italy, and Switzerland, and that England retained the colonial possessions that she had captured, can hardly be considered surprising, especially when it is remembered that the inclusion within France of Avignon and Montbéliard, of Annecy and Chambéry, which had not formed part of the ancient kingdom, was recognised, and that the troops which were occupying Paris were withdrawn forthwith. There is no place for defeat in the philosophy of chauvinism. Although the latter word had not been coined in the days of the first Napoleon the spirit existed, and to that spirit it had seemed only right and proper that the whole of Europe should serve as the footstool of France. Now, when the tide of victory had turned, patriots of that kidney could only explain facts by alleging

treachery—and when the peace was signed by a politician
with so equivocal a past, it was not unnatural that he should
be suspected of having sold his country. The jingo nationalist is always the first to denounce his fellow countrymen as
traitors.

But Talleyrand was not ashamed of his work. He had
never set great store by public opinion and he could afford
now to despise the views of those who thought that they
might retain the conquests at the price of having disowned
the conqueror. He had never cared about those conquests,
and had always foreseen in them a source of weakness rather
than of strength. He could therefore surrender without a
qualm possessions that he had not coveted. Caring chiefly
for the welfare of France he made the best terms that he
could for his country, and, accepting them cheerfully, he
laid the foundation of confidence in the new Government
and prepared the way for the greater task that he had yet
to perform at the Congress which was to settle the affairs of
Europe.

Chapter Ten

THE CONGRESS OF VIENNA

I

THE distrust with which Talleyrand was regarded by the more fervid supporters of the restored monarchy is not surprising, but the decision to confine his activities to foreign affairs was one of the first, and not one of the least, of the mistakes that Louis XVIII committed. Count Ferrand, one of the more reactionary of the new Ministers, who was known at one time as 'the white Marat,' was not slow to realise that Talleyrand was the most dangerous opponent of the ideas which he represented. Typical of the Royalist mentality was the importance attached by Ferrand and others to inducing the King to affix to all his proclamations the words 'in the nineteenth year of our reign.' Talleyrand fought against the phrase and succeeded in eliminating it from the proclamation of Saint Ouen, but it appeared in the Charter. He knew the minds of his fellow-countrymen which he had been studying all his life. They were willing now to be rid of Napoleon, but they still looked back with pride, if without regret, upon the epoch of glory, and they were loth to pretend that during the days when the eagles and the tricolour swept invincibly over Europe the fat old gentleman at Hartwell had really been the King of France.

Talleyrand was allowed no hand in the final drafting of the Charter, and his protests against the limitations imposed upon the freedom of the press went unheeded. In this

matter, as in every other where he took any part, he foresaw
and sought to remove the causes which were to prove fatal
to the Restoration.

Nobody understood more clearly the errors that were
being committed, nobody deplored more sincerely the
reactionary and undemocratic tendencies of the time, than
the liberal-minded autocrat who was so largely responsible
for restoring the monarchy. Alexander blamed Talleyrand.
He himself had always doubted the wisdom of bringing
back the Bourbons, he had thought of establishing a new
dynasty, he had been willing to contemplate a republic. It
was Talleyrand who had over-persuaded him; it was Talleyrand who had insisted on the Bourbons as the only satisfactory solution; and already the Liberals of Paris, known
and respected by Alexander, were coming to him with complaints and reproaches. Impulsive and volatile, the Emperor
was swift to turn against the man whose advice he blamed
himself for accepting, and when, with the King of Prussia,
he left Paris for the triumphant visit to London he did not
even take leave of one who in the days of crisis had been his
most trusted counsellor and his host.

In a letter which Talleyrand addressed to the Emperor
after his departure he deplored the coolness which had
arisen between them and defended the policy which he had
advocated. 'Liberal principles are in accordance with the
spirit of the age, they cannot be avoided; and, if Your
Majesty will take my word for it, I can promise you that
we shall have monarchy combined with liberty; that you
will see men of real merit welcomed and given office. . . . I
admit, Sir, that you have met many discontented people in
Paris, but what is Paris after all? The provinces, they are the
real France—and it is there that the return of the House of
Bourbon is blessed and that your happy victory is proclaimed.' The Emperor did not apparently reply to this

letter, and events at the Congress of Vienna were destined still further to widen the breach.

2

While the victorious monarchs were being feasted and fêted in London, Talleyrand set himself to the serious task of determining his policy and drafting his instructions for the coming Congress. 'The rôle of France,' he writes in his memoirs, 'was singularly difficult. It was very tempting and very easy for the Governments which had so long been hostile to keep her excluded from the major questions affecting Europe. By the Treaty of Paris France had escaped destruction, but she had not regained the position that she ought to occupy in the general political system. Trained eyes could easily detect in several of the principal plenipotentiaries the secret desire to reduce France to a secondary rôle.'

The first task, therefore, to be accomplished at Vienna was the re-establishment beyond all doubt or question of France's position as one of the great Powers of the world. In order to make certain of achieving this purpose 'it was necessary above all,' to employ once more Talleyrand's own words, 'that the French representative should understand, and should make it understood, that France wanted nothing more than she possessed, that she had sincerely repudiated the heritage of conquest, that she considered herself strong enough within her ancient frontiers, that she had no thought of extending them, and, finally, that she now took pride in her moderation' (*elle plaçait aujourd'hui sa gloire dans sa modération*).

Convinced of the importance of these general principles he proceeded to draw up written instructions for his own guidance. This document has rightly attained some degree of celebrity. If ever a text-book is compiled for the education of diplomatists these instructions should find prominent place in it. No better model could be found of concision and perspicuity. In some thirty pages of print is contained a complete introduction to all the European problems of the day, and a lucid indication of the policy to be pursued with regard to each of them by the French plenipotentiary at the Congress.

For more than twenty years Europe had been at war. During that time there had been many changes, both as regards the causes for which the nations were fighting and the sides upon which they fought. The enemies of one year had become the allies of the next, and alliances so rapidly formed had been dissolved with equal rapidity. Territories had changed hands, dynasties had been overthrown, new monarchs had been set up, old ones had been sent into exile, new kingdoms had been called into existence, frontiers that had held good for centuries had disappeared. Changes more remarkable than magic had succeeded one another with bewildering celerity, but now the wand of the magician was broken, the fabric that he had created was in pieces, and it was the arduous duty of ordinary men to reassemble the parts.

'The first question to decide,' wrote Talleyrand, 'is who, that is to say, what states, shall take part in the Congress, and the next is to settle the various subjects with which they must deal. Then comes the question of the manner and method of procedure, the order in which these matters shall receive attention, the form to be given to the decisions arrived at, and the way in which such decisions shall be enforced.' To all these questions the answer is returned, plain and decisive. Wherever doubt arises it is solved by application of the principle of legitimacy. This principle is to serve as a guide and a test in every difficulty.

Having dealt briefly with every question that will demand attention, from the future equilibrium of Europe to the slave trade, and having briefly indicated his policy with regard to each, he finally reduces the main interests of France to four, and thus enumerates them in order of importance:

(1) That Austria shall be prevented from making one of her princes King of Sardinia.
(2) That Naples shall be restored to its former ruler.
(3) That the whole of Poland shall not pass to Russia.
(4) That Prussia shall not acquire the whole of Saxony.

Talleyrand was successful in maintaining the French point of view with regard to each of these four questions. The last two were to prove the most difficult and to come nearest to destroying the harmony of the Congress.

Talleyrand had always held the view that the partition of Poland had been a crime and that its reconstruction was desirable. That belief he re-affirms in the Vienna instructions. 'The re-establishment of the Kingdom of Poland would be a benefit and a very great benefit; but only on the three following conditions:

(1) That it should be independent.
(2) That it should have a strong Constitution.
(3) That it should not be necessary to compensate Prussia and Austria for the parts they would lose.'

All these conditions were, at the time, impossible of fulfilment. Having shown that this is the case Talleyrand reluctantly concludes that the continuation of the arrangement existing before the war, that is to say, of the partition, is the best solution. But it will be only temporary. 'By remaining partitioned Poland will not be destroyed for ever. The Poles although not forming a political entity will always form a family. They will no longer have a common country, but they will have a common language. They will, therefore, remain united by the strongest and most lasting of all bonds. They will, under foreign domination, reach the age of manhood which they have not achieved in nine centuries of independence, and the moment when they reach it will not be far distant from the moment when, having won their freedom, they will all rally round one centre.'

The vision was clear, the words were prophetic, and the future that he foresaw was accomplished in a hundred years.

3

Having thus prepared his own instructions, nothing remained but to select his companions. Three other pleni-potentiaries were appointed—the Duke of Dalberg, of German origin, who had been closely associated with Talleyrand in all the intrigues and diplomacy connected with the restoration; Alexis de Noailles, an aide-de-camp of the Count d'Artois; and the Marquis de la Tour du Pin, whom we have seen in exile in America and as a prefect of Napoleon. In selecting these assistants Talleyrand was thinking more of Paris than of Vienna. So far as the real work of the Congress was concerned he relied upon him-self and upon the able assistance of La Besnardière, a permanent official of the Ministry for Foreign Affairs. The others were to act as links with Paris, not only to keep him informed of the intrigues that were going on there but also —especially in the case of Alexis de Noailles—to act as the informant of the extreme Royalists and to report to his enemies what Talleyrand wished them to learn.

In Paris he left as Acting Minister for Foreign Affairs his old friend Jaucourt, with whom he had been intimate before the Revolution, who had made one of the society at Juniper Hall, and who had now for long been married to that Madame de la Châtre who had, even then, been the object of his affections. Talleyrand could rely upon him implicitly both to carry out the policy he desired and to keep him informed of all developments.

There remained one other not unimportant member of the French Mission to Vienna for whose presence Talleyrand in his memoirs accounts as follows:

'It also seemed to me important,' he writes, 'to dispel the prejudices which France of the Empire had aroused in the high and influential society of Vienna. To do so it was necessary to make the French embassy as agreeable as possible, and I therefore asked my niece, Madame la Comtesse Edmond de Périgord, to be good enough to accompany me and to do the honours of my house. Her tact and superior intelligence enabled her to attract and please people, and she was very useful to me.'

Thus began a relationship which was to continue for the remainder of Talleyrand's life. He was sixty, she was twenty-one. A woman of great beauty, distinction, and charm, highly educated and of semi-royal birth, she devoted the twenty-four most important years of her life to the man who was her husband's uncle and had been her mother's lover.

Before he left Paris Talleyrand had an interview with Castlereagh, who was also on his way to the Congress. This exchange of views was eminently satisfactory to both. Talleyrand was again striving, as he had ever striven, and as he was to strive to the end, for a better understanding between France and England. So eager were his expressions of good will that Castlereagh reported that he found it necessary 'rather to repress the exuberance of this senti-ment and to prevent its assuming a shape which, by exciting jealousy in other states, might impair our respective means of being really useful.'

The one interest which the two men had in common, and which was to enable them to work harmoniously together, was a genuine desire to establish the peace of Europe upon a lasting basis.

4

The Congress that assembled at Vienna in the autumn of 1814 attracted to that city all that was most brilliant in Europe. Not only did the leading statesmen of every country attend, but in most cases the reigning princes accompanied them. It was calculated that the royal palace served as lodging at one moment to two emperors and as many empresses, four kings, one queen, two heirs to thrones, two grand-duchesses, and three princes. Minor royalties were more numerous. The courtiers followed in the train of their sovereigns. The flower of European nobility, the richest, the most distinguished, the most beautiful, all who played any part either in the political or in the social sphere flocked to Vienna. The majority were not there for work. They never had worked and never meant to. The eighteenth-century tradition of pleasure still lingered. It was strangely appropriate that the octogenarian Prince de Ligne, the very soul of the eighteenth century, should have come there and been much in evidence, that he should have made the jest about the Congress that is best remembered: '*Le Congrès ne marche pas, mais il danse*,' that he himself should have danced there and made love, arranging midnight rendezvous to the last, and that in the midst of all that frivolity he should have died before the Congress dispersed. When his end was near he remarked with a smile that he was glad to be providing the Congress with yet another spectacle, the funeral of a Field-Marshal and Knight of the Golden Fleece.

There was an endless series of balls and banquets, hunts, shooting-parties, and musical rides. There were theatrical performances, some given by the most celebrated professionals of Europe, others performed by aristocratic amateurs. There was a medieval tournament in which these paladins of the nineteenth century aped the customs of their ancestors, contending in armour for their ladies' favours, and acquitting themselves so ably that one prince was carried unconscious from the lists. Masked entertainments were frequent, and glamour was lent to them by the knowledge that any mysterious stranger might be the ruler of a vast kingdom, that any domino might conceal a queen. The English Ambassador, a half-brother of Lord Castlereagh, who made himself slightly ridiculous by his ostentation, attempted a fancy dress ball, in which everybody was to appear in Elizabethan costume. This was a failure, as only the English dressed up. More successful on grounds of originality was the effort of Sir Sidney Smith, the hero of Acre, who told such tedious stories that the Prince de Ligne called him Long Acre. He organised what the foreigners believed to be a picnic but which would have been more accurately described as a subscription dinner and dance. After the dinner Sir Sidney delivered a lengthy speech which, to those unaccustomed to English manners seemed a novel and amusing departure, and the profits of the evening were devoted to the benevolent purpose of emancipating Christian prisoners in Algeria. It was altogether a very English entertainment.

Among the many who came to Vienna on this occasion for no better reason than that it was the fashion to do so was the Count de la Garde-Chambonas, who wrote a complete volume devoted solely to the social side of the Congress. He went everywhere, met everybody of importance, and it is thus that he describes his first visit to the French Embassy: 'It is a memorable thing in a man's life to be able to approach closely to an actor who has played a principal part on the world's stage. . . . I reached the embassy early. There was nobody there except M. de Talleyrand, the Duke of Dalberg, and Madame Edmond de Périgord. The Prince bade me welcome with the exquisite grace that had become a second nature to him, and taking hold of my hand with the kindliness reminiscent of a bygone period, he said: "I had to come to Vienna, Monsieur, in order to have the pleasure of seeing you at my home."

'I had not seen him since 1806, but I was struck once more with the intellectual sublimity of the look, the imperturbable calm of the features, the demeanour of the pre-eminent man whom I, in common with all those for-gathered in Vienna, considered the foremost diplomatist of his time. There were also the same grave and deep tone of voice, the same easy and natural manners, the same in-grained familiarity with the usages of the best society, a belated reflection, as it were, of a state of things which existed no longer, and of which one beheld in him one of the last representatives. He seemed to dominate that illustrious assembly by the charm of his mind and the ascendancy of his genius.'

On another occasion the same chronicler was present at the Prince's levée. It was his sixty-first birthday, and several admirers were assembled in his bedroom at the moment when his head emerged from between the heavy curtains of the bed. 'Wrapped in a plaited and goffered muslin peignoir, the Prince proceeded to attend to his luxuriant hair which he surrendered to two hairdressers who, after a great deal of brandishing of arms and combs, ended by producing the ensemble of wavy hair with which everybody is familiar. Then came the barber's turn, dispensing at the end a cloud of powder; the head and the hands being finished they proceeded to the toilet of the feet, a somewhat less recreative detail, considering the by no means pleasant smell of the Barège water employed to strengthen his lame leg. When all the ablutions of water and perfume were terminated his head servant, whose only function consisted of superintending the whole, came forward to tie his stock into a very smart knot. I am bound to say that all these transformations were carried out with the ease of a *grand seigneur* and a nonchalance never overstepping the good form which only permitted us to see the man without having to trouble about his metamorphosis.

'At table M. de Talleyrand not only showed his natural grace and urbanity but he was in reality more amiable than in his reception-rooms. It was no longer that habitual silence which, as has been said, he had transformed into the art of eloquence just as he had transformed his experience into a kind of divination. Though less profound his talk was perhaps all the more charming. It came straight from the heart and flowed without restraint.'

5

Although the chief concern of the Congress appeared to be the search for amusement, business was in fact being transacted, and in six months a great deal was done. Talleyrand had arrived on 23rd September, and had soon discovered that although the official opening of the Congress was due to take place on 1st October the representatives of the four great Powers, Russia, Prussia, Austria, and England, had already been in conference together. The exclusion of France from these counsels was exactly as Talleyrand had foreseen and exactly what he was determined to prevent, and he lost no time in stirring up the resentment of the smaller nations and assuring them of his support. France alone the great Powers might afford to ignore, but France at the head of the rest of Europe became at once a formidable antagonist.

Talleyrand was careful not to complain, or to humble himself by craving admittance, but he allowed the line he was adopting to become known, with the result that on 30th September he received an invitation from Metternich to attend a private conference in the afternoon. A similar invitation was addressed to the Spanish representative with whom Talleyrand had been collaborating.

Talleyrand arrived punctually but the others were already there. Castlereagh, at the head of the table, appeared to be presiding. There was a vacant chair between him and Metternich which Talleyrand occupied. He immediately inquired why he had been summoned alone and not with the other French plenipotentiaries. Because it was thought best at the preliminary conferences to have present only the heads of Missions. Then why was the Spaniard, Labrador, there who was not head of his Mission? Because the head of the Spanish Mission had not yet arrived in Vienna. But why was Prussia represented by Humboldt as well as Hardenberg? Because of Prince Hardenberg's infirmity. (He was almost stone deaf.) 'Oh, if it's a question of infirmities we can all have our own, and make the most of them.' They would raise no objection in future, they assured him, to two representatives attending from each Mission. Talleyrand had won his first point—a small one— but in the art of diplomacy, as in the art of war, details are of importance, and every foothold gained contributes towards the desired position of superiority.

Castlereagh then read a letter from the representative of Portugal demanding the reason of his exclusion from a conference where the representatives of France and Spain

were admitted. His case was a strong one; Talleyrand and
Labrador supported him; a decision was postponed until the
next meeting.

'The object of to-day's conference,' said Castlereagh, 'is
to acquaint you with what the four Powers have done since
we have been here,' and turning to Metternich he asked him
for the protocol. It was handed to Talleyrand who, casting
one glance at it, immediately pounced upon the word
'allies.'

It compelled him to ask, he said, where they were. Were
they still at Chaumont, or at Laon? Had not peace been
made? If they were still at war, whom was it against? Not
Napoleon, he was at Elba; surely not against the King of
France—he was the guarantee of the duration of peace.
'Let us speak frankly, gentlemen; if there are still any
"allied powers" this is no place for me.'

The other Ministers found little to say in reply. They
disclaimed any sinister motive in making use of the peccant
word which they had employed only for convenience and
brevity. 'Brevity,' retorted Talleyrand, 'should not be purchased at the price of accuracy,' and returned once more to
the study of the protocol. Presently he laid it down with the
words: 'I don't understand,' and then picking it up again
pretended to be making a great effort to follow the sense of
it. 'I still don't understand,' he finally exclaimed; 'for me
there are two dates and between them there is nothing—the
30th of May when it was agreed to hold the Congress, and
the 1st of October when the Congress is to open. Nothing
that has taken place in the interval exists so far as I am
concerned.'

Once more the other Ministers accepted defeat. They
attached, they said, little importance to this document and
were prepared to withdraw it. It was accordingly withdrawn
and no more was heard of it.

A more important document was then produced which explained the decision arrived at by the Powers and the policy which they wished to pursue. It was suggested that all the subjects to be dealt with by the Congress should be divided into two categories, that each category should be handed over to one of two committees, and that not until these committees had finished their work should the full Congress be opened. The real object of this proposal was to leave in the hands of the great Powers the settlement of all the more important questions. Talleyrand saw at once the danger. So long as the former Allies worked in harmony he and his Spanish colleague would be in a minority of two to four and all their wishes would be overruled. He therefore said that the proposal was an entirely new one and that he must have time to consider it. To settle everything before opening the Congress seemed to him to be putting at the end what ought to come at the beginning. He received some support from Castlereagh, and the discussion then became general without any decision being reached.

Somebody mentioned the King of Naples, meaning Murat. 'Of what King of Naples are you speaking?' Talleyrand coolly inquired, and added, 'We do not know the man in question.' The effrontery of such a question and such a statement coming from one who had been for years in the service of Napoleon must have staggered even the trained diplomatists gathered round that table. Yet it was part of the supreme irony of the situation that there was not one of them except the representative of England who was in a position to remind Talleyrand of his past. The Prussian could not forget that his master had once humbly thanked Napoleon for leaving him a fragment of his kingdom, the Russian had been a witness of the adulation with which his master had overwhelmed Napoleon at Tilsit, the Austrian had been proud to conduct his master's daughter to

Napoleon's bed. Who were they to question the orthodoxy of one who represented His Most Christian Majesty, who alone of all the monarchs had never even treated with the usurper? On another occasion when the Emperor Alexander, referring to the King of Saxony, spoke bitterly of 'those who have betrayed the cause of Europe,' Talleyrand replied with justice, 'that, Sire, is a question of dates.'

6

The result of the attitude adopted by Talleyrand at this first conference was to affect profoundly all future developments. Gentz, who had been present as secretary, entered in his diary: 'The intervention of Talleyrand and Labrador has hopelessly upset all our plans. They protested against the procedure we have adopted and soundly rated us for two hours. It was a scene that I shall never forget.' When it is remembered that those who submitted to such treatment were the representatives of the four dominant Powers of the world whose troops had lately occupied Paris and were shortly to occupy it again, some estimate can be formed of the magnitude of Talleyrand's achievement.

Here it is not proposed to follow step by step the diplomatic manœuvres of the next three months. With the smaller nations at his back Talleyrand had succeeded on 1st October in getting, as it were, his foot into the door of the European council chamber. From that position he never withdrew, and very soon those who were already ensconced there were glad enough that he should come in and shut the door behind him, leaving his former supporters in the passage. He appeared to have failed in his first endeavour to secure a Congress of all the plenipotentiaries, but he had in reality won his own admission into the select conclave which consisted in future of five instead of four.

Once having established his position in that small and omnipotent society his next move was to destroy its solidarity and by dividing it into two halves to ensure that his own adhesion would give superiority to either half. Thus from being the representative of the one Power whom all Europe had united to conquer he became at a turn of the wheel the determining factor in the future settlement.

It was only a few days after the conference described in detail above that he found himself closeted with Metternich and casually made use of the word 'allies' in conversation. Metternich remembered his lesson: 'Don't speak of allies,' he said, 'they no longer exist.' 'There are people here,' replied Talleyrand, 'who ought to be allies in the sense that they ought to think in the same way and desire the same things. How have you the courage to put Russia like a belt round your principal and most important possessions, Hungary and Bohemia? How can you allow all the patrimony of an old and good neighbour (the King of Saxony) to be given to your natural enemy (Prussia)?'

In these words Talleyrand raised what were to prove the two thorniest questions of the Congress, and were narrowly to avoid bringing about a renewal of war. Alexander wished to create for himself a kingdom out of the whole of Poland; Prussia hoped to swallow up the whole of Saxony as a punishment to its king for his fidelity to Napoleon. Austria was naturally opposed to the aggrandisement on these lines of her two neighbours, and Castlereagh, more clear-sighted than Parliament or his own Cabinet, who were inclined to think that these matters did not concern England, foresaw that such a settlement would not conduce to the permanent peace of Europe. He was, however, not so strongly opposed at first to the satisfaction of Prussia's ambition because he still harboured resentment against so good an ally of Napoleon as the King of Saxony had been, and he was affected by the argument that a powerful Prussia would act as an effective barrier against Russia. Talleyrand was at some pains to dispose of this argument in a memorandum which he wrote and published on the question of Saxony. He pointed out that the rulers of Russia and Prussia were on such intimate terms that they had nothing to fear from one another. It was therefore far more probable that Prussia would rely upon Russian support in furthering her schemes in Germany while Russia would be assisted by the good will of Prussia in pursuing her attacks on the Ottoman Empire. This prophecy was fulfilled. The good relations then existing between the rulers of the two countries were maintained by their descendants to their mutual benefit and it was not until the end of the century that this understanding was destroyed. In October 1814 Talleyrand wrote that if Prussia got her way 'she would in a few years form a militarist monarchy that would be very dangerous for her neighbours.'

During the remainder of the year, while the carnival of Vienna continued with unabated gaiety, relations between the principal Powers grew steadily worse. It had at first been the custom for the Ministers to meet in the morning and the Sovereigns in the afternoon, but as the tension increased the Sovereigns, less accustomed to concealing their sentiments, found it impossible to bear each other's company so often. Each side was intriguing to strengthen their position. Talleyrand and Metternich thought they had won the King of Prussia but Alexander asked him to dinner and their work was undone. Alexander made advances to Talleyrand at a ball at Count Zichy's, pressed his arm amicably, begged him to call on him and to come without ceremony. ('*En frac, de reprendre avec lui mes habitudes de frac.*') He then suggested a bargain. 'Be nice to me over the question of Saxony and I'll be the same to you over the question of Naples.' Talleyrand replied that Alexander's views on Naples must surely be the same as his own. So Alexander turned towards England and at the British Embassy ball 'danced polonaises with Lady Castlereagh and country dances with Lady Matilda,' a gesture which nobody suspected of having any but a political significance.

The New Year saw the culmination of Talleyrand's tireless efforts, the completion of his task. On 3rd January there was signed a secret treaty between England, Austria, and France. The three Powers undertook to act together 'with perfect disinterestedness' in order to carry out the Treaty of Paris; if they could not succeed by peaceful means they would each put into the field a force of 150,000 men to defend whichever of them might be attacked. Bavaria, Holland, Hanover, and Sardinia should be invited to accede to the treaty.

Talleyrand may be pardoned the note of triumph in the announcement of his success to Louis xviii. 'The coalition is dissolved. . . . France is no longer isolated in Europe. . . . Your Majesty possesses a federal system which fifty years of negotiations might not have constructed. You are acting in concert with two of the greatest Powers and three states of the second rank, and will soon be joined by all the states whose principles and politics are not revolutionary. So great and so fortunate a change can only be attributed to that protection of Providence which has been so plainly visible in the restoration of Your Majesty.'

Perhaps it would have been more becoming to have terminated his despatch with the expression of this lofty sentiment. He went on, however, as follows: 'After God, the main causes of this change have been:

'My letters to M. de Metternich and Lord Castlereagh and the effect produced by them.

'The suggestions that I made to Lord Castlereagh concerning an agreement with France, which I reported in my last letter.

'The pains that I took to calm his suspicions by showing complete disinterestedness on the part of France.

'The peace with America.'

Even after the treaty was concluded a final effort was made by the northern Powers to lure France away from her new friends, and it afforded Talleyrand an opportunity of displaying both his sincerity and his statesmanship.

The idea, already mooted, was once more brought forward of compensating the King of Saxony in the Rhineland. So feeble a neighbour naturally appeared to most Frenchmen far more desirable than the King of Prussia. Those who had reluctantly abandoned that territory saw a hope of regaining it, and Talleyrand admitted that for purposes of ambition and conquest he would favour the plan; 'but that as his sincere desire and that of his Court was to put a restraint upon any extension of the existing boundaries of France he was against the project.' 'This example of statesmanship, rare in history, won Castlereagh's warm appreciation,' is the comment of the latter's biographer.

The altered attitude adopted by each of the signatories of the treaty soon produced an effect upon the Congress. In December war had seemed probable but the knowledge that the three Powers were prepared to fight served, as such knowledge usually does serve, to improve the prospects of peace. On 5th January Castlereagh was able to report to his Government. 'The alarm of war is over.'

Although Talleyrand cannot be accused of excessive modesty there was one boast that he might have made and from which he refrained. The policy which he had been pursuing at the Congress and which he had brought to such a successful conclusion was no new scheme which he had contrived to meet the occasion, no topical adaptation to suit the fancy of his latest master, but was the same policy for which he had worked all his life. He had welcomed it before the Revolution, he had striven for it by the side of Mirabeau, he had pursued it under the Feuillant Government and under the Girondins, from exile he had urged it upon Danton, during the Directorate he had endeavoured to return to it, and under the Consulate he had promoted it at the Peace of Amiens; he had remembered it at Erfurt and supported it against Napoleon in good and in evil days. This policy, the alliance with England and with Austria based upon the common interest of those three Powers in the maintenance of peace and in the avoidance of any alteration of existing frontiers, he believed to be in the best interests of France as well as of Europe. At Vienna he had triumphed; but already the restless exile of Elba was preparing to undo his work and to unite once more the enemies of France whom Talleyrand had succeeded in dividing.

7

Although much remained to be decided the months of January and February passed peacefully at Vienna. The questions of Poland and Saxony were settled by compromise. Both the Emperor of Russia and the King of Prussia got less than they wanted, but both had to be contented with what they could get.

The future of Naples presented some difficulty, for Austria had guaranteed Murat in the possession of his kingdom by formal treaty and the treaty had been recognised by the British Government. The position of Metternich was rendered the more delicate by the fact that he had been the lover of, and was apparently still in love with,

Caroline Murat. Indignantly Louis xviii protested in a letter to Talleyrand that the Emperor of Austria was worse than Mark Antony who had at least made a conquest of Cleopatra himself and had not allowed his policy to be affected by the love affairs of his Minister.

Castlereagh's difficulties in the matter were increased by the attitude of certain Whig Members of Parliament who cherished a sentimental admiration for the dashing cavalry leader. This was not shared by the Duke of Wellington, and Talleyrand recorded with disapproval that both Wellington and Castlereagh detested in Murat the man rather than the usurper. He deplored their indifference to his beloved principle of legitimacy which he considered that they seemed hardly to understand, adding the acid comment that the policy pursued by the English in India naturally debarred them from a proper appreciation of it.

The finesse of Metternich aided by the folly of Murat eventually settled the matter without much assistance from Talleyrand who, however, received a handsome pecuniary reward from the restored Bourbons for the services he had rendered.

One other negotiation with which Talleyrand was entrusted by Louis xviii was concerned with the marriage of his nephew, the Duke of Berry, to a sister of the Czar. For the second time he had to approach that monarch on behalf of a suitor for his sister's hand, and for the second time he was unsuccessful.

One morning early in March before Talleyrand had risen, his niece, Madame de Périgord, was sitting by his bedside discussing the prospects of the day, and particularly the rehearsal of some theatricals in which she was to take part. A letter was brought in from Metternich: Talleyrand, saying that it was probably to inform him of the hour at which the Congress would meet, asked her to open it.

She did so and exclaimed on looking at it: 'Bonaparte has left Elba—oh, uncle, and my rehearsal!' 'Your rehearsal, Madame, will take place all the same'—was the quiet reply of the Prince, who thereupon set about the usual preparations for his leisurely toilet.

It was the fashion at first in diplomatic circles at Vienna to affect complete confidence on the receipt of this sensational intelligence. Pozzo di Borgo prophesied that if Napoleon dared to set foot in France he would be hanged on the first tree, and Talleyrand himself was of opinion that he would more probably attempt to collect a following in Italy before making any attack upon France.

It was, however, soon realised that the centre of interest had shifted from the Austrian capital and that work more important than the negotiation of treaties was awaiting the Duke of Wellington. The necessity for concluding without further delay the business of the Congress sent Talleyrand, together with Wellington and Metternich, on an urgent mission to the King of Saxony at Pressburg in order to induce him to accept the settlement which had already been agreed to by the other Powers.

At Pressburg, there was living that same Madame de Brionne who had loved Talleyrand when he was young and had attempted to obtain a cardinal's hat for him before the Revolution. She was old and she was dying. For a quarter of a century she had severed all connection with one whose political activities she so strongly condemned. When he had been in Austria as the Minister of the victor of Austerlitz in 1805 she had refused to receive him, but now that he was in the service of the legitimate King of France she consented to do so.

Wellington, Metternich, the King of Saxony, and all the problems of the international situation at that great crisis were forgotten as the old man knelt at the feet of the older

woman whom he had once loved and asked her forgiveness.
He felt her tears falling upon him and heard her voice: 'So,
you are there once more. I always believed that I should see
you again. Deeply as I have disapproved of you I have never
ceased for one moment to love you.' The man whose imperturbable self-control had become a legend was so overcome with emotion that he could find no words and was
compelled to leave the room and to seek the fresh air in
order to recover himself. When he returned they were able
to talk composedly of the past and the present. A few days
later she was dead.

Before the Congress dispersed it was important that those
who had taken part in it should make some public announcement of the policy that they meant to pursue in the new
situation created by the return of Napoleon. Talleyrand
took credit to himself for the terms of the proclamation
which was issued and which made it plain that it was against
Napoleon only, and not against France, that the wrath of
Europe was directed. The usurper was denounced as the
enemy and disturber of the peace of the world and was
handed over to public vengeance. In his memoirs Talleyrand is at pains to justify the term 'usurper,' explaining that
in the past, while Napoleon's brothers were usurpers, he
himself was a conqueror, but that now he had become a
usurper too. Talleyrand would apparently have approved
of Napoleon's statement that he had originally found the
crown of France in the gutter and had picked it up on the
point of his sword, but why the ten months' residence of
Louis xviii at Paris should have so materially altered the
rights and wrongs of the situation it is not easy to understand.

Whatever may be thought about Talleyrand's arguments
with regard to the meaning of words it is plain that at this
moment he had sufficient sense of political realities to know

that it was impossible for him ever again to serve under his former master. But Napoleon, whose weakness—and perhaps whose strength—lay in his refusal to recognise impossibilities, saw no objection to employing again the man whom he had often blamed himself during the past year for not having condemned to the gallows. 'It is he, after all,' said Napoleon, 'who best understands this age and society, both the Governments and the peoples. He deserted me—but I had myself deserted him somewhat abruptly. . . . We were not always of the same opinion, but more than once the advice which he gave me was sound.'

At Lyons, midway in his triumphant progress, Napoleon issued an edict of amnesty from which the name of Talleyrand was one of the few omitted, but from Paris he despatched messengers to Vienna charged to enlist the services of the man whose property he had already sequestrated. The envoys that were selected were Montrond, Talleyrand's intimate friend, and Flahaut, his son. The latter got no further than Stuttgart where he was arrested and reconducted to the frontier, and Montrond, although he arrived in Vienna, was equally unsuccessful. Upon one subject the mind of Talleyrand was made up, as were those of all the Sovereigns and responsible Ministers in Europe—whatever the future might produce, whatever policy they might be forced to pursue, they would have no further dealings with Napoleon.

It was not until 9th June that the final act of the Congress was signed. On the following day Talleyrand left Vienna.

Chapter Eleven

THE SECOND RESTORATION

I

D URING the eventful days that elapsed between Napoleon's landing at Cannes and his defeat at Waterloo two main considerations occupied the minds of European statesmen. The first was how best to secure his defeat and the second was whom to put in his place after he had been defeated. While Louis XVIII, fatuously confident in the strength of his divine right, shambled with ponderous dignity from one Flemish town to another, those who had been responsible for his restoration and who felt that partly owing to his ineptitude their efforts had been in vain, were casting about for another solution to the problem.

There is no evidence to show that during this period Talleyrand ever wavered in his allegiance. But when the future of Europe seemed once more to have been thrown into the melting-pot it would have been contrary to the principles which had guided him all his life to exclude the possibility of any outcome save the one that he preferred, or to shut the door in the face of anyone who approached him with a proposition.

To Montrond, despite the long friendship that united them, he had given no word of encouragement, but when others who had been associated with him in the past, but who, owing to their Liberal or even Jacobin antecedents, had been excluded from public life since the Restoration, began to make their appearance at Vienna, it was only

262

natural that he should receive them and be prepared to discuss the future of his country upon any basis save the recognition of Napoleon. Lord Clancarty, who had been left in charge of the English Mission, reported such developments with alarm. Castlereagh's reply was characteristic both of his sound sense and of his insular aloofness. 'I agree with you,' he wrote, 'that Talleyrand cannot be relied on, and yet I know not on whom His Majesty can better depend. . . . The fact is, France is a den of thieves and brigands, and they can only be governed by criminals like themselves.'

But whomever Talleyrand may have been seeing in Vienna, and with whatever possibilities he may have been playing, he was not afraid to perform the most ungrateful task of a loyal friend in time of adversity, namely the demonstration to the sufferer of his own responsibility for his misfortunes. The office, delicate at all times, becomes dangerous when the person in question is a king, and Talleyrand in order to carry it out with becoming courtesy adopted the device of putting his own words into the mouth of another.

In one long despatch which he addressed to Louis XVIII before leaving Vienna he outlined with considerable frankness the mistakes that the King had made during the past year and gave him the soundest advice with regard to his future conduct. At the same time he slightly sweetened the pill by giving the impression that he was merely reporting the views of the Emperor of Russia. In the first place he pointed out how the good will of Alexander had been alienated. The Blue Ribbon which had been granted to the Prince Regent had been withheld from him, his intercessions on behalf of Caulaincourt had been ignored, no concession had been made over the religious difficulties that arose in connection with his sister's betrothal to the Duke of Berry, and the Charter had been drawn up on lines far less liberal than he desired.

He then proceeded to analyse the support which Napoleon was finding in France. It consisted of the army and of all the old revolutionary factions. The army Louis could hardly have hoped to win, but the leaders of the democracy realised that Napoleon was in fact their greatest enemy. These people, Talleyrand insisted, had abandoned any idea of a republic, they were not opposed to the legitimate dynasty, but what they could not bear was their exclusion from all participation in politics. Rather than that they were prepared to risk the horrors and hazards of a revolution. Now it was Napoleon's main object to make the present struggle appear a national war and it was for the Allies to defeat this purpose by making it plain that they were fighting against Napoleon only and had no desire to impose their will upon France. Alexander was fully alive to the importance of this issue and in a recent conversation with Clancarty he had insisted upon the danger, supposing they restored Louis XVIII, of a similar catastrophe occurring again at a time when the Allies were far less prepared to meet it, when they were not all collected in one town, and when they had not nearly a million men on a war footing. He had then gone so far as to propose that the Duke of Orleans would be the best alternative—a Frenchman, a Bourbon, and one who had served the constitutional cause in his youth and worn the tricolour cockade, 'which,' Alexander added, or Talleyrand made him add, 'as I often said at Paris, ought never to have been given up.'

Having thus warned Louis of the danger Talleyrand went on to advise him how best to avoid it. In the first place he should issue a declaration promising constitutional reform. In the second place he should not await his return to France in order to form a new Government. Thinly cloaking once more his own opinions by attributing them to Alexander he insisted upon the mistake of employing only men who

had emigrated and had therefore been out of touch with
France for the last twenty years. It was particularly regret-
table that the most unpopular of all these men was known
to be the one to whom Louis was most strongly attached—
the Count de Blacas; and he went so far as to state frankly
that the activities and the influence of the Count d'Artois
and his sons had done no good service to the restored
monarchy.

What effect such plain speaking produced upon the mind
of the King we cannot tell. His reply was to urge Talleyrand to join him without delay. Surrounded as he was by
the most loyal and therefore the most reactionary of his
supporters he doubtless felt the need of one who was
capable both of putting forward the more moderate point of
view and of supporting it against all opponents.

2

By the time that Talleyrand reached Brussels the battle of
Waterloo had been fought and won. It was the Prince de
Condé, grandfather of the ill-fated Duke d'Enghien, who
greeted him with the details of that event, and at the same
time congratulated him upon the success that France had
achieved at Vienna, 'with a grace,' he wrote, 'that I shall
never forget.' Gratified by praise from such a quarter, and
fully conscious of the value of his own achievement, he
pressed on to join the King who had left Ghent after receiving the news of the battle and had travelled as far as Mons
on the road to France.

When Talleyrand arrived there some misunderstanding
arose between him and the King, the most detailed account
of which is contained in the memoirs of Chateaubriand.
Any information from such a source concerning Talleyrand
must be regarded with suspicion owing to the mutual dislike

which existed between the two men, and when the incident is one in which the pen of a great literary artist might be tempted to enhance the drama such suspicion will be increased. According to Chateaubriand Talleyrand having arrived at six in the evening was soon surrounded by a court of flatterers, and when it was suggested that he should pay his respects to the King he replied haughtily that it would be time enough to do so on the morrow. The King, naturally resenting such conduct, was nevertheless persuaded by Chateaubriand to allow him to act as an unofficial mediator, and he accordingly visited Talleyrand and pressed him to reconsider his decision, without success. The King then decided to leave Mons at three in the morning. On learning that he was doing so Talleyrand leapt from his bed and, having made the hastiest toilet of his life, intercepted the royal carriage as it was actually leaving the gates of the King's lodging. Louis then consented to grant him an interview and having listened to all he had to say calmly recommended him to take a cure at some watering place, and having thus signified his dismissal proceeded on his journey. No explanation is attempted as to why either the one or the other should have behaved so foolishly.

Talleyrand's own account of the interview agrees that it took place when the King's carriage was already waiting, but makes no mention of the hour. He immediately expressed his deep regret that the King should be regaining France in the wake of the British army, and strongly urged him to take a different route, no matter which, so long as he crossed the frontier at some point where there were no foreign troops to protect him. He suggested that Lyons would be the best place to aim at, and that, having arrived there, he should establish himself in complete independence of the Allies. As the King refused to accept this advice he tendered his resignation.

3

Whichever of the two accounts may be the more correct the one fact that emerges from both is that Talleyrand was not prepared to resume his former position as though nothing had happened nor to allow his master to suppose that the Hundred Days were merely an unfortunate incident that was best forgotten.

He was determined that for once the Bourbons should be compelled to overcome their proverbial reluctance to learn anything from events. For six months he had been serving to the best of his ability and with conspicuous success both France and Louis. There, at Vienna, he had been in touch with the public opinion of Europe, and he knew that unless he could impress upon the King something of what he had learnt there the second Restoration would last no longer than the first. He had accordingly drawn up a memorandum which he handed to the King before they separated at Mons.

In this document he first defended his own conduct both in concluding the Treaty of Paris and in the handling of affairs at the Congress. He proceeded without any disguise or apology to criticise the manner in which France had been governed meanwhile. While the principle of legitimacy was triumphing at the Congress it was being attacked at home. This was mainly due to the fact that those who supported it confused legitimacy with absolutism. 'The spirit of the times in which we live demands that in great civilised states supreme power shall only be exercised with the consent of bodies drawn from the heart of the society that it governs.' To fight against that opinion was to fight against universal opinion, and the fact that many who were opposed to it had recently surrounded the throne had gravely injured the Government. The reason why the principle of legitimacy had fallen into disrepute was because some people believed that it connoted absolutism, and recent actions of the Government had encouraged that belief. In the old days legitimacy had the support of religion and people could believe in divine right, but religion now had lost the great power it once possessed and in the modern world legitimacy like everything else must stand or fall by the test of utility. Its advantages were obvious, but if people came to think that the abuses outweighed the advantages it could not survive.

Further, it was a mistake to suppose that the royal power ever had been absolute in France. In the past it had been limited by the action of the magistrature, of the clergy, and of the nobility. These bodies no longer exercised the same influence. Indifference to religion had penetrated all classes and had become general. Sovereign power must therefore have the support of public opinion, and in order to have it must work in harmony with public opinion. Certain guarantees were indispensable. Liberty of the individual, liberty of the press, an independent judiciary, and responsibility of Ministers: these, briefly, were the points upon which he insisted in 1815; these, roughly, were the points upon which he had laid stress in his election address to the clerics of Autun in 1789.

These views, he respectfully informed the King, were not peculiar to one country but were held by all, as he had discovered at Vienna where it had been generally regretted that Ferdinand VII should have been restored to the throne of Spain without having been compelled to grant a Constitution. It was of the first importance that His Majesty should have due regard to the opinions of other Powers, for England, alone among them, genuinely desired his return to the throne; Russia was hostile, Austria was tepid, and Prussia thought of nothing save her own aggrandisement. The declaration, however, which Louis had already

issued on his own initiative had made the error of under-
lining the fact that he was being restored by foreign soldiery;
he should therefore lose no time in issuing another designed
to win over to his side all that weight of public opinion which
had hitherto supported Bonaparte.

This brief summary of a lengthy document should suffice
to show how calm, how clear, and how statesmanlike was
the mind of the man who wrote it; and it seems the more
remarkable when we remember that it must have been composed as he went jolting over the broken roads of Europe
from Vienna to Brussels, taking short rests at bad inns,
that it was completed almost within earshot of the cannon
of Waterloo, and presented to the restored monarch in the
intoxicating hour of victory.

But Louis, deaf to the voice of reason, fearful for the
fate of his own favourite, M. de Blacas, and glad to be rid
of a Minister whom he could never like, placidly pursued
his way as far as Le Cateau, where his next halt was made.
Talleyrand remained at Mons, and, whatever his real feelings
may have been, presented the appearance of being well
content with the way that things had fallen out. Count
Beugnot met him at dinner at the Mayor's. 'M. de Talleyrand,' he writes, 'showed on that occasion a quality which I
did not know he possessed, that of being an excellent companion. He was in a charming humour and vented his wit
in amusing anecdotes and pungent phrases. I had never
known him so frank and pleasant. Seeing and hearing him
one would certainly not have thought that he was a Minister
who had been disgraced a few hours before. Was he yielding to the pleasure of being freed from conducting the
affairs of France at a time when they were more complicated
and difficult than ever? Or was he, perhaps, hiding under
those apparent high spirits the regret and the anger by which
he was secretly devoured? The second explanation is

certainly the more probable: but then what sort of man really is M. de Talleyrand?'

Postponing the solution of this problem which puzzled so many of his contemporaries Beugnot devoted himself to the task of reconciling the fallen Minister with his master. He claims to have succeeded in this endeavour by securing the advocacy of Talleyrand's uncle, the aged Cardinal, for whom he always had the deepest respect and who happened to be in Mons at the moment. Vitrolles says that it was a letter from Wellington that persuaded him, but whatever may have been the causes, and they were probably numerous, he eventually pocketed his pride, rejoined his master at Cambrai, and proceeded to act as though there had never been any question of his resignation.

A council was held forthwith and Talleyrand did not hesitate to make plain his position. He had prepared, with the aid of Beugnot, the draft of a proclamation which he thought that the King should issue, and in which the mistakes of his previous Government were recognised and the intention expressed of correcting them in the future. It was the duty of Beugnot, whose memoirs furnish the authority for this incident, to read the proclamation to the Council. When he had concluded the King, whose features betrayed his emotion, commanded him to read it again. After the second reading the Count d'Artois was the first to speak. He complained bitterly of the terms of the proclamation. It made the King confess to having been guilty of mistakes, and to having been led away by his affections. It represented His Majesty as begging the pardon of his people and promising to behave differently in future. Such language, which meant either nothing or too much, was humiliating to royalty.

Talleyrand immediately replied. He defended the language used. The King had made mistakes; he had allowed his affections to mislead him.

'Is it to me that you indirectly refer?' demanded the Count d'Artois.

'Yes, since Monsieur has put the question in that way; Monsieur has done much harm.'

'The Prince de Talleyrand forgets himself.'

'I fear so, but the truth carries me away.'

This was strange language for a time-server to use when addressing the heir to the throne, the heir of an aged and ailing monarch. It was more than the Duke of Berry, his impetuous son, could bear and the authority of the King, his uncle, was necessary in order to call him to order and to prevent the council from degenerating into a brawl. The discussion passed on to another subject but the proclamation acknowledging faults committed was eventually signed by the King and issued from Cambrai on 28th June. Wellington, who was already negotiating terms with those who for the moment exercised authority at Paris, was well pleased with the terms of this proclamation which facilitated his task. He was, as ever, the most conciliatory of conquerors, and the only point upon which he and Talleyrand differed was the return of the works of art looted by Napoleon's armies to the countries to which they belonged. Strange are the manifestations of national prejudice. This condition imposed by the Allies, which seemed, and still seems, to most Englishmen an act of obvious equity, was more bitterly resented by the French than any other action taken as a result of the second occupation of Paris.

4

No greater misfortune can befall a master of political intrigue than to be absent from the scene at the moment when the crisis arises. This had been Fouché's ill-fate at the time of the first Restoration. He was determined not to let it occur again and during the days that followed Waterloo, while the defeated Emperor waited irresolutely at Malmaison, Fouché, Duke of Otranto, made himself master of the situation in Paris. Now, the grave objection to Fouché from the point of view of Louis xviii was that he had voted for the death of Louis xvi. Far as the restored King was prepared to go in forgetting the past he had never yet been asked to receive a regicide.

Wellington, whose genius lay in summing up the practical needs of any situation and in taking the necessary steps without loss of time, was already in communication with Fouché. He saw that only through the compliance of Fouché could Paris be occupied without further fighting, which he was, as ever, anxious to avoid. It was accordingly arranged that on the evening of 5th July, Wellington, accompanied by Talleyrand and Pozzo di Borgo, should meet Fouché at Neuilly in order to discuss the situation. Louis xviii when informing the Baron de Vitrolles that he had authorised the interview added that he had told his emissaries while doing their best for his cause to remember his feelings—'I asked them to be gentle with me, and reminded them that it was my virginity.' Vitrolles, a better Royalist than the King, was not amused by the jest and immediately repaired to Talleyrand's room to await his return. It was a long vigil. The dawn had broken before the carriage was heard on the cobble-stones and the limping step of the statesman in the corridor. 'Well, well, Monsieur de Vitrolles,' he exclaimed, while two valets set about the task of undressing him, 'your Duke of Otranto told us nothing at all. What do you think of that?' Poor Vitrolles was equally annoyed by the meagreness of such information, and by the suggestion that he had some proprietary interest in the Duke of

Otranto. He hurried off during the morning to Fouché and asked him why he had said nothing to the King's emissaries. 'What would you have me say,' he replied, 'to people who say nothing to me?' and Vitrolles had to be content with this abridged version of the all-night sitting.

In fact Fouché had spent most of the time in describing the difficulties of the situation, difficulties which were largely of his own creation, and in exaggerating the strength of the Liberal and the Republican parties in order to increase the importance of the services that he was prepared to render. Talleyrand understood him, and it was arranged that they should meet again that day at dinner with the Duke of Wellington. They dined in the pretty house at Neuilly which had belonged to Murat. Once again Fouché began to paint in the most lurid colours the situation in Paris and the strength of the opposition to the Bourbons, until Talleyrand finally cut him short with a firm offer—a complete amnesty for all his friends and the Ministry of Police for himself. It was good enough. Fouché lost no further time in accepting it, and forthwith they two drove off together to the King for Fouché to kiss hands on his appointment. Chateaubriand, who had a longer memory than politicians can afford, saw the two as, Talleyrand leaning on Fouché's arm, they passed through the royal ante-chamber. It seemed to him a vision of Vice supported by Crime. 'The loyal regicide, kneeling, laid the hands which caused the head of Louis xvi to fall between the hands of the brother of the royal martyr; the renegade bishop stood surety for the oath.'

On 8th July Louis xviii once more returned to his capital. He was received by the Parisians without the slightest enthusiasm. On the following day there appeared the official announcement of Talleyrand's appointment as President of the Council and Minister for Foreign Affairs.

5

Talleyrand's Ministry was composed, as was to be expected, of moderate men who had served under the last regime. He did not forget his friends. While retaining for himself the Ministry for Foreign Affairs together with the Presidency of the Council he assigned the Ministry of Finance to the Baron Louis and the Admiralty to the faithful Jaucourt.

For the history of this short-lived Government we rely largely upon the records left in their memoirs by Pasquier, the Minister of Justice, and Molé, the Minister of Transport. Pasquier was one of those familiar figures in political life who, entirely without distinction, yet seem to render themselves indispensable to Governments, whose very mediocrity secures them from committing great errors and who fill one office after another with complete lack of imagination and with unimpeachable competence.

Molé was of a different type. He belonged to his age and might have stepped from the pages of one of the romantic novels that were then fashionable. Strikingly handsome, he was descended from one of the oldest families of the nobility of the law. As a child of twelve he had seen his father dragged away to trial and the guillotine, and had walked beside the stretcher upon which his mother had been carried to prison. Early privations had impaired his health as seriously as misfortune had embittered his mind. He had served Napoleon without enthusiasm, and he states as his principal reason for taking office under Talleyrand the desire to divert his mind by hard work from brooding over certain melancholy experiences connected with affairs of the heart.

The first task of the new Government was to summon a Parliament. So far as the Upper Chamber was concerned Talleyrand, still faithful to his admiration for the English

Constitution, desired it to be hereditary, and despite the wishes of the King, who would have preferred an assembly over which he could exercise greater influence, an hereditary Chamber was decided upon, and the nomination of peers was left to the Government.

The exercise of such important patronage was a great responsibility, but Talleyrand took it lightly. Vitrolles has described the scene as he saw it. 'I arrived one morning at the house of M. de Talleyrand and found him alone with M. Pasquier. He was walking up and down while M. Pasquier sat with his pen in his hand. "You see," he said, "we are busy making peers. The Chambers will soon meet. We don't know what influence we shall have in the Chamber of Deputies and we must be sure of the support of the Chamber of Peers."

'Then, continuing to walk up and down, the Prince mentioned names just as they occurred to him, as he might have done if it had been a question of invitations to a dinner or a ball.' As the other members of the Government dropped in they were all asked to suggest names. Vitrolles himself mentioned one or two, including that of a distinguished sailor. Talleyrand was pleased with the suggestion—'That will please the navy,' he said, and asked the Minister for that department to suggest a few more admirals.

To the surprise and indignation of the virtuous Vitrolles the list of peers drawn up in this frivolous fashion was approved without change or comment by the indolent King. On the evening of the day that it received the royal signature Talleyrand casually informed the company collected in his drawing-room that the announcement would appear in the *Moniteur* on the following day. Not unnaturally those present were interested and excited. Nobody knew but that he himself, or his nearest relative, might have suddenly been promoted to the position of a peer of France. 'Tense expecta-

tion was depicted on every face,' writes Molé. 'That of
M. de Talleyrand, on the other hand, seemed to me more
of a mask than ever. It was as if he were genuinely sorry for
people capable of becoming so excited over such a trifle.

' "Good heavens," he said to his questioners; "you'll see it
in the paper. I can't exactly remember myself, I believe
there's a Monsieur so-and-so"; and he named myself and
three more persons present.' This was the first that Molé had
heard of the matter, and he was, he says, never more amazed
in his life.

Later Talleyrand informed Vitrolles that two names had
been omitted, those of the Count de Blacas and M. de la
Châtre. 'And who do you think reminded me of the
omission? Why, it was Madame de Jaucourt, who was dining with me.' Now Madame de Jaucourt in the days of
Juniper Hall had been Madame de la Châtre, but she had
long since divorced her husband and married her lover. It
was kind of her to remember the interests of the former at
such a moment. Vitrolles comments acidly: 'M. de Talleyrand was much amused by this incident.' The question,
however, was whether the two names could be included in
the official list. The King had gone to bed according to his
invariable habit, at eleven o'clock, and even the intrepid
Vitrolles dared not disturb him. So Talleyrand persuaded
him to take the lesser risk of inserting the names in the list
on his own authority; a decision which subsequently received
the royal approval.

While thus light-heartedly creating a hereditary peerage
Talleyrand spared no effort in order to ensure that the
elections for the Lower Chamber should return a majority
well affected to the restored monarchy. He succeeded
beyond his hopes and beyond his wishes. Popular elections,
even with the restricted franchise then exercised in France,
are always capable of producing surprises. Instead of a

Chamber being returned with a respectable working majority in favour of the Government and a fairly representative opposition, the Royalists succeeded in sweeping the country. Bonapartists, Republicans, Jacobins were wiped out, and Talleyrand's Government of moderate men, who had served under the Empire, found themselves faced by an elected Chamber of extremists who regarded them with the gravest suspicion. Ministers who had been forced by circumstances on Louis xvIII had now to rely upon the support of deputies whose views were much more royalist and reactionary than those of the King. They were caught between the hammer of a monarch to whom they were personally uncongenial and the anvil of a popular assembly which differed from them profoundly in principle.

Fouché was the first to fall. He had created for himself a powerful following in the most exclusive circles of the Faubourg St. Germain. He had even, old and ugly as he was, won the hand of a maiden belonging to one of the noblest families. The King himself had witnessed the marriage contract. The Duke of Otranto believed that his position was secure and that belief was his fatal and his final error. The affection that he had inspired in the hearts of the aristocracy had its origin in fear. They had looked to Fouché as the one man who could protect them from the Jacobins, but now that the Jacobins had ceased to be a menace they remembered that Fouché had been a Jacobin himself. Almost his last act contributed to his own downfall for he was compelled to draw up a list of those whose conduct during the Hundred Days could not be forgiven. It was a strange document, for few of those whose names appeared on it had been more guilty than the man who compiled it. 'One must do him the justice,' said Talleyrand, 'to recognise that he has omitted none of his friends.' Previously we have compared the function of Fouché to that of an exterminator of rats who, if he is wise, leaves sufficient stock behind him to render his further employment necessary. This time none had been spared. The task of the rat-catcher was completed: his services were no longer required.

Talleyrand had never liked Fouché. Now he no longer feared him. The method that he chose for informing him of his fate was characteristic. Vitrolles has described the scene. 'The Council was coming to an end in Monsieur de Talleyrand's house. He was half-sitting on his writing-table between the two windows of his room. His bad leg was hanging and the other one was supported on the floor. All the Ministers had shut their portfolios; some were seated, others were standing by the round table, and I was in a large arm-chair between the door and the fireplace.

' "Gentlemen," said M. de Talleyrand in a manner calculated to attract attention, "I have now at my disposal the best appointment that the King can give."

' "What post is that?" said M. Pasquier, turning round.

Talleyrand then proceeded to expatiate on the humiliations of a Minister's position in France and the unpleasant necessity of negotiating with the Allied Sovereigns. "There is still one country and one only where the King's Minister can retain the advantages of his rank and exercise real influence. And that Minister is he who shall represent France in the United States."

Silence fell on the Council. Others might be uncertain as to the meaning of the words, but Fouché understood. It was his sentence of exile, the end of his career. His eyes flashed hatred at Vitrolles whom he knew for his enemy. But Talleyrand breaking the uncomfortable silence calmly proceeded: "America is such a beautiful country. Do you know that country, Monsieur de Vitrolles? I know it, I have travelled through it and lived in it; it's a superb country. There are rivers there such as we have never seen. The

Potomac, for instance, nothing more beautiful than the Potomac! And then those magnificent forests full of those trees . . . what are they called?"

‘ "Daturas," suggested Vitrolles.

‘ "That's it, forests of daturas." ’

A lot poor Fouché cared about the Potomac or the forests of daturas. The beauties of nature had never been one of his weaknesses, and as he passed from the scene of history he must have carried with him a bitter hatred for the old rival who had so delicately and with such exquisite pleasure administered the coup de grâce.

6

No doubt Talleyrand had hoped by throwing Fouché to the wolves to satisfy their appetites for a time and obtain a respite for himself. This hope was doomed to disappointment. The situation described above rendered his position increasingly difficult. Without the support either of the King or the Chamber he could not survive. He had an additional and a powerful enemy in the Emperor Alexander who had never forgiven him for the part he had played at Vienna.

It is possible that by the exercise of his unfailing charm Talleyrand might have regained the confidence of his old friend. He made little effort to do so. Both Pasquier and Molé are agreed that he seemed to be suffering at this period from a curious mental lassitude which rendered him incapable of comprehending or coping with the situation. Both writers attribute his failure to the same cause.

Among the honours that had fallen to him as a result of the Congress of Vienna had been the offer of a duchy from the restored rulers of Naples. He had refused it for himself but had asked that it might be bestowed upon his nephew.

and it was thus that his niece-in-law, Madame Edmond de Périgord, became the Duchess of Dino. With this young lady, despite the difference of age and despite the official and the unofficial relationship, he was now passionately in love. At Vienna, according to rumour, she had been attracted by a younger rival. Compelled to return to Paris she had begun, according to the fashion of the day, to pine away with melancholy. Afraid that she might die or leave him, Talleyrand had allowed her to return to Vienna. But the concession had affected him deeply and it was unfortunate that at this moment when such heavy responsibilities weighed upon him he should have been a prey to the pains of love and the pangs of jealousy.

The drama ended happily for Talleyrand. Molé, to whom we are indebted for these details, says that the ambition of the lady was 'to govern some famous and really powerful man. Nature had fitted her to play such a rôle, and to play it not without brilliance.' On this occasion she 'sacrificed her love to her ambition.' But the sacrifice was made too late to save the Government.

While his mind was principally occupied with matters of this nature it is not surprising that Talleyrand was incapable of devoting to affairs of state the attention they demanded. 'I feel I ought to write to the Emperor of Russia,' he said one day to Madame de Rémusat, 'but it's a bore and I should much prefer to go and play whist with Madame de Laval, who is expecting me. You must write the letter for me.' She did so, and the result was disappointing.

It is at least doubtful, however, whether any efforts that Talleyrand could have made would have won back for him the good will of Alexander. The latter was also under the influence of a woman, and Madame de Krudener had so filled his head with exalted notions concerning the divine rights of kings and the truths of the Christian religion that there was little hope of any impression being made upon him by one who was an ex-revolutionary and a married bishop. When Talleyrand invited the Duke de Richelieu, the most broad-minded and high-principled of the emigrant aristocracy to take office, he refused on the ground that his long absence from France unfitted him for such responsibility. But as this excuse did not prevent him from forming a Government himself two months later, those were probably right who attributed his refusal to the influence of Alexander. He was on intimate terms with the Czar who had given him a home during the emigration and made him Governor of the Crimea.

Talleyrand could read the signs of the time. He had dealt with situations far more complicated. The dismissal of Fouché had availed him nothing. When his agents in the Chamber pointed out to the deputies, plain country gentlemen from the provinces, the counterpart of the Tory squires who filled the Restoration Parliament, how great a service he had performed in getting rid of Fouché, they were met with the reply: 'Yes, the King was right to send away Fouché, but when will he send away the other one?'

'What other one?'

'Why, M. de Talleyrand himself.'

No Government can last for ever. To select the right moment for resignation is one of the most difficult tasks that confronts the politician. Terms of peace had not yet been concluded. They were bound to be painful and humiliating for France. Talleyrand saw no reason why his Government, distrusted by Parliament and disliked by the King, should incur the additional odium of signing an unpopular treaty. The tone of his notes to the Allies grew perceptibly haughtier and less accommodating. Finally he presented an ultimatum to the King. In view of the difficulty of the task before them, and of the lack of support that they

met with in the Chamber, they must insist upon the formal
and unequivocal assurance of His Majesty's support, and
failing to obtain it they must tender their resignations. Far
from being taken aback by such peremptory language, the
old King, whose imperturbability was truly royal and almost
great, replied calmly, after one moment's silence: 'Very
well then, I will take a new Government.'

It was Talleyrand's turn to be astonished. He had
expected protests, he had probably been prepared to yield
to persuasion; but the way in which his resignation was
accepted, with unruffled composure and without a comment
took, for once, the wind from his sails. It was not thus that
Napoleon behaved at a crisis—nor Barras, nor Danton, nor
Mirabeau. 'The King seemed enchanted to get rid of us,' he
said afterwards with a smile.

His regret at going was tempered by the reflection that
the moment had been well chosen, and by the belief that
his exclusion from office could not be of long duration. He
made two mistakes. He exaggerated, as Ministers are apt
to do, the value of his own services, believing that they
would soon prove to be indispensable. He also underestimated the ingratitude of the Bourbons. He did not think
that a family, for whose restoration he had twice been mainly
responsible, would offer him no further employment during
the fifteen years that they retained the throne.

Chapter Twelve

RETIREMENT

I

COMPULSORY retirement from public life puts a test upon the dignity of a politician. The result is usually disappointing. This is less to be wondered at in the case of men who have no interests beyond the political horizon. But even those whose leisure can be crowded with broad intellectual and varied social activites are often too reluctant to relinquish the noisy and exhausting scene of their hard-won and short-lived political triumphs. So deep and tenacious is the hold that this particular form of excitement takes upon the minds of men, that there are few indeed whose assurances of the pleasure with which they withdraw from the arena can be received without suspicion of their sincerity.

In the case of Talleyrand the fall from power was softened by every circumstance that could detract from its bitterness. It was accompanied by no disgrace. It left to others the uncongenial duty of signing peace treaties with victorious enemies. The post of Grand Chamberlain, which was shortly afterwards conferred on him, was a dignified sinecure bringing with it 100,000 francs a year and assuring to its holder a permanent footing at Court and a prominent position at every important ceremony. This income, added to the wealth he had already accumulated, enabled him to live and to entertain upon the lavish scale which he considered suitable to his position. He would continue to play in the eyes of the world the leading part to which he had been so long accustomed, and his salons would continue to be filled with the familiar crowd, who, with the same vigilance, would still watch for, hang upon, and repeat his every word and gesture.

Nor had he any reason to believe that the policy for which he stood was to suffer as the result of his downfall. Louis did not turn, as he might with good excuse have done, to the extreme Royalists to form a Government. Still wiser than his own supporters, he was determined not to be ruled by the hotheads who formed the majority in the Chamber, and who were prepared to prove themselves, in their turn, almost as bloodthirsty as the Jacobins in the days of the Terror. The new Government was headed by the Duke de Richelieu, who refused to be driven from the path of moderation; and Decazes, as Minister of Police, became not only the King's favourite but also a powerful advocate of the cause of sanity and conciliation. During the next twelve months Europe witnessed the curious spectacle of a restored monarch attempting, rather feebly, to defend his old enemies from those who were determined to avenge his wrongs.

The first and the most illustrious to pay the penalty was Marshal Ney. Louis had groaned when he heard of his arrest, but the Royalists had cheered. He demanded to be tried by the House of Peers. Talleyrand wisely declined to sit in judgment on him. He had no particular affection for Ney, but he doubtless saw as clearly as Louis did how great would be the reaction in the heroic Marshal's favour after his death.

Fear, the most common cause of cruelty, was the motive power behind those who were demanding that extreme penalties should be inflicted on all their opponents. The astonishing ease with which Napoleon had effected the overthrow of the first Restoration made many tremble for the security of the second. It was a cloak and dagger period.

Some of Balzac's stories which describe it are apt to strike the modern reader as too sensational. But he was writing of what he had seen. Dark conspiracies, secret societies, midnight meetings of desperate men, impossible plots— these were the order of the day; and real as a great deal of the danger may have been, it was many times exaggerated in the imaginations of the fearful.

When conspiracy was in the air it was not unnatural that the nervous and the credulous should look for the hidden hand of the arch-schemer in every manifestation of discontent. It was disappointing when one conspiracy after another was proved to be the work of obscure individuals, involving nobody of any importance. In vain the arrested conspirators were urged to reveal the names of their powerful supporters. A certain Didier, who was executed for having organised an ineffective rising at Grenoble, was reported to have said before his death: 'Let the King keep the Duke of Orleans and M. de Talleyrand as far from the throne and from France as possible.' The only evidence of the statement, however, was that of the General who had put down the rising, who had tried and brutally punished all concerned, and who afterwards was shown to have been guilty in his reports of such wild exaggeration that his testimony was generally discredited. Even if Didier used the words suggested they proved nothing, and the sentiment would have been echoed by half the population of France.

Nevertheless Talleyrand's conduct at this time may have been partly influenced by the knowledge that such suspicion was bound to attach to him and by the desire to convince the Royalists of his loyalty to their cause. Such motives for aligning himself with the party of the Count d'Artois and the extremists were powerfully reinforced by the natural antipathy of a fallen Minister towards his successor.

These were his excuses for temporarily appearing on a

side with which he could have had scant sympathy. It availed him little for he became further estranged from the King, with whom in reality he had so much in common, but who was strongly influenced by the desire to be served by Ministers who were personally agreeable to him. The King had esteem for Richelieu and he was deeply devoted to Decazes. Of Richelieu Talleyrand said that he had been selected to govern France because he was the Frenchman who knew most about the Crimea, and Decazes he described as resembling a fairly good-looking barber's assistant. These witticisms, and as many others as Talleyrand indulged in at the expense of Ministers, were faithfully reported by them to their master. Decazes had inherited the efficient police system of Fouché, and made full use of it for keeping his enemies under observation. Whether Talleyrand was entertaining in the Rue St. Florentin, or arranging his library at Valençay, or drinking the waters at Bourbon l'Archambault, reports of all his movements and most of his sayings were regularly received by the Minister of Police, who as regularly laid them before the King.

While Talleyrand thus succeeded in permanently alienating any good will that Louis might have felt towards him, he made little progress in his attempts to gain the confidence of the extreme Royalists. The intelligence that could charm Napoleon, outwit Metternich, and defeat Fouché was thrown away on the stolid country gentlemen who formed the majority in the 'Incomparable Chamber.' Against the wiles of the subtlest intriguer there is no weapon so effective as impenetrable stupidity.

His credit therefore fell with all parties during the year that followed his fall from office. It was not enhanced by an agreement which he forced his wife to accept, whereby in return for a pension she was to live abroad and trouble him no longer.

2

He continued to play his part at Court, and in June of
this year he was present at the reception of the young
Princess of Sicily who came to marry the Duke of Berry.
He drove out with the King from Fontainebleau to meet
her at certain cross-roads in the forest. It was the very spot
at which twelve years earlier he had stood with Napoleon
when they greeted Pope Pius VII, who was coming for the
coronation. During the drive Louis was extremely affable.
'His conversation,' wrote Talleyrand, 'never flags and is
always interesting.'

But the King's affability was not a proof of his favour.
The violent abuse of the Government in which Talleyrand
frequently indulged and which, with a curious lack of
caution in one proverbially prudent, he poured forth without any discrimination before many who were bound to
repeat it, did him harm, not only with those whom it
offended, but also with unprejudiced witnesses, who concluded from such behaviour that his faculties were beginning
to fail. 'He has prodigiously gone to pieces,' wrote Von
Goltz, the Prussian Minister. 'There is nothing more to
be done with him,' said Wellington, and even young James
Gallatin, the son of the American Minister, found time to
note in his diary, which was principally devoted to amorous
adventures, that: 'Prince Talleyrand is such an intriguer, so
absolutely false that nobody trusts him.'

The climax was reached at a dinner-party at the British
Embassy on 18th November. Talleyrand was at this time
living under a regime according to which he ate and drank
nothing until the evening. It was noticed that, as a result,
he was inclined both to eat and drink more than was good
for him at the one meal he was permitted. He would become
flushed at its conclusion and would talk more freely than

was his custom. He was fond of dining at the Embassy; he felt more at home there than anywhere, and he believed that England more than any other Power desired his return to office.

After dinner was over and the guests had left the dining-room, he led one or two of the Frenchmen into a recess where he began to inveigh against the Government. There was nothing peculiar about a fallen statesman denouncing his successors, but the British Embassy was hardly the appropriate place for an attack upon the King's Ministers by a Frenchman still holding a high Court appointment. Pasquier was there, and Pasquier, who had been Minister of Justice under Talleyrand, now occupied the office of President of the Chamber. He overheard enough of the conversation to make him anxious to escape, but Talleyrand fastened upon him and compelled him to listen. The arrival of some new guests, however, seemed to give him the opportunity he wanted, and he was hastily beating a retreat when Talley-rand shouted after him, in tones loud enough for the whole room to hear, a violently worded insult at the expense of the Minister of Police, Decazes, the King's favourite. Pasquier replied with dignity—this is his own account of the incident—'that Talleyrand might think what he liked, but that so long as the King had a Minister of Police nobody had the right to refer to him in such language.' He there-upon left the room but Talleyrand shouted after him: 'And the Chamber of Deputies allows itself to be run by the Minister of Police.' This was a direct insult to Pasquier in view of the office that he held, and it was fortunate that, having left the room, he was able to ignore it.

But the news spread rapidly. Talleyrand knew that it would. A moment's reflection, a slight fall in temperature, convinced him that he had acted foolishly and that his enemies would lose no time in taking advantage of his folly.

He knew the importance of spreading the right rumour and of making sure that the drawing-rooms of Paris should first receive his own version of the tale. He hurried therefore from the Embassy to the house of Madame de Laval. It was there that in January 1809 he had told the story of his famous scene with the Emperor, and he now again turned to the same organ of publicity as the best calculated to serve his interests in that small but powerful world of opinion which consisted of fashionable society. But his task was too difficult. No nation sets higher store by decorum than the French. In 1809 it was Napoleon whose behaviour had been ill-bred, but in 1816 it was Talleyrand who had grossly insulted a Minister of the Crown under the roof of a Foreign Ambassador, and although many of the Royalists shared his opinions nobody could excuse his conduct.

The scandal spread like wildfire through Paris and every fresh report of the incident exaggerated the details. The contemptuous term that Talleyrand had applied to Decazes was magnified into a criminal libel. The story was carried beyond Paris; all over France it was the only subject of conversation, and versions of it appeared in the English press. Of these Talleyrand felt obliged to take notice and he caused to be published in London a letter addressed by himself to Lord Castlereagh. Phrased in admirable English this letter so minimises the incident that it cannot carry conviction, and the appeal made in it to Mr. Tierney, who had been present, to confirm its accuracy does not appear to have met with any response.

The French Government felt compelled to take action. A high dignitary of the Court could not be allowed to insult with impunity the King's Ministers. Some were for severe measures and suggested depriving Talleyrand of his office. Pasquier says that Molé was the chief of this party. Others thought that a private reproof from the King would meet

the case. Pasquier insinuates that this was his opinion.
Richelieu chose a middle course. On the morning of 21st
November, three days after the eventful night, the First
Groom of the Chamber called at Rue St. Florentin with a
message to the effect that the Grand Chamberlain was for-
bidden to present himself at Court until further notice.

Disgrace of this nature might have extinguished one whose
political and social position was based upon feebler or more
recent foundations. It made little difference to Talleyrand, but
it was felt and resented. Talleyrand was anxious from the first
to make his peace with Pasquier, and when Molé, who was
asked to act as intermediary, reported that Pasquier had no
wish to resume their former intimacy, the news came as a blow.

'Madame Edmond de Périgord was at her uncle's when I
returned. On learning that Pasquier was throwing over the
patronage of M. de Talleyrand her rage was such as I do
not remember having seen in a woman, even in the street.
Her face was livid and she was trembling from head to foot.
Instead of replying to her abuse I turned my back to her
and with an impassive face continued to address M. de
Talleyrand as if we had been alone. This made her weep
with rage and she looked ready to devour me. At the same
time I read in her uncle's face and appearance that he never
could forgive me any more that he could Pasquier. We separated coldly and politely, as one salutes with a drawn sword.'

But despite one or two defections of this nature, the
salon in the Rue St. Florentin remained as crowded and as
distinguished as ever. The Government was not popular
with the Royalists and just as the courtiers had left Versailles
to do homage to Choiseul in disgrace at Chanteloup so,
by the irony of political fortune, the house of Talleyrand
became the rendezvous for those who were most opposed to
the policy of conciliation which he had always advocated and
which his successors were endeavouring to put into force.

Nor was his banishment from Court of long duration.
In February of the following year, three months after the
date of the offence, Richelieu, with characteristic magnan-
imity, advised the King to revoke it. He thereupon resumed
his functions, the King received him with his customary
politeness, no reference was made to the unfortunate
incident, and the relations between monarch and Grand
Chamberlain were restored to their old footing of guarded
and distrustful civility.

3

In the five volumes of Talleyrand's published memoirs
the fourteen years that divide 1815 from 1830 are referred
to only in an appendix of twenty pages that deal with two
incidents, Savary's accusation and Maubreuil's assault, both
of which had their origin in events of an earlier period.
From the age therefore of sixty-one to seventy-six his part
was one of a spectator. The stage was filled by lesser actors,
the play was tame and dull. It merited all the scorn that
lay in the drooping corners of his mouth as he remembered
the tremendous drama of the past and the rôle that he had
played in it. Nevertheless, so lasting is the fascination of the
footlights, there was not a moment during all those years
when he would not gladly have accepted an invitation to
quit the auditorium and to remount the boards.

But his existence was agreeable. The winters were passed
in Paris, the summers at his château of Valençay. He grew
more and more attached to the home that he had visited so
little during the crowded years that lay behind him. There
were many improvements to be carried out there, the first
being to remove such traces as the Spanish Princes had
left of their occupation. The unwilling visitors had proved
bad tenants. One of them had devoted his leisure to design-
ing wolf-traps, had turned his bedroom into a workshop, and

had covered the walls with specimens of his craft. On one occasion they had nearly burnt down the whole château as the result of holding an auto-da-fé of the complete works of Voltaire and Rousseau.

Talleyrand took a keen interest in the local affairs of that quiet countryside, where the post from Paris arrived only twice a week. Having been for so long an absentee landlord he was determined to compensate by benevolence for the years of neglect. He endowed the church with a belfry, he set up an almshouse, inaugurated a girls' school, opened a pharmacy where the poor could obtain medicaments without payment, and finally he became Mayor of the little town, retained the office for six years and when he relinquished it continued to act as a member of the municipal council.

His life in the country, however, was hardly what an Englishman would describe as country life. He retained his custom of rising late and spending some hours over his toilet. Dinner, in the early afternoon, was the main event of the day, and the fare that was provided at Valençay was equal in excellence to that of the Rue St. Florentin, where his table was reputed to be the finest in Paris. The celebrated cook, Carême, whose ambition it was to 'raise his profession to the status of an art,' pays a tribute, in his memoirs, to all that he learnt in the kitchen of the Rue St. Florentin, where he laid the basis of his European reputation and where his talents were brought to the notice of the Emperor of Russia and Lord Charles Stewart so that the gourmets of St. Petersburg and London vied with one another for the privilege of securing his services.

We owe to Lady Shelley the following account of a meal at Talleyrand's house. 'During the whole repast the general conversation was upon eating. Every dish was discussed and the antiquity of every bottle of wine supplied the most eloquent annotations. Talleyrand himself analysed the dinner with as much interest and seriousness as if he had been discussing some political question of importance.'

After dinner the Prince would drive in the long avenues of his vast estate. He would give orders for improvements and plantations, and would see to it that the woods were stocked with game and the rivers with fish for the entertainment of his sporting friends. So far as outdoor pleasures were concerned lameness and age restricted his activities to driving, but life within the château was rendered as cheerful as possible by every form of entertainment. Charades and private theatricals usually celebrated great occasions. Reading aloud was popular. While remaining faithful to the great masters of the seventeenth century he did not neglect contemporary literature. He was too much a child of the eighteenth century fully to appreciate the Romantics, but on being lent the first published volume of Lamartine's poetry, which appeared anonymously, he lay awake until four in the morning reading it, and prophesied a great future for the unknown author.

He was always reluctant to go to bed and the lights of Valençay burnt into the small hours of the morning. Every man loves to exercise his own talents and one whose conversation had long been acknowledged to be his supreme gift, who had found a willing audience so many years ago in the drawing-rooms of Madame Dubarry, was sure never to lack listeners now when his talk in addition to its natural charm provided exclusive and authentic information concerning the history of Europe for half a century.

It was therefore not surprising that there was seldom a shortage of visitors. If there had been the members of the household would have filled the gap. A doctor, an almoner, a tutor, musicians, agents, and lawyers were always in attendance, giving to the place something of the appearance of a little Court, and recalling the quasi-royalty which had once pertained to the Prince of Benevento.

Whatever other form of distraction the château had to offer, an evening seldom passed without the Prince being drawn to the card table. 'What a sad old age you are preparing for yourself,' he observed to a young lady who could not play cards; and during these long years of inactivity many were the hours that whist and piquet assisted him to pass agreeably.

Although the greater part of his time was thus spent between Paris and Valençay hardly a year passed without an expedition further afield. He had long since formed the habit of visiting, during the summer months, Bourbon l'Archambault, a small watering-place in the centre of France. In more strenuous times, when he had been a Minister of Napoleon, his health had required the change and repose that the place afforded. Delightfully situated in a slight hollow among gently rolling hills, the little spa had won his affection and he benefited from the treatment that he received there. He was always happy at Bourbon. In the old days his secretaries had marked how lightly he threw off the cares of office when he arrived there and how gracefully the formidable statesman would become a pleasant holiday companion with the humblest of them. His letters confirm such evidence. He always writes cheerfully from Bourbon. Whatever he may be thinking of the Government of the day, he finds there other things to amuse him. On one occasion he complains that 'nobody writes to Bourbon'—and adds—'however, we have got some new paralytics who arrived recently. There is not, this year, a single rheumatism of our acquaintance.'

Although he remained singularly faithful to Bourbon, he frequently made the experiment of visiting some new locality during the annual excursion. For three years in succession from 1817 he visited the Pyrenees; in 1825 he spent the summer in Switzerland, the end of the year at Marseilles and the beginning of the next at Hyères, and in 1829 he went to Aix-la-Chapelle.

He did not travel alone. Henceforward until the end of his life the Duchess of Dino was always at his side. At Valençay, at the Rue St. Florentin, and afterwards at the French Embassy in London she acted for him as hostess. Her natural dignity and her long experience of courts and of diplomatic society equipped her admirably for the task. And she enjoyed it. Count Molé, who at first disliked her but later fell under her charm, believed, as has been stated, that her dominant passion was to play an important part in the life of a prominent statesman. This theory accounts partly, but only partly, for her devotion to Talleyrand. During the fifteen years of his exclusion from public life there were other and younger statesmen who would not have disdained an Egeria who brought beauty, intelligence, wealth, and independence, owning in her own right vast estates in Germany where she exercised semi-royal prerogatives. Hostile as well as friendly critics pay tribute to her large dark eyes which were said to be the loveliest in France; and the rapidity of her mind, the swiftness with which she took a point was the quality which particularly astonished and delighted Talleyrand.

Her husband, Edmond, had long since ceased to play any part in her life. He was a spendthrift and his debts were a continual source of anxiety to the family. The marriage had been one of convenience from the first, and as no tenderness had ever united the young couple so now no rancour apparently divided them. She had borne him two sons who would carry on the ancient name and presumably inherit the wealth of their great-uncle. She had not lived in the same house as her husband for many years but in 1820 there was a somewhat ostentatious reconciliation. Later in the same year she bore a third child, a daughter, who received the name of Pauline.

Madame de Souza wrote to her son, the Count de Flahaut,

in August, 'M. de Montrond has come back from Valençay
bored to such a point that one yawns even to hear him speak
of it. Madame Dorothea has become mystical. Poor
Edmond is a pitiable spectator of this pregnancy conferred
by the grace of God. He fears his uncle may force him to
stay in bed when Dorothea is delivered. He sees their minds
so inclined to believe in miracles that for all he knows he
may be asked to suckle the infant.'

Edmond's troubles were soon over. When he had
recognised the child as his he returned to his own way of
living with no doubt a fresh lease of credit for the accumula-
tion of debts. The true parentage was generally attributed
to Talleyrand, and his devotion to the little girl, the delightful letters that he wrote to her long before she could read
them, his care of her education and anxiety for her health,
all suggest that he believed himself to be her father. There
seems to be no reason to doubt it, although in view of the
difference of ages and his previous relations with the
Duchess of Courland many people would prefer to persuade
themselves that the whole affair between Talleyrand and
Dorothea was platonic. Such self-persuasion no doubt
afforded some consolation to a large number of extremely
respectable and highly conventional people who frequented
their society both in France and in England.

There was more often than not a third on their travels.
The Countess Tyszkiewicz, whom Talleyrand had met at
Warsaw in 1807 and whose pretty niece, the Countess
Potocka, had visited Paris in 1812, remained his faithful
admirer until the end. She took a house in Paris in the same
street as his, and she had her own apartments in the west
wing at Valençay. She was only eight years his junior and
so no shadow of jealousy was likely to mar her relations with
the Duchess of Dino. When the three of them travelled
together they sometimes moved in separate detachments, as

inns on the road were too small to accommodate them all
with their retinue of attendants. On such occasions Talleyrand would arrive last so that the hotel-keeper would have
received full instructions for his comfort before his arrival.

4

If there be truth in the saying that a man may be judged
by his friends, those who take the least favourable view of
Talleyrand's character will find it difficult to account for the
presence of some of those who, during his latter years, were
most frequently in his company. The most prominent of his
country neighbours was Royer-Collard, a man who, if he
had not been a Royalist and a Catholic, might almost be
described as the John Bright of French politics. The
austerity of his virtue, both in private and in public life,
was the subject of general admiration. His loyalty to the
throne and the sincerity of his religious faith were equalled
only by the independence of his mind and by his complete
indifference to self-interest. He said once that the sight of a
married priest gave him a sensation of nausea, and Talleyrand's first suggestion of paying a call was coldly repelled
on the ground that Madame Royer-Collard's health would
not permit her to return it. But Talleyrand was not to be
put off so easily. He came all the same and on arriving after
a twelve-miles drive on an execrable road his first words
were: 'Sir, you are indeed a difficult man to approach'—
(*Monsieur, vous avez des abords bien sévères*). From that day
forward relations between the two houses became intimate.
To the astonishment of many, who revered Royer-Collard
as much as they abominated Talleyrand, a strong and lasting
friendship sprang up between the two. A few years before
Talleyrand's death Royer-Collard wrote to him: 'You know
the place that you have occupied in my life for many years,

a place that nobody else can fill. You are the only remaining one of the race of giants.'

Amable de Barante was a man of the same type as Royer-Collard, whose political biography he wrote. As a young auditor he first met Talleyrand at Posen during the Prussian campaign of 1806. It was his duty to go on to Warsaw to make the necessary billeting arrangements. Talleyrand bespoke his good service with the result that he reserved for him a large private house that contained the only bed with curtains in Warsaw. The friendship begun under such favourable auspices lasted until death, and it was Barante, the austere historian of the Dukes of Burgundy, who pronounced Talleyrand's funeral oration in the House of Peers.

Another friend, whose acquaintance he first made in 1822, was young Monsieur Thiers. The public lives of the two cover a century of French history. They formed a striking contrast in conversation. The animated little bourgeois, bursting with eagerness and volubility, and the phlegmatic aristocrat, with his long disdainful silences and polished epigrams, were each in their way admirable representatives of the two centuries to which they belonged. Thiers complained once that when he wished to talk politics Talleyrand would turn the conversation on to the subject of women. 'But,' replied Talleyrand, 'women are politics.' He called Thiers 'an urchin of genius.'

It may have been an article of the latter's which defended the painting of Delacroix that first secured him an invitation to the Rue St. Florentin. Delacroix, like many great painters, was provoking more opposition than approval. His methods, revolutionary at the time, were denounced by the pundits, but, despite their denunciation, his pictures were frequently purchased by the State. Government patronage of art is generally on conservative lines, and some of those who wondered at the exception made in favour of Delacroix noticed also his striking resemblance to the old Grand Chamberlain who, even when out of office, continued to exercise influence.

The young Duke de Broglie, whose first vote in the House of Peers was given against the condemnation of Marshal Ney, was another regular member of Talleyrand's circle. He had married the daughter of Madame de Staël. His principles were those of an English Whig, and, during a long life, he was never suspected of acting from any but the loftiest motives.

The society therefore that Talleyrand collected round him was as respectable as it was distinguished. Perhaps it was not so gay nor quite so amusing as that which the Abbé de Périgord frequented before the Revolution. It was certainly less mixed and more moral than that which was entertained by the Minister for Foreign Affairs and his mistress in the days of the Directory. But times had changed. The eighteenth century was over, little Princess Victoria was growing up in England and already immorality was frowned upon in the best society.

5

Meanwhile the strength of the restored Bourbon monarchy was being gradually undermined by the activities of its keenest supporters. Just as the Revolution had been frustrated by the Jacobins so the Ultras were determined to destroy, in their blind folly, the hopes of the royal family whom they served. In vain Louis XVIII endeavoured to restrain them. His influence was weakened by the fact that it was his brother and his heir upon whom they relied for support.

The Minister who seemed most capable of assisting the King was Richelieu, who combined a great name with considerable ability and complete lack of personal ambition. But he had one quality which, while deserving the moralist's approval, will always be a doubtful asset to the politician. There are many who say, when they are conducting affairs

of state, that they would far sooner be enjoying the ease of
private life. Few mean it. Richelieu did. However pure a
man's patriotism may be, he will not perform best the task
that is distasteful to him. Richelieu was always longing for
the hour of his release. He hated intrigue. He was ever
more ready to show generosity to an opponent than to do a
job for a friend. The highest compliment that he could pay
to a supporter was to offer him nothing in the way of office
or honours, thus showing his confidence in the man's
integrity—a compliment which, even by the most dis-
interested, was sometimes accepted without enthusiasm.

When Richelieu threatened resignation the argument
most frequently employed by those who sought to dissuade
him was that if he went he would be forcing the King to
send for Talleyrand. During the years that Louis continued
to reign Talleyrand was always the undesirable alternative.
While the fall of Napoleon was followed by a remarkable
outburst of genius in the spheres of literature and art, there
seemed to be a singular lack of talent in the arena of politics.
The Ultras could produce no man of marked ability; the
Doctrinaires were what their name denotes and nothing
more; and Richelieu looked in vain among his own supporters for a successor. It was inevitable therefore that when
a change of government was suggested men's minds should
turn towards Talleyrand, whose competence and experience
so far exceeded that of all his contemporaries. Nor could
anyone accuse him of suffering from Richelieu's failing—
the dislike of office. He shared the view of those who considered his return to power inevitable, and spared no pains
to ensure that it should take place at the earliest moment.
What he hoped to achieve was a Ministry that should include
all parties. To this end he continued his efforts to win the
confidence of the Ultras and at the same time made overtures
to Decazes which were well received despite the violence of

his previous attacks. But unfortunately for his hopes there were two people whom he could not win, the leader of the Ultras and the patron of Decazes.

At the end of the year 1818 Richelieu resigned and Molé went with him. Decazes was left master of the situation. It was generally expected that he would advise the King to send for Talleyrand, but whether because Louis himself refused to adopt this course or whether because, as Molé suggests, Decazes and his friends were afraid that, having once placed Talleyrand on their backs, they might find him too difficult to dislodge, the decision was taken to make General Dessolles President of the Council.

The new Government had an uneasy existence of less than twelve months. They sought to win the support of the Bonapartists and the Liberals, but although the President of the Council had been a General of the Empire, and although Decazes used all his arts to please the middle classes, they only succeeded in uniting the extremes of Right and Left in opposition. Molé was so little pleased with them that he confided to Richelieu his regret that Talleyrand had not succeeded him. Throughout the year it was expected that Talleyrand would be invited to strengthen the tottering Ministry by joining it, while Ministers themselves believed that their opponents were plotting with Talleyrand to bring about their fall. At the end of the year the General resigned, and the favourite who was already the power behind the Government as well as behind the throne, openly assumed the highest office. This was the end of Talleyrand's hopes of a coalition with Decazes who, during the few months that he remained in power, seemed more inclined to turn to Richelieu for assistance.

But the ministerial days of Decazes were numbered. The fight that he and his master had fought against the forces of reaction was doomed to failure. On 13th February 1820

the Duke of Berry was assassinated at the opera. The
Duchess, while her husband was breathing his last, pointed
an accusing finger at Decazes, and cried: 'It is he who is the
real assassin.' The hysteria of a distraught woman became
the accepted view of the political party that had long been
opposing the policy of the favourite. Feeling was so violent
that the Royalists plotted to coerce the monarch and to
impose upon him by force a Minister of their own choosing.
Their choice was Talleyrand and some may regret that the
plot did not materialise. Believers in the divine right of
kings compelling the descendant of St. Louis to accept as
Minister the renegade priest and married bishop who had
defended the proceedings of 10th August 1792, would
have provided a memorable incident for those who appreciate the irony of history.

How far the conspiracy went, and how deeply Talleyrand
was involved in it are questions which, owing to insufficient
evidence, must remain unanswered. Vitrolles is said to
have been the principal conspirator, but Vitrolles was
deeply in the confidence of the Count d'Artois and it was
the action of the latter which defeated the scheme. He
went himself to Richelieu, against whom he had persistently
intrigued, and implored him on patriotic grounds to return
to office. Richelieu was ill in bed, but despite his extreme
reluctance, when the Count gave him his word of honour,
'the word of a Prince to a gentleman,' that he would loyally
support him, he consented to resume the burden. Louis
sadly parted with Decazes whom he made a duke and sent as
Ambassador to London, and the hopes of Talleyrand were
disappointed once more.

Richelieu's second administration lasted less than two
years. The 'word of a prince' was soon broken. The old
alliance between extremists on both wings rendered the
attempt to govern on moderate and constitutional lines

impossible. When it became plain, towards the end of 1821, that Richelieu would resign, Talleyrand, untaught by experience, believed again that his time had come. He sought out Molé whom he wished to include in his Cabinet. All the places were already allotted. Molé listened to his plans without allowing him to see that 'I was humouring his ambitious dreams in the way one treats women or children.' His chances were, in reality, slighter than ever. In addition to the factors that had previously defeated him there were two new features of the situation unfavourable to his hopes. The first was the influence of Madame du Cayla, who had replaced Decazes in the King's affections, and the second was the increased suspicion with which he was regarded as the friend of England and the advocate of a pro-English policy. When therefore Richelieu resigned it was Villèle who succeeded him. Villèle had appeared in Paris as a member of the Incomparable Chamber and had been an Ultra from the first. He was on the best of terms with the Count d'Artois. 'The two brothers have embraced,' commented Molé, 'and Louis xviii seems to have resigned in favour of Charles x.'

6

The appointment of Villèle was the turning point in the history of the Restoration. It marked the final triumph of the Ultras, the slamming of the door on constitutional government. For Talleyrand it meant not only the end of his own hopes of office under the existing regime but also the beginning of a new period of liberal opposition. He had sought the support of the Ultras as a stepping-stone to power. He had failed to obtain it, but if he had succeeded we may be sure that he would not have used power for purposes of reaction. He knew to what end such policy was bound to lead. In 1817 he wrote that the two solid bases of lasting peace were legitimacy and reasonable liberty. 'Everything that is done on those principles will be in accord with the ideas of the age, and one must always move, and move prudently, with one's age.' From 1821 onwards the restored monarchy was moving not with but against the ideas of the age. Therefore it was doomed to fail. Talleyrand knew it, and acted accordingly.

In the summer before the fall of the Richelieu Government a bill was introduced which considerably restricted the liberty of the press. To oppose such a measure at such a time was to court unpopularity. Yet Talleyrand stayed in Paris on purpose to speak and to vote against the bill. When announcing his intention to do so in a letter to the Duchess of Courland, he added: 'One must be true to the doctrines one has professed all one's life.'

In the speech which he made on this occasion he again laid stress on the importance of acting in harmony with the spirit of the age. His two main propositions were, first, that the liberty of the press was a necessity of the age, and, second, that a Government endangers its existence when it refuses obstinately and for too long to permit what the age proclaims to be necessary. He applied this principle to the Revolution, daring even to maintain that despite its errors it had accomplished much that was good. The Revolution, he said, was in accord with the age when it proclaimed religious liberty, equality before the law, liberty of the individual, trial by jury, and liberty of the press; but it was no longer in accord with the age when it set up a single chamber, when it destroyed royal authority, and when it tortured conscience. In the most famous passage of his speech he used words strangely suggestive of those that an American President was to use long afterwards and make famous. 'In our time it is not easy to deceive for long.' Forty years later Abraham Lincoln discovered that one could not fool all the people all the time. 'There is someone,' Talleyrand went on, 'who is cleverer than Voltaire, cleverer than Bonaparte, cleverer than any of the Directors, than any Minister in the past or in the future; and that person is everybody (*tout le monde*). To engage, or at least to persist, in a struggle in which you may find everybody interested on the other side is a mistake, and nowadays all political mistakes are dangerous.'

At no time was Talleyrand so open to the charge of being false to his political principles as when he sought to curry favour with the Ultras at the expense of Louis XVIII's more moderate Ministers. That he did attempt to do so in order to return to power is undeniable, but no overt act or public utterance can be cited in evidence against him. On the contrary, at the very moment when Richelieu was tottering to his fall, when for the first time it seemed, as it proved, certain that the voice of the Ultras would decide the selection of the next Minister, Talleyrand came boldly forward and proclaimed his unshaken faith in the principles that he had upheld in 1789. In that famous year of great ideals he had not been an idealist, but he had laid hold upon all that he could find in the programme of the reformers that was compatible with common sense. To the gospel of common sense he remained true. The language of common sense he had always spoken, and after his long experience and deep study of events that language, as he spoke it, seemed full of the deepest political wisdom, and fraught with prescience.

Talleyrand maintained that he had never abandoned anyone until they had first abandoned themselves. During the years that followed the gulf dividing him from the Bourbon kings became steadily wider. It might, however, well be argued that it was they, not he, who were responsible, that his position was stationary while they were always moving towards the right, away from the principles upon which their restoration had been based.

One of Villèle's first actions was to introduce a measure by which all offences connected with the press were no longer to be referred to a jury but to be dealt with by magistrates of the royal courts. Again Talleyrand spoke against the bill. He was followed by the Duke of Fitz-James who made a very violent personal attack upon him, referring bitterly to the course he had pursued during the Revolution and under the Empire. All eyes were fixed on Talleyrand who leant forward in his seat listening with the closest attention but without betraying the slighest emotion. Occasionally he would take a note, but when the speech was finished he tossed his notes away, turned to a neighbour and nonchalantly observed that really M. de Fitz-James had a great deal of talent; that there were perhaps a few things in what he had said which were a little harsh (*des petites choses un peu acerbes*), but that otherwise it was a very good speech.

In 1823 France went to war with Spain in order to assist King Ferdinand, once Talleyrand's unwilling guest at Valençay, to break the promise that he had given to his own people that he would govern as a constitutional monarch. Chateaubriand, who was Minister for Foreign Affairs at the time, claimed all the credit for having brought about one of the least defensible wars in history. Talleyrand disliked war and he disliked interfering in the domestic affairs of other nations. In the speech which he prepared for the debate on this question, he claimed to have opposed Napoleon's Peninsular policy from the first and to have earned his disgrace by his opposition. Chateaubriand has described in his memoirs how, while listening to this speech, he felt almost stunned by Talleyrand's power of falsehood, how his eyes followed him as he returned impassively from the tribune to his seat, and how he felt torn between a kind of horror and a kind of admiration.

We have previously had occasion to question the accuracy of Chateaubriand's testimony where Talleyrand is concerned. Unfortunately for the apostle of truth as against the master of falsehood we know for certain that the speech which it shocked him so to hear was never delivered. The debate was closured before Talleyrand was called, but, according to the custom of the French Upper Chamber at the time, undelivered speeches were printed in the records, and it was presumably in this manner that Chateaubriand became acquainted with the text.

Soon afterwards Chateaubriand quarrelled with his colleagues, as he quarrelled with everybody, and resigned his office. He was appointed for a short time Ambassador to Italy but he played no further part in politics. On hearing somebody remark that Chateaubriand had grown very deaf, Talleyrand observed: 'He only thinks he is deaf because he can no longer hear anyone talking about him.'

7

Chateaubriand, sixteen years younger than Talleyrand, was to outlive him, but meanwhile the circle of his contemporaries was being annually reduced in numbers. Choiseul, the earliest of his friends, between whom and himself during more than half a century affection had survived many differences of opinion, died in 1817. 'He was the last,' wrote Talleyrand, 'of the people with whom I was brought up. Of that generation I remain almost the only survivor: it is most sad.'

The same year saw the deaths of Madame de Staël and of Dupont de Nemours. Of the latter Talleyrand wrote: 'I have been associated with him since my early youth. The losses that befall me every day attach me the more to the people that I love.'

The year 1821 besides disappointing Talleyrand's political hopes brought to him many private sorrows. In August died the Duchess of Courland. He had loved her passionately. At an age when passion might have passed from both their lives it flared up again in him and it was her own daughter who had inspired it. It is not pleasant to think of the sufferings of one who sees herself replaced in the affections of the man she loves by her own child. Madame de Boigne writes of the Duchess's 'despair' but she appears to have given no outward sign of it. She continued in regular and affectionate correspondence with Talleyrand till the last and after she was dead he wrote: 'I shall mourn for her until my last day, which I see approaching now without regret.'

His uncle, the aged Cardinal, died in October, and in December he lost Madame de Rémusat whose friendship he had made in the early, glorious days of the Consulate, when together they were attendant upon Bonaparte and Josephine during their triumphant tour through Belgium. No cloud had ever cast its shadow over that happy, half-amorous friendship of nearly twenty years.

It was autumn in Talleyrand's life. All round him the leaves were falling; now and then some great tree came down with a crash that resounded through the forest. In this same year, 1821, Napoleon died at St. Helena. When the news was reported in the crowded drawing-room of Madame Crawford—it was the ephemeral centre of Parisian fashion, and Wellington was there at the time—a momentary hush fell on the chattering groups. 'What an event!' was the inevitable if inadequate comment that broke the silence; but from a corner of the room the deep voice of Talleyrand made answer: 'It is no longer an event, it is only a piece of news.'

Richelieu died a year later. The Bourbons whom he had

served so faithfully would not even go to his funeral. Never in this world has honesty been worse rewarded. Talleyrand, who had done him no honour during his life, believed that his death was a public calamity and gave him, perhaps grudgingly, an epitaph that was quoted through Paris at the time, and is still remembered: '*C'était quelqu'un*' (He was somebody).

Louis XVIII died in 1824. His death effected no change in the political situation. Since he had fallen under the influence of Madame du Cayla, who was herself under the influence of the Ultras, his views had ceased to differ from those of his successor. He was buried without the omission of a single ceremony that ten centuries of feudal tradition had accumulated round the throne of France. After the coffin had been lowered into the vault four dukes cast upon it the colours of the four companies of the Guards. The crown, the sceptre, and the hand of justice were thrown after them. Then followed the spurs, the breastplate, the sword, the shield, and the gauntlets which the warrior king would have worn if ever he had led his armies to battle. But the last homage of all was performed by the aged Grand Chamberlain, who with great dignity limped to the edge of the open vault and lowered the standard of France over the coffin.

Talleyrand had an equally important part to perform at the coronation of Charles X, which took place in the following May. By all accounts he performed these duties with singular distinction. Charles X was crowned in the cathedral at Rheims. Talleyrand had been present there at the coronation of Louis XVI in 1775. Much had happened since then.

The leaves were falling. The Emperor Alexander, still young in years but old in disillusion, died in 1852. No reconciliation had ever taken place between him and Talleyrand.

In 1826 the funeral of Talma, the great actor who had refused to the last to receive the offices of the Church, was made the occasion for an anti-religious demonstration, a significant symptom of the way in which the wind was beginning to blow in a country where clerical influence was becoming daily more dominant.

Canning, who had been on friendly terms with Talleyrand, died in 1827, not before he had, in response to Chateaubriand's policy in Spain, 'called the new world into existence to redress the balance of the old'—a development which, as we have seen, Talleyrand had himself suggested some thirty years earlier.

In 1828 another death occurred which was a cause of regret to Talleyrand. A friend was surprised one day to hear him deplore the demise of the Duke of San Carlos. Talleyrand explained. 'You see, the Duke of San Carlos was my wife's lover; he was a man of honour and gave her good advice, which she needed. Now I don't know into whose hands she may fall.'

8

In 1827 there occurred an incident which created considerable stir in Paris at the time. Every year on the anniversary of the execution of Louis xvi a religious ceremony took place in the basilica of St. Denis. Talleyrand, in virtue of his office, naturally assisted at this function. This year, after the ceremony was over, and the Grand Chamberlain had conducted the members of the royal family to their carriages, an unknown man suddenly forced his way through the throng and advancing on the Grand Chamberlain dealt him a blow in the face with the palm of his hand. The old man—he was seventy-three, and very lame—fell to the ground. Those standing round hurried to his assistance, helped him to rise and supported him to his carriage, while his assailant was apprehended by the police.

The name of the man was Maubreuil. He had been in prison for an attack made on the Queen of Westphalia, wife of King Jerome, during the unsettled days of 1814, when Talleyrand was head of the Provisional Government. The attack had been made on the high road, where he had held up her carriage and had got away with a large sum of money in gold and much valuable jewellery. He had claimed when arrested to have been acting as an agent for Talleyrand who, he further alleged, had commissioned him to murder Napoleon. That Talleyrand could have given such a commission to such a man no sensible person, even at the time, believed. Maubreuil, who was an unbalanced and violent man of notoriously bad character, admitted that he had never had a personal interview with Talleyrand who had always acted through an intermediary. It is possible that some third party in that dark underworld which was the police system of the time may for some private purpose have persuaded this scatterbrained swashbuckler that Talleyrand was making use of his services. At his trial he delivered a violent diatribe not only against Talleyrand, whom he accused of poisoning Mirabeau amongst other crimes, but also against many of the most distinguished people of the time, including the Emperor of Russia, whom he described as 'the son of a murderer and a murderer himself.' The individual suffering from a grievance who accuses well-known people of crimes, is still not an uncommon phenomenon in the law courts. Whether the asylum or the prison is the proper place for such people is an open question. Maubreuil was sent to the latter for two years.

On the day of the assault Paris hummed with the news, and the gossip-mongers hurried round to the Rue St.

Florentin to express their condolences and collect their
material. Talleyrand might have been suffering from shock
—it was an unpleasant experience for a man of his age—
but he was swift to devise his plan of campaign. A gentleman cannot have his face slapped, but anybody may be
the victim of a murderous assault. It was important as
ever that the right version should be the first to get abroad.
So the doors of the Rue St. Florentin were open to all
callers. They found the old Prince stretched upon a couch,
his head swathed in voluminous bandages. He was ready to
explain to all what had happened and insisted that it had been
an attempt at assassination. Clenching his fist and imitating
the action of one who strikes down from above, he kept
repeating the phrase: 'He felled me like an ox.'

Although the accounts of those who had witnessed the
scene did not tally exactly with his who had been the victim
of it, still there was a feeling of general sympathy for one
who, whatever wrong he might have committed in the past,
was becoming more and more every year a traditional and
legendary figure among the society into which he had
survived, a relic of, and a link with, the past.

Pasquier, who had not spoken to him since the scene at
the British Embassy, called to inquire, and the two old men
were reconciled. Pasquier's heart had no doubt been
touched by the misfortune of his former friend, but Pasquier
was also one whose principal business it was to detect any
alteration in the weathercock. In 1827 the wind was
beginning to vary. The elder branch of the Bourbon family
were slow to notice such changes. The Duke of Orleans was
living in England, a country where Talleyrand had always
had friends, and the Count de Montrond was spending
more time than ever on that side of the Channel, gambling
and drinking very ostentatiously, and—less ostentatiously—
keeping in touch.

Chapter Thirteen

THE LONDON EMBASSY

I

Louis xviii once said of his younger brother: 'He conspired against Louis xvi, he has conspired against me, some day he will conspire against himself.' The prophecy came true, and this last conspiracy, to which Charles x devoted the greater part of his reign, was the most successful. His Ministers, although they were all drawn from the ranks of the Ultras and were convinced reactionaries, could never be Ultra or reactionary enough for the extreme right wing of their own party. Extremists, to whatever camp they belong, are the disease germs in the body politic. They can never create, but when the general health of the body is weak, they can bring destruction. They are reckless as to the means they employ, and because their passion-blinded eyes can discern no difference between the most moderate and the most violent of those who differ from them, they are ready to combine with the latter in order to defeat the former. So during the reign of Charles x the extreme Royalists, whom even the reactionary measures of Villèle could not satisfy, combined with the Liberals to render the task of Government impossible, and in doing so they felt, more often than not, that they had the secret approval of the King himself.

Interference with the liberty of the press, against which Talleyrand had warned the restored monarchy in 1814, in 1821, and in 1822, continued to exercise a fatal fascination for Ministers. In 1826 Villèle brought forward a law by which nothing might be printed that had not been submitted to the Government for approval five days before publication. Casimir Périer said that they might as well simply suppress printing in France for the benefit of Belgium. Chateaubriand even, now one of the extreme reactionaries, said it was a law of barbarism. Talleyrand's comment was terse: 'It is not French, because it is silly.'

The alliance between the extreme Royalists and the Liberals drove Villèle from office after six years. He was succeeded by Martignac, who attempted to pursue a similar policy, and who was defeated by similar means. The King, who had rendered Martignac's task impossible by withholding his loyal support, then decided to choose a Minister after his own heart. Jules de Polignac was a fanatic. He had risked his life—and nearly lost it—for the Royalist cause in the days of the Consulate. His faith in his master's divine right was unfaltering, and he believed that if he relied upon divine guidance he could not fail. His mind was always made up, even when he had no idea what he was going to do. After the revolution which he had provoked was in full swing, he assured the King that it was only a riot—and added that if he should prove to be wrong he would give his head in expiation of his mistake. 'Not much of a present that,' was the comment of the Duchess de Gontaut when Charles informed her of the pledge.

The Polignac Ministry took office in August 1829. Talleyrand spent that autumn at Valençay, returning for a short visit to Paris and leaving again at the end of November for Rochecotte, a small château in Touraine which he had given to the Duchess of Dino in 1825. Hither in December came Thiers accompanied by Armand Carrel, that brilliant young writer and politician whose life of promise ended miserably in a duel seven years later. Thiers

and Carrel were determined to fight the Government. They
could only do so through the press, but the policy of intimida-
tion was beginning to produce its effect upon editors, and
they could find no organ of publicity that was bold enough
to suit their taste. So they had decided to produce a paper
of their own. Funds were all that they lacked, and it was for
funds that they had come to Talleyrand.

We can picture the scene. Candlelight during the long
December evenings in the charmingly situated château on
the banks of the Loire: the two young men eagerly pouring
forth their plans and prospects before the impassive veteran
of conspiracy whose weary, sunken eyes would turn now
and then from their animated faces to that of his lovely
hostess bending over her needlework. Carrel was twenty-
nine, Thiers thirty-two, Dorothea thirty-five, and Talleyrand
seventy-seven. Perhaps the old man's mind travelled back
to nights of conspiracy before Brumaire, when young
General Bonaparte talked as eagerly as they did now, and
was as full of plans and prospects and hope.

They won their cause. The money was forthcoming.
The new review was to be called the *National*. The first
number appeared in January 1830, and for the next seven
months it continued to be a thorn in the side of the Government.

2

At the end of July the storm burst. The importance of
the part played by the *National* was recognised in the
celebrated Ordinances issued by the Polignac Ministry
which, besides dissolving the newly elected Chamber before
it met and interfering with the freedom of election, sought
to abolish once and for all the liberty of the press. Paris
sprang to arms. Once more the tocsin sounded and the
tricolour flag was hoisted over the towers of Notre-Dame.

Charles x continued to hunt at St. Cloud as Louis xvi had hunted at Versailles on 5th October 1789. The Duke of Orleans lurked unobtrusively in the suburbs. In the Rue St. Florentin, in the very heart of the town, Talleyrand played whist, watching and listening. When the sound of street fighting, of bells ringing, and of cheering drifted through his window, he exclaimed: 'Hark, we are winning.' 'We, who are we?' they asked. 'Hush,' he replied, 'not a word, I will tell you to-morrow.'

His house commanded the Rue de Rivoli and the Place de la Concorde. During these eventful July days he spent much time looking out of the window. The Duke de Broglie saw him from the street and on going inside found the British Ambassador and many of the leading Liberals. Madame Adelaide, the Duke of Orleans' sister, went for an adventurous walk with Madame de Boigne. The two ladies, heavily veiled, each took an arm of the latter's butler. As they passed the Rue St. Florentin the Princess preferred to take the centre, in order the better to escape observation. 'I don't want the lame old man to see me,' she said, 'he is so intelligent that he is capable of recognising me from his window.'

On 29th July Talleyrand sent a message to the Duke of Orleans to the effect that he should come to Paris at once and put himself at the head of the movement. The Duke accepted the advice. On the 30th Charles x left Saint Cloud for Rambouillet. 'It is not I who have abandoned the King,' said Talleyrand, 'it is the King who has abandoned us.'

On the 31st, early in the morning, representatives of the group who were controlling events from the Hôtel de Ville came to the Palais Royal to offer the leadership to the Duke of Orleans. Again he hesitated. Again the future of France hung in the balance while a messenger hurried down the

Rue de Rivoli to ask the advice of the aged statesman in the
Rue St. Florentin. 'Let him accept,' was Talleyrand's
laconic reply. The Duke acted upon it. He went to the
Hôtel de Ville. At the suggestion of Lafayette he was
accepted by the mob. The July Revolution was over and
the reign of Louis-Philippe had begun.

3

The first objective of a new Government which has
come into being as the result of a revolution must be to
obtain the recognition and, if possible, the support and
friendship of Governments older and better established.
Revolution was hardly the password to popularity among
the Governments of Europe in 1830. The originator of the
Holy Alliance was dead, but its spirit survived, and the
Emperor Nicholas was a far less compromising and more
practical exponent of autocracy than the Emperor Alexander had ever been. From Vienna the opinions of Metternich dominated Italy and Central Europe, and if the King
of Prussia ever hesitated to accept the views of Metternich
it was only when he preferred those of Nicholas. The
restored Bourbon still sat uneasily on the throne of Spain,
and a Tory Government still ruled in England.

An usurping monarch, waving the tricolour, singing the
Marseillaise, himself the son of a regicide, could find little
hope of an enthusiastic reception from any of the contemporary Courts of Europe. But while no prospect was
exactly pleasant the outlook towards England was more
promising than any other. True, the Government was
Tory, but the Prime Minister was the Duke of Wellington,
than whom no man knew better what France had suffered
in the way of provocation, and none had done more, when
he had the opportunity, to promote the cause of conciliation.

A new king had recently come to the throne of England, a sailor of unassuming manners and supposedly liberal sentiments. Nor was it for the House of Brunswick to criticise if another country chose to call a younger branch of the royal family to the throne, in flattering imitation of the English people who had done the same thing a hundred and forty years before.

If recognition were once accorded by England the Government of Louis-Philippe could feel confident that the example would soon be followed by other Powers. It was important therefore to induce England to lead the way, and, even after that point had been gained, it was Talleyrand's opinion that England should remain the pivot of France's foreign policy. Throughout his life he had consistently clung to the desirability of the Anglo-French alliance. These were the views that he had impressed on Mirabeau in 1791, these were the views that he expressed to Louis-Philippe at their first interview after the latter's accession to the throne in August 1830.

Louis-Philippe accepted this advice, but if the policy was to be successful much would depend upon the personality of the French representative in England. There was needed a man of great political experience, of consummate diplomatic skill, who should have had some previous acquaintance with the prominent people in English public life, and who should, if possible, combine liberal opinions with aristocratic manners, for an Ambassador who was not a gentleman would be equally at a disadvantage in London whether Tories or Whigs were in office, whether the Prime Minister were the Duke of Wellington or Lord Grey.

All these qualifications were united in Talleyrand and in nobody else. His age was an objection. 'He looks horribly old,' wrote Greville, who had seen him that summer; Guizot said that his face resembled that of a dead lion, and

Molé, now Minister for Foreign Affairs, had written some months previously, forgetting for once his prejudices: 'Monsieur de Talleyrand attracts me as everything does that is passing away, and that threatens to disappear for ever. What memories are connected with this historic old man. The spirit and the principles of the 18th century, the grace and courtesy of the old Court are united in him with the independence of judgment that belongs to our age and with the recklessness of the Revolution. His place will not be refilled; the circumstances of these times are so petty that there is no longer room for greatness.' This tribute paid to Talleyrand in a moment of emotion would not have been repeated a few months later when the Minister for Foreign Affairs found grave reason to complain of the conduct of his principal Ambassador.

But at that time Molé offered no objection to the appointment, and such reluctance as Talleyrand himself expressed was overcome. The Duchess of Dino was pleased. She had always coveted a high official post, and she had waited long for it. Madame de Boigne, who disliked her, suggests that she had some more intimate reason for wishing to leave France at this moment, some love affair which she was anxious to end.

It was realised that there might be some disillusionment in the hearts of those enthusiasts for liberty who had risked their lives at the barricades during the glorious days of July, when they found that the dawn of the new era was to shed its first rays of preferment upon the hoary head of the old diplomatist who had never been a favourite with enthusiasts of any school. But the good will of foreign Governments was considered to be of greater importance for the moment than the illusions of native enthusiasts. The appointment was made, and in September the first Ambassador of the first King of the French arrived in London.

4

When Talleyrand heard the guns at Dover saluting his
arrival as French Ambassador, he could not help remembering, so he tells us in his memoirs, how he left the shores of
England thirty-six years before. Exiled from his own
country, he had been refused hospitality where he had most
right to expect it, and had been driven across the Atlantic
to face the hazards and hardships which awaited a penniless
and discredited emigrant in a new continent. Now he was
returning 'animated by hope and above all by the desire to
establish at last that alliance between France and England
which I have always considered as the most solid guarantee
of the happiness of the two nations and of the peace of the
world.

'. . . These were the reflexions that occupied my mind as
I travelled through beautiful England, so rich and so
peaceful, and arrived in London on 25th September 1830.'

He had never borne any grudge against the English for
the treatment he had received at their hands. He had
acquitted them of responsibility for conduct which had been
due to false reports concerning him spread by his enemies
among the French emigrants. It was easy enough for a
Frenchman to be anglophile in 1830, but there were few
who had cared to express such sentiments in 1806, at the
height of the war, at the date of the Berlin decrees, when
Napoleon was concentrating the whole of his genius and all
the resources of France upon the destruction of Great
Britain. Yet even then Talleyrand, the time-server, had been
fearlessly consistent. We have the unprejudiced testimony
of Ferdinand von Funck, a Saxon officer, to that effect.
'Talleyrand liked the English nation,' he wrote in 1806, 'he
regarded Pitt's policy as the most astute and at the same time
the most logical a statesman had ever pursued. He often

enlarged on the subject without reserve, as indeed he was in general not as guarded in his speech as one might have expected of such a circumspect statesman. . . . When he saw an opportunity of paying the English a compliment he never failed to take it. He praised their customs . . . he liked talking about his stay in their country, and this always frankly and cordially, though always giving reasons for his commendations so that it was impossible to discern any set purpose behind them.'

It was a very different country that this lover of England was revisiting in 1830 from that which he had left in 1794. Never perhaps have thirty-six years effected so complete a change in the outward aspect and in the inward mind of a whole nation. It is hardly too much to say that the complete process of alteration from the eighteenth to the nineteenth century had taken place in that period. He had known the London of Horace Walpole and he came back to the London of Charles Greville. When he was last there Pitt and Fox had been at the height of their powers; now the young Disraeli was already older than Pitt had been when he became Prime Minister, and the young Gladstone was coming of age. He had left the London of knee-breeches and powdered hair, he returned to the London of frock-coats and top-hats. White's Club, down the steps of which he would have been kicked as a rascally Jacobin in 1794, elected him an honorary member. The famous bow window had been built over those steps in the interval and had already seen its greatest days, for the brief reign of Brummel was over, and the dandies of the Regency were no more. Boswell had been alive when he was last in London. The whole life-work of Keats, Shelley, and Byron had taken place during his absence and in this, the year of his return, the first publication of Tennyson saw the light. Those who were alive at his first visit could remember the reign of Queen

Anne, those who were alive at his second could live into the reign of George v.

It is interesting to find him describing London as 'much more beautiful' then he had left it, an opinion corroborated by an American who, returning to London in this same year after an absence of nineteen years, said that it had become 'a thousand times more beautiful' than it was. Talleyrand was surprised that the sun should be shining in September and that all the members of the Government should be out of town—phenomena which would have caused less astonishment, then and now, in one better acquainted with the climate and the customs of the country.

The new Ambassador was well received by the Duke of Wellington and by Lord Aberdeen, who was Foreign Secretary. With the former he had for long been on friendly terms, for the two men understood one another. They were both great gentlemen of the old school. They were both intensely practical and they both hated any kind of humbug or cant. Aberdeen had been brought up in the tradition of Pitt and under the wing of Castlereagh. No Government, it was said, could be too liberal for him, provided it did not abandon its conservative character. He belonged to the European as opposed to the nationalist line of British Foreign Ministers and it had been mainly due to his advice that Wellington had overcome his scruples about recognising the Government of Louis-Philippe.

5

Revolution is a symptom of grave political disease, and, unfortunately, it is contagious. The events of July in Paris produced similar outbreaks in several other countries of Europe. The first to which the infection spread was Belgium. The causes of discontent had nothing in common with those that had led to the upheaval in France. In the latter country one of the principal grounds of complaint had been the increasing influence of the Catholic Church. In Belgium, on the other hand, the Church was behind the revolution, and was engaged in stirring up that spirit of nationalism which was to prove the bane of the nineteenth century.

It had been the policy of Castlereagh at the Congress of Vienna to set up in the Low Countries a state that should be strong enough to remain independent both of France and of Prussia, and yet not so strong as to offer any menace to the tranquillity of England. Pitt had gone to war with France not out of horror at the principles of the Revolution, but because the French Revolutionaries had incorporated Belgium with France, and had, in Napoleon's graphic phrase, held Antwerp like a pistol at the head of England. Castlereagh knew that whenever again a great Power of Europe should send armed forces across the frontier of Belgium, without the consent of England, then England would have to go to war as inevitably as if those forces had landed in Kent.

The mistake made by the statesmen who met at Vienna in 1814 was to overlook, or to under-rate, the new spirit of nationalism which had hardly troubled the repose of the eighteenth century and which the disastrous career of Napoleon had done so much to inflame. They had therefore seen little objection to incorporating Belgium with Holland in one state under the rule of the House of Orange. Unfortunately, however, the Belgians and the Dutch, although living in such close proximity, have little in common. Still more unfortunately, racial antagonism was reinforced by religious hatred. The Belgians had always been Catholics, whereas the whole tradition of Holland was bound up with the history of the Protestant revolt. In August 1830 the pent-up passions of fifteen years broke loose. It began with a riot in Brussels and before it had ended Europe was convinced that, whatever else might be the outcome, the two countries could never be united again.

It was with this matter that the mind of Talleyrand was principally occupied as he drove through the quiet autumn fields towards London on 25th September. He had recently received the latest news of the revolution in Belgium, and he realised how serious an obstacle it placed in the way of that better understanding with England which he desired to effect. All the sympathies of the French people would be with the Belgians, who spoke the same language, professed the same religion as they did, and whose revolution they had so plainly inspired. The English, on the other hand, might be expected to support the House of Orange and the Protestant Dutch; while the Government, together with other Governments, would naturally deplore any interference with the settlement of Europe that had been agreed upon at Vienna.

The affairs of Belgium formed the principal subject of the first conversations between Talleyrand and the British Government. During the four years of his mission to England the Belgian question remained the most important in the domain of foreign affairs. Of the five volumes that contain his memoirs two are devoted to his official and semi-official correspondence on this subject. There it is possible to follow from day to day his skilful and successful handling of a problem that often threatened to produce a European war.

It is not proposed here to follow those negotiations step by step. At every turn in them Talleyrand was guided by one unchanging principle, the determination to maintain the peace of Europe, of which he was certain that the surest guarantee was a good understanding between England and France. He described the world of his day as being governed

by two contending forces. On the one side was the principle
of autocracy, firmly maintained by the powerful Empires of
Russia and Austria and supported by Prussia; on the other
side was the power of public opinion which ruled in England,
and which now was to rule in France. This alone was
sufficient to justify the alliance of those two countries, and
while their armed forces might be less formidable than
those of their opponents, they were strengthened by the
fact that their cause had supporters in every country.

6

Talleyrand was not a convenient Ambassador from the
point of view of the Government that he represented. An
Ambassador should be, in fact as well as in theory, the
subordinate of his Minister for Foreign Affairs. When the
Ambassador is a bigger man than the Minister the instrument becomes top heavy. Not only was Talleyrand a far
more important person in the eyes of the world than any of
Louis-Philippe's Ministers, not only did he surpass them
in talent and experience, but he also had his own particular
methods of conducting business that were neither in accordance with diplomatic usage nor with democratic ideas.

He had always preferred the service of women as agents
and intermediaries. Before leaving Paris he had arranged
to correspond regularly with Madame Adelaide, and she
was to lay all his letters before the King, her brother, over
whom she exercised more influence than did anyone else.
His other principal correspondent, to whom he wrote almost
as often, was the Princess de Vaudémont. She was a daughter
of Madame de Brionne and had remained one of his dearest
friends throughout all the vicissitudes of his career. Even
now his letters to her were often couched in terms of
gallantry, and all that they contained of political importance

was communicated by her to the Palais Royal, where she was on a footing of intimate friendship.

Molé was a proud and sensitive man. He was one of those Ministers who are always on the look out for slights and insults, and are always on the point of resignation. This private correspondence carried on between the Ambassador and the King behind his back not unnaturally annoyed him. When, however, he resigned on account of it the King persuaded him to remain in office.

Molé was anxious that the Conference which it was decided to hold on the Belgian question should take place in Paris. Talleyrand was determined that it should be held in London, which was also the desire of the British Government. Molé explained to the English Ambassador in Paris that his real reason for putting forward this proposal was Talleyrand's unpopularity in France. His appointment had already been severely criticised and if such an important negotiation were entrusted to him the position of the Government might be endangered. Here Molé was guilty of conduct as incorrect and as unconventional as any with which Talleyrand could be charged. The British Government could hardly be expected to give much consideration to the argument of a French Minister for Foreign Affairs who complained of the unpopularity of his own Ambassador. The English view therefore prevailed. It was agreed to hold the Conference in London. Talleyrand was appointed to act as French representative and shortly afterwards the resignation of Molé and his colleagues was accepted.

The British Government did not outlive the French one for more than a fortnight. The long supremacy of the Tory Party came to an end in November 1830. The Duke of Wellington was succeeded by Lord Grey as Prime Minister; and Lord Aberdeen was replaced by Lord Palmerston as Secretary of State for Foreign Affairs.

A few weeks earlier Lord Grey, in the privacy of Howick, had classed Talleyrand with Castlereagh and Brougham as the three greatest rascals in the world. He belonged to that type of high and narrow-minded Whig who found it difficult to change his opinions, so that although he made Brougham Lord Chancellor and always got on very well with Talleyrand, he probably retained his views of both unaltered. So far as foreign affairs were concerned the sympathy which he naturally felt with the liberal Government of France was somewhat tempered in practice by the influence exercised over him by the Princess Lieven who, always combining diplomacy with affection, missed no opportunity of upholding the interests of her master, the Emperor of Russia, in her intimate relationship with the Prime Minister of England.

Palmerston was in the full bloom of his exuberant manhood. He was a newcomer at the Foreign Office. As Aberdeen had been the disciple of Castlereagh, so was Palmerston the disciple of Canning. He had a cheerful contempt for foreigners. To him the doyen of European diplomacy, 'this almost fabulous old man,' was merely 'Old Tally,' whom he did not scruple to leave in a waiting-room for an hour or two, treatment which a gentleman would hardly have accorded to the humblest individual approaching his eightieth year. One who could remember the Court of Louis xv must have found it difficult to brook the behaviour of this flamboyant Harrovian with his dyed whiskers and striped pantaloons. But patience, the fruit of long experience, and tolerance born of scorn, enabled him to suffer with equanimity the indignities to which he was subjected, and never to allow his personal irritation to interfere with his political plans. That Palmerston was not able to do the same is the only failing for which Talleyrand afterwards criticised him. There appeared in London a cartoon entitled 'The lame leading the blind,' in which Palmerston was shown as being led by Talleyrand. Palmerston's vanity was deeply wounded; that he of all men should be suspected of subservience to a foreigner was more than he could bear. His behaviour to Talleyrand underwent from that date a change for the worse, but in spite of it Talleyrand describes him in his memoirs as one of the cleverest, if not *the* cleverest man with whom he ever had to deal.

7

It was the duty of these ill-assorted colleagues to stand together in the Five-Power Conference on Belgium against the representatives of the three absolutist states. The sittings were long and proved a high tax on the strength of Talleyrand. At the first two meetings agreement was reached on the important points of recognising the independence and the neutrality of Belgium. Palmerston, in a letter to Granville, now Ambassador in Paris, wrote that Talleyrand had 'fought like a lion,' and by claiming more than he expected had got all that he desired.

The next question was to find a king for the new kingdom. The Belgians offered the throne to Louis-Philippe's younger son, the Duke de Nemours. Louis-Philippe with some reluctance was induced, largely by Talleyrand's insistence, to refuse the offer. There were other claimants— Princes of Sicily and Bavaria, a son of Eugène Beauharnais, and even some local magnates.

Talleyrand favoured from the first the candidature of Prince Leopold of Saxe-Coburg. He was the widower of Princess Charlotte, George iv's only child, and was therefore likely to be regarded by other countries as an English candidate. This difficulty Talleyrand believed could be overcome by his marrying the daughter of Louis-Philippe.

In a conversation with Palmerston on this subject he so manœuvred that it was Palmerston who first mentioned the name of Leopold. 'I showed some astonishment,' wrote Talleyrand, 'as though this idea had never occurred to me; but my astonishment had slightly the air of a happy discovery.' The more Palmerston believed the idea to be his own the more he liked it. Finally it proved to be the proposal that prevailed and Leopold in due course, with Talleyrand's full approval, became the first King of the Belgians.

It was one thing, however, for the Powers to decide, and quite another to get their decision accepted. Holland refused to listen to them, and although they had agreed to a settlement among themselves, the question of coercing Holland presented difficulties. The King of Holland was the brother-in-law of the King of Prussia, the Prince of Orange was the brother-in-law of the Czar. While France was ready enough to enforce the settlement by arms, these monarchs were naturally reluctant to let loose at the throats of their relatives the revolutionary armies of the usurper.

It was a dangerous year, 1831, in Paris. Every moment the new monarchy seemed about to fall. Shrewd observers predicted the return of the Bonapartes, and, if the young heir of Napoleon had not died shortly afterwards, their predictions might have come true. The representative of a tottering Government is always in an unenviable position, and Talleyrand's task was rendered the more difficult by rumours of war abroad as well as of revolution at home. Disturbances had broken out in Italy, in Portugal, and in Poland. There was the prospect of a dynastic war in Spain. Through all these difficulties Talleyrand steered his way with infinite patience and consummate skill, virtually directing from London the foreign policy of the French Government.

Molé had been succeeded by Laffitte as principal Minister and Laffitte had been followed by Casimir Périer. The latter by firm measures did much to retrieve the errors of the former. He worked in harmony with Talleyrand, whom he appreciated, and sent his son, father of the future President of the Republic, to serve in the Embassy in London. Talleyrand, reporting favourably on the young man, wrote: 'I check his zeal, because in our career zeal is only harmful'—and at the same time he expressed the belief that 'the greatest danger in times of crisis comes from the zeal of people who are inexperienced.'

When the recalcitrant King of Holland sent troops into Belgium Talleyrand obtained the approval of the Conference for military intervention by the French. The Dutch ran away from the French as fast as the Belgians had run from the Dutch, and the next difficulty was to persuade the French to retire neither having enjoyed the glory of battle nor taking with them the fruits of victory. Coupled with the demand for an indemnity was the claim to demolish the fortresses which had been set up in Belgium by the Congress of Vienna to serve as watch towers from which the Powers could descend upon France to deliver chastisement whenever merited. They had been deeply resented and the occasion seemed opportune for their destruction. In all these matters it was Talleyrand's duty to perform the delicate task of representing his country to the Powers and of using all his influence to moderate the demands of his own Government. 'In general,' he wrote, '—and this was my greatest difficulty—at Paris people judged affairs only from an exclusively French point of view.'

Opinion in England was hardening against France as the result of her military operations in Belgium. On 29th September during a debate in the House of Lords a violent personal attack was made on Talleyrand by Lord Londonderry. 'That ass Londonderry,' as Greville called him, was the unworthy half-brother of Castlereagh. He had acted as Ambassador at Vienna during the Congress where by his ostentation and his violence—he once had a fight with a cabman—he had frequently rendered himself ridiculous. With such experience of diplomacy he should have known better than to make a personal attack on the representative of a friendly Power.

Talleyrand, however, did not lack defenders. Lord Goderich, the spokesman of the Government, administered the official reproof. He was followed by Wellington, who, like Londonderry, was in opposition and was supporting his attack on the Government. Characteristically he did not allow such considerations to prevent him from saying what he thought. He reminded the House that 'that illustrious individual who had been so strongly animadverted upon by his noble friend near him had enjoyed to a very high degree the confidence of his noble friend's deceased relative. . . . He had no hesitation in saying that in every one of the great transactions that took place at the Congress of Vienna and in every transaction in which he had been engaged with Prince de Talleyrand since, from the first to the last of them, no man could have conducted himself with more firmness and ability with regard to his own country or with more uprightness and honour in all his communications with the Ministers of other countries. They had heard a good deal of Prince de Talleyrand from many quarters; but he felt himself bound to declare it to be his sincere and conscientious belief that no man's public and private character had ever been so much belied as both the public and the private character of that illustrious individual had been.'

Lord Holland, later in the debate, paid a further tribute: '. . . forty years' acquaintance with the noble individual who had been alluded to, enabled him to bear his testimony to the fact that, although those forty years had been passed during a time peculiarly fraught with calumnies of every description, there had been no man's private character more shamefully traduced, and no man's public character more mistaken and misrepresented, than the private and public character of Prince de Talleyrand.'

When these speeches were reported to him the old man was moved to tears. It was not only the generosity of their language that touched him, but the thought that he had never received such recognition in his own country. Even now, when he was exhausting the last hours of his life in the service of France, there was not a soul in Paris who would have said as much for him. When news failed to come from across the Channel he would fall into a fever. 'At my age,' he explained, 'one's nerves are easily upset.'

To an Englishman who believes that Talleyrand was a true patriot and a wise statesman, to whom neither contemporaries nor posterity have done justice, it is a source of some satisfaction to remember that it was in the British House of Lords that there were paid to him these glowing tributes by two men of singular honesty of outlook and clarity of perception, one a convinced adherent of the party that was beginning to be called Conservative, and the other a genuine Liberal in every sense of the word.

8

Glimpses of his life in London are to be obtained from the journals of Creevey and Greville. He appears only to have talked French although during his previous visits to England and to America he had acquired considerable knowledge of the language. 'What an idiot I am,' wrote Creevey, 'never to have made myself a Frenchman. To think of having such a card as this old villain Talleyrand so often within one's reach and yet not to be able to make anything of it. I play my accustomed rubber of whist with him.'

Greville spoke French, but he was deaf and found Talleyrand difficult to understand owing to 'his mode of pumping up his words from the bottomest pit of his stomach.' But Greville collected a few of them and tells us of the affection with which he always spoke of Fox, delighting to dwell on his simplicity and gaiety, his childlike qualities, and his profundity. Reminiscences of Madame Dubarry who 'had some remains of beauty up to the period of her death,' of the mysterious Count de St. Germain who was believed to be the Wandering Jew, of Mirabeau, of Benjamin Franklin, and of all the other celebrities of the last fifty years were ready for those who were prepared to listen. 'It is strange to hear M. de Talleyrand talk at seventy-eight,' Greville comments. 'He opens the stores of his memory and pours forth a stream on any subject connected with his past life. Nothing seems to have escaped from that great treasury of bygone events.'

But even in recollections of the past he met his match in Brougham. Creevey describes conversation between the two at Stoke. 'Sefton and I were more astonished at Brougham than ever. By his conversation with old Talleyrand it appeared most clearly that Vaux (although he was a child at the time) had been intimately acquainted with every leading Frenchman in the Revolution, and indeed with every Frenchman and every French book that Talleyrand mentioned. He always led in this conversation as soon as Tally had started his subject.'

The same Lord Sefton sat next to Talleyrand at a banquet at St. James's Palace. King William IV had one weakness which was not inappropriate in a monarch who ruled over England while the *Pickwick Papers* were being written. He hated to see water drunk at his table, he never set a bad example in this respect himself and after dinner he was fond of making speeches which were always irrelevant, often indiscreet and sometimes indecent. On this occasion, all the Cabinet Ministers and Foreign Ambassadors being present, he made two speeches. The second, after the ladies had left, 'travelled over every variety of topic that suggested itself to his excursive mind and ended with a very coarse toast and the words "Honi soit qui mal y pense." Sefton said he never felt so ashamed; Lord Grey was ready to sink into the earth; everybody laughed of course, and Sefton said to Talleyrand: "Eh bien, que pensez vous de cela?" With his unmoved and immovable face, he answered only: "C'est bien remarquable."'

The following is Greville's final verdict: 'The years he passed here were probably the most peaceful of his life, and they served to create for him a reputation altogether new, and such as to cancel all former recollections. His age was venerable, his society was delightful, and there was an exhibition of conservative wisdom, of moderate and healing counsels in all his thoughts, words, and actions very becoming to his age and station, vastly influential from his sagacity and experience, and which presented him to the eyes of men as a statesman like Burleigh or Clarendon for prudence, temperance and discretion. Here therefore he acquired golden opinions and was regarded by all ranks and all parties with respect, and by many with sincere regard.'

9

The premiership of Casimir Périer did much to restore the waning prestige of the Orleans Monarchy. In some directions he showed himself almost needlessly aggressive and Talleyrand particularly deplored the despatch of French troops to Ancona in reply to similar action taken by the

Austrian Government. He was, as ever, opposed to any gesture likely to cause alarm and distrust in foreign countries. The Ancona expedition, with regard to which he was not consulted, was regarded with severe disapproval by the British Government, and his position in London was therefore rendered more difficult.

Further obstacles were put in his way by the intrigues of the Count de Flahaut who was guilty at this period of far from dutiful conduct towards one to whom he owed so much.

That Talleyrand was genuinely fond of Flahaut seems proved by the letters which he addressed to him over a period of thirty years, but it is doubtful whether the affection was ever reciprocated. In his childhood and youth Flahaut's mind had been poisoned against Talleyrand by his mother, and the work that she had begun had been completed by his wife. When Flahaut fled to England after Waterloo, where he had acted as aide-de-camp to Napoleon, it had been a great achievement on his part, penniless and an exile, to win the hand of an English heiress, whose father, Admiral Lord Keith, had spent his life in fighting the French. The match had been bitterly opposed, but Meg Mercer, as her friends called her, was a woman of most determined character, and the Admiral eventually capitulated before her insistence and the charm of Flahaut, which worked almost as irresistibly upon men as upon women.

To obtain the admiration of women is the ambition of most men, and those who achieve it easily are apt to believe that their success is in some way a proof of their intelligence, forgetting that it is not always intellectual superiority that makes the strongest claim on feminine regard. There is no reason to think that Flahaut's brain was above the average, but both his mother and his wife were remarkable women and there had been many others, during the interval between the cradle and the altar, who had done their utmost to persuade him that there was not his equal upon earth.

Public life during the Restoration had been closed to one who had been too faithful to the Emperor, but after the Revolution of July all the Bonapartists began to look for employment, and Flahaut felt that at last his talents would find scope. He was in London in 1831 and at first worked harmoniously with Talleyrand, but he presumed to hold views of his own on foreign policy and was not prepared to abandon them at the bidding of anyone. He saw no grave objection to the acceptance of the Belgian throne by the Duke de Nemours, and he later advocated a scheme for the partitioning of Belgium between France and other Powers, according to which England was to be compensated by the port of Antwerp. Talleyrand was horrified at the plan, particularly at the suggestion that England should be given a foothold on the mainland of northern Europe, but Flahaut was loth to relinquish it until the situation was simplified by his appointment as Ambassador at Berlin. Such promotion should have satisfied the claims of a man little over forty whose previous experience had been only military, but neither Flahaut nor his wife was content. They considered themselves admirably suited to the French Embassy in London and they could not forgive its occupant for standing in their way.

This was the main cause of the estrangement which sprang up between father and son, and it was undoubtedly increased and embittered by the violent animosity that divided Margaret de Flahaut and Dorothea de Dino. It was difficult for the two women to be friends; they were too nearly of an age; their interests were too obviously opposed, and they were both too active and too intelligent to admit inferiority.

Flahaut did not stay long in Berlin and henceforward all

his activities and those of his wife were directed to the undoing of those to whom they refer in their correspondence as 'the uncle and the niece.' The violence of their feelings is surprising. Flahaut refers to his father as 'that vile old man' and to Dorothea as 'that horrid little serpent,' 'that lying little devil'—saying of her 'I don't think she writes to all her former lovers but she does to a great many and she will stick at nothing to serve her purposes and malice.' So exaggerated was his idea of his own importance that he informed his wife that the King wished to make him Minister for Foreign Affairs and was only prevented from doing so through fear of displeasing Talleyrand.

The hostility of this couple was a factor to be reckoned with. Madame de Flahaut had powerful friends in London. She was on intimate terms with Lord and Lady Grey and with their son-in-law, Lord Durham; and she spread rumours that Talleyrand was plotting with Wellington behind the backs of the Whigs. In Paris she established a salon and Flahaut himself was a close friend of the young Duke of Orleans, the heir to the throne.

In May 1832 Casimir Périer fell a victim to cholera. It was immediately suggested that Talleyrand should take his place. Charles de Rémusat, the son of his old friend, came to London on purpose to persuade him, bringing messages from many of his prominent friends in Paris urging him to accept. 'One ought not to be obstinate,' he wrote about this time, 'except when one ought to be; but when one ought to be, then one ought to be unshakable.' On this question he was as firm as a rock. He had already made a success of his English mission. He hoped to make a greater success of it still. 'At every epoch,' he wrote, 'there is some good to be done or some harm to hinder; that is why, if one loves his country, one can, and in my opinion one ought to, serve it under all the Governments that it adopts.' He knew that he was serving his country well in London, and therefore he meant to remain there until, at least, the Belgian question was settled. 'I will not think about my age until the ratifications have been received.'

In June 1832 he left London on leave. The King and his Ministers all impressed upon him before his departure the importance that they attached to his return. It was generally felt in London that good relations with France and indeed the avoidance of war depended upon Talleyrand's presence. From the social as well as from the political point of view he and the Duchess of Dino had created for themselves a remarkable position in English society. 'The Revolution of July,' wrote a French observer, 'is sometimes rather middle class in Paris, but, thanks to M. de Talleyrand, it has a very grand air in London.' Prosper Mérimée, who prided himself on being a judge of such things, wrote at the same period, having met Talleyrand for the first time: 'I cannot sufficiently admire the profound sense of everything he says, the simplicity and the comme-il-faut of his manner. It is the perfection of an aristocrat. The English, who have great pretensions to elegance and good taste, come nowhere near him. Wherever he goes he creates a court and his word is law.'

During his visit to France, from June to October, he went once more to Bourbon for the waters, and stayed at Rochecotte with his niece. On his return to London he found the Belgian question still unsettled. The King of Holland had possession of Antwerp and refused to surrender it. Once more military intervention was necessary, and once more France was the only Power that was prepared to intervene. Agreement having been reached with Palmerston, French troops crossed the frontier in November; and in December Antwerp capitulated.

This was really the end. The King of Holland did not

officially accept the situation until some years later, but his reluctance to do so was no longer of any importance. Talleyrand said with truth that Belgium could date her existence as an independent state from the day of the capitulation of Antwerp.

The period of gestation had been long. It was over at last. No statue of Talleyrand stands in Brussels, but few countries have ever owed more to a single statesman than Belgium owes to him. Her independence, her frontiers, her reigning House, the guarantee of her neutrality—for each of these features of her existence he had worked untiringly and with success. It was mainly due to him that her birth was not accompanied by a European war, and that more ink than blood was spilt at her baptism.

10

By the end therefore of the year 1832 the main object of his mission was accomplished and he began to contemplate retirement. On the last day of the year the Princess de Vaudémont died, and he described himself as inconsolable at the loss of one whom he had known for fifty years and with whom his relations had never varied.

His friend Dalberg died a few months later, and Lafayette in the following year. He had never admired the latter and had always referred to him as Gilles the Great. He had written of him in his memoirs: 'In a novel the author gives some intelligence and a distinguished character to the principal personage; fate takes less trouble: mediocrities play a part in great events simply because they happen to be there.' Yet he felt the death of the other veteran. Madame de Dino's explanation was perhaps correct: 'It seems that after the age of eighty all contemporaries are friends.'

He could not help thinking of Lafayette and the mad days of 1789, when he conversed with Lord Grey and heard accounts of the new House of Commons. That strange man Cobbett, whom he had met in America long ago, had been elected for a strange place called Oldham that had been enfranchised by the Reform Bill. Cobbett had suspected Talleyrand of being a Jacobin then. The two men had trodden very different roads in the interval and we cannot tell what the new Member of Parliament thought of the old Ambassador. But to the latter it seemed that the scenes of his youth were being enacted again. Once more the aristocrats were playing with democracy. Did Lord Grey and his noble friends know what they were doing? Did they realise that they had sealed the doom of their own order? He was pessimistic as to the future of England. He felt more keenly here than elsewhere that he had survived into a world to which he did not belong. His work was finished. Why should he put up with the bad manners of Palmerston any longer?

He went again to France on leave in 1833, and returned again to duty with increased reluctance. He would have liked to form a definite alliance with England but his overtures were not well received. Affairs in the Peninsula were troublesome. Two reactionary claimants were in opposition to two supposedly liberal Governments. Palmerston having arranged treaties with the latter invited France to adhere. It was beneath the dignity of a great Power to adhere to treaties arranged by others. France would come in as a principal contracting party or not at all. A heated diplomatic controversy ensued, out of which after prolonged argument and many weary sittings Talleyrand emerged victorious. The Quadruple Alliance was signed in April 1834, and it was regarded in France as a triumph for Talleyrand.

II

But the summer of 1834 was a sad one for diplomatic circles in London. The Lievens were going away. The arrogance of Palmerston, who had insisted upon sending as Ambassador to Russia the one man in England whom he knew the Czar would not receive, had resulted in the recall of the Russian Ambassador from London. For twenty-two years Princess Lieven had been one of the leaders of London society. The prospect of returning to St. Petersburg filled her with despair. Dorothea de Dino had provided her during the last four years with the kind of rivalry that she enjoyed. Creevey describes them as furnishing the principal entertainment at a large house party—'the female Lieven and the Dino were the people for sport. They are both professional talkers—artists quite, in that department. We had them both quite at their ease, and perpetually at work with each other; but the Lieven for my money! She has more dignity and the Dino more grimace.'

The one emotion that they shared was hatred of Palmerston, and as the day drew nearer for the departure of the Lievens a bond of sympathy united the two women. Madame de Dino felt that the time had come for Talleyrand's mission also to be concluded. She noticed that when they were going on leave in 1832, the King had said: 'I have charged my Ambassador in Paris to tell your Government that I insist on keeping you here.' In 1833 he had said: 'When are you coming back?' In 1834 he asked: 'When are you leaving?' The sailor King was no diplomatist, and the clever woman probably read more into the blunt old man's words than he had ever intended. She saw in this diminishing cordiality the influence of Palmerston, and, more jealous of Talleyrand's dignity than he was himself, she could not bear that he should continue to be subjected to the impertinence of his inferior.

Lady Cowper, Palmerston's intimate friend and soon to be his wife, sought to excuse his conduct on the ground that it was due merely to bad manners and to overwork. She was anxious to prevent the impression getting abroad that he had driven Talleyrand as well as the Lievens away from England.

But Madame de Dino was not to be convinced. She had been happy in England. In one of the letters—almost love letters—which she wrote to Thiers during the first two years of her stay—she had said that if the climate were better and the cost of living lower she would like to live in England for ever. But the Reform Bill had changed everything. When the Houses of Parliament were burnt, later in this year, she thought it 'ominous.' 'Those old walls,' she wrote, 'would not dishonour themselves by lending shelter to the profane doctrines of the time.'

She felt things deeply. A libellous publication entitled 'Monsieur de Talleyrand' appeared in July. She could not bear to read it, but Talleyrand read it himself and said that it was 'so silly, so untrue, so dull, and so badly invented that he would not have given five shillings to have prevented its publication.'

In August he left London. He had not decided whether he would return; but Dorothea had. She set her arguments before him in a long letter, 'for,' she wrote, 'I irritate you a little sometimes by talking, and then I stop before I have said all I think; so let me write to you.' She went on to argue that the object of his mission was accomplished, that he could render no further service in England when the political future was so uncertain and where, owing to the break up of the diplomatic corps and the bad manners of the Foreign Secretary, life was no longer agreeable. 'If, like you, one belongs to history one should think of no other future save that which history prepares. You know that history judges the end of a man's life more severely than the beginning. . . . Declare yourself old, lest people should find that you have aged, say nobly to the world: "The hour has struck." '

Talleyrand still hesitated. Every man is reluctant to sign his own death warrant. Resignation at the age of eighty-two must mean the end. Delicate from youth, his health in old age was remarkable. The weakness of his legs now necessitated his being carried over the shortest distances, but otherwise he was vigorous and all testimony concurs as to the clearness of his memory and the youthfulness of his mind. Nevertheless as the autumn went on he began to yield before the arguments of his niece, reinforced by the promptings of his own reason. It was she who finally drafted his letter of resignation, Royer-Collard corrected the draft, and with a weary shrug of his shoulders the old man signed it, and brought his long political life to an end.

Chapter Fourteen

THE LAST TREATY

I

W<small>HEN</small> Talleyrand signed his resignation in November 1834 he had still three and a half years to live. It would seem that during these years he enjoyed as great a measure of happiness as ever falls to the lot of those who reach extreme old age. His health was failing and his limbs were crippled, but his senses of sight and hearing were undiminished, and the pleasures of conversation remained with him to the end. He had survived his generation; the companions and the loves of his youth were dead; but he never lacked congenial society, and there was always at his side the woman to whom he had been devoted for twenty years, who, at the age of forty, retained her beauty, and whose daughter, the child Pauline, his 'guardian angel' as he called her, shed an atmosphere of innocence and pure affection over the closing days of his life.

Dorothea de Dino began to keep a journal in 1831, and from 1834 she wrote in it regularly. Her pages provide an almost daily record of her life and Talleyrand's during this period. They lived as before principally in Paris during the winter and at Valençay in the summer. Shorter visits were paid to Rochecotte, where she became the hostess and he a guest; and in the summer of 1835 she left him for a few months, during which she travelled in Germany and Switzerland.

Whether in Paris or in the country they entertained on a

lavish scale, setting an example of hospitality which the subjects of the bourgeois monarch were slow to imitate. Henry Greville, the young brother of Charles, was an attaché at the British Embassy. During the first nine months that he was in Paris Talleyrand's was the only house to which he received an invitation. He dined there frequently, was an enthusiastic admirer of his host's conversation, and has left in his journal a detailed account of a visit that he paid to Valençay in the autumn of 1834.

'The day begins,' he wrote, 'with déjeuner à la fourchette at half-past eleven, after which the company adjourn to the salon and converse until two o'clock when the promenades begin. Dine at half-past five, and go to bed at any hour; but the early dinner hour makes the evening interminable. . . . The Prince is uncommonly well and seems as happy as possible au sein de sa famille. Every evening at nine o'clock he drives for an hour, and on his return plays his rubber of whist until eleven o'clock, when the post arrives from Paris. . . . He was very proud of a definition he had made of "l'Amour"—"L'Amour est une réalité dans le domaine de l'imagination." '

Some days they hunted the stag and on others they shot. Visitors came and went. Lady Clanricarde, Canning's daughter, a brilliant talker and a great favourite with Talleyrand, was there at the time, and the Duke of Orleans paid a short visit although he was strongly dissuaded from doing so by the Count de Flahaut.

Montrond, 'le beau Montrond' of other days, had recently left the château after an unpleasant interview with Dorothea. She had never liked him, and now more than ever she deplored his manners and his morals and the influence which she believed him to exercise over the mind of Talleyrand. His bitter tongue had grown no kinder with the years. It was said of him that his wit lived on human flesh. He refused to compromise with the taste of the nineteenth century, and continued to ignore the ban which had been laid upon the indecent and the profane in polite conversation. Worse still, he was beginning to prove a cantankerous and quarrelsome guest. Nothing was good enough for the old voluptuary. He cursed the servants, complained of the food and the wine, and, on his arrival in Paris, spread satirical comments on the dullness of the company and the poverty of the entertainment.

The Princess de Lieven was another who found life at Valençay insufficiently exciting. She was an unhappy woman. Exiled from the throne that she had made for herself in London, she refused to return to Russia, whither duty and her husband called her, and lingered on in Paris absorbed as ever in social and diplomatic intrigue, but without any definite position to lend dignity and significance to her activities. She had not yet formed the liaison with Guizot which was to close her cycle of romance.

At Valençay she insisted on changing her bedroom three times in a week. Neither reading nor needlework could distract her. The post from Paris was all that she waited for and her irrepressible yawns were terrible to behold. She was attached, however, to Dorothea de Dino who, although her junior, treated her as a spoilt child. Their rivalry had brought them together, but the younger woman had broader interests and, while sharing all those which bound the other to the town, could herself be happy in the country. Her books, her garden, her children and the ever-present anxiety with regard to the health of her uncle, were sufficient to occupy her mind.

At the end of 1835 there occurred the death of the Princess de Talleyrand. She had not seen her husband for more than twenty years and such affection as had once united them had vanished long before. Yet Dorothea

hesitated to tell him the news. She had found him ill
and depressed on her return from Switzerland, and in no
mood to receive a melancholy announcement. But when the
news was broken he neither showed nor expressed the
slightest concern. 'That simplifies my position,' was his
only comment, and all that day he wore a smile and sometimes hummed a tune. It did not occur to him to simulate
sorrow or to disguise satisfaction. Hypocrisy had never
been one of his vices. Financially he benefited by his wife's
death for he had made her a generous allowance. Another
consideration was probably present to his mind. He was no
longer a married priest.

2

So long as there was breath in Talleyrand's body he could
not abandon political intrigue. He still exercised great
influence. Madame Adelaide still corresponded with him
regularly and the King still listened to Madame Adelaide.
In the long rivalry between Thiers and Guizot, which was
now beginning, the Rue St. Florentin was on the side of
Thiers. The Prince had liked the voluble little man from
the first, and his friendship with Dorothea had at one time
attained definitely sentimental proportions.

When Thiers formed a Government in February 1836
it was popularly supposed that Talleyrand was responsible;
when he fell from power in August of the same year, it was
generally believed that Talleyrand had withdrawn his support. Thiers was urging armed intervention in the affairs
of Spain. The King refused his consent. Talleyrand shared
the views of the King. He had opposed intervention in
Spain under Napoleon; he had opposed it under Louis XVIII;
he continued to oppose it under Louis-Philippe.

Thiers was succeeded by Molé, whose first action on
assuming office was to write to Talleyrand. 'As the new

Cabinet had been formed upon a question and with ideas which M. de Talleyrand had wisely made his own, the new Ministers should be able to congratulate themselves on his approval, and for himself he trusted that it might be so, as he relied upon M. de Talleyrand's counsel and opinion.' The next day Madame de Dino received a letter, almost flirtatious, from Guizot, informing her of his inclusion in the Ministry. Well might she write in her journal 'the friendship of the King for M. de Talleyrand and the confidence with which he honours him forbid any Minister to be on bad terms with him.'

But despite the high estimation in which he was held by all, despite the influence which he exercised in public life, despite the ease and comfort, the grace and charm of his existence, Talleyrand's mind was not at peace. To the younger people of the age he was already a legendary figure. He had always despised the opinion of his contemporaries, but he could not be equally indifferent to the verdict of posterity. He knew that that verdict was being written while he yet lived, and although he was still too proud and too indolent to plead his cause, to enter a defence, to draw up an elaborate apologia, it is plain that he, who all his life had never cared for what people might say of him, was beginning to feel some anxiety as to what would be thought of him after his death.

Balzac had paid him a tribute in *Le Père Goriot*, referring to him as the man who had prevented the partition of France at the Congress of Vienna, a man to whom crowns were owed and at whom mud was thrown, a tribute the value of which was only slightly diminished by its being placed in the mouth of a criminal. Balzac was invited to Rochecotte. Dorothea was not pleased. She found him vulgar. 'Clever no doubt, but without verve or ease in conversation. . . .

He examined and observed us most minutely, especially M. de Talleyrand.' But Talleyrand knew how important was the good opinion of this stout, overdressed, inquisitive little man. He laid himself out to win it. Balzac was impressed. 'M. de Talleyrand,' he wrote, 'is astonishing. He had two or three outbursts of prodigious ideas (jets d'idées prodigieuses). He pressed me to visit him at Valençay and I shan't fail to do so if he lives.'

On another occasion he opened his heart to Lamartine. He had been one of the first to appreciate Lamartine's poetry. 'Nature has made you a poet,' he told him, 'poetry will make you an orator, tact and reflection will make you a politician. . . . I knew the Mirabeau of the past, try to be the Mirabeau of the future. He was a great man but he lacked the courage to be unpopular. In that respect I am more of a man than he; I abandon my reputation to all the misunderstandings and all the insults of the mob. I am thought immoral and machiavellian, I am only calm and disdainful. I have never given evil counsel to a government or to a prince; but I do not share their fall. After shipwrecks there must be pilots to save the victims. I have presence of mind and I guide them to some port; little matter what port provided that it shelters them. . . . I have braved the stupidity of public opinion all my life; I can brave it for forty years in the grave. Remember what I am prophesying to you, when I am dead. You are one of the few men by whom I wish to be understood.

'There are many ways in which a statesman can be honest. I see that my way is not yours; but you will value me more than you think one day. My pretended crimes are the dreams of imbeciles. Has a clever man ever the need to commit a crime? Crime is the resource of political half-wits. . . . I have had weaknesses, some would say vices— but crimes, *fi donc.*'

Long afterwards when Lamartine was playing a leading part in the Revolution of 1848 he doubtless remembered the counsels of moderation that the old statesman had impressed upon him, for it was his eloquence that maintained order in Paris, and it was his wisdom that insisted upon despatching without delay a circular note to the Powers proclaiming the pacific intentions of the new Government.

Talleyrand's efforts were not confined to winning the good opinion of men of letters, important as he knew that their testimony would be in the future. We have seen from Charles Greville how favourable was the impression he made on all circles in London, and Henry Greville is equally enthusiastic in praise of his manners, his conversation, and his kindness shown towards a humble attaché in Paris.

It is even more interesting to find that he could still win over the good opinion of a woman strongly prejudiced in his disfavour. The charm before which the dislike, distrust, and disapproval of Madame de la Tour du Pin, Madame D'Arblay, Madame de Rémusat, and Madame Potocka had collapsed long ago was still potent in the octogenarian.

Lady Granville, the British Ambassadress, was a good woman, a great lady and an attractive letter-writer. Her opinion of Talleyrand was that of most of her contemporaries, and in her early letters from Paris 'old lizard' was the most complimentary term in which she referred to him. But one morning he called on her. 'Did I tell you,' she wrote to her sister, 'Talleyrand paid me a long visit on Wednesday morning? I never knew before the, as Mr. Foster says, power of his charms. First of all it is difficult and painful to believe that he is not the very best man in the world, so gentle, so kind, so simple, and so grand. One forgets the past life, the present look. I could have sat hours listening to him.'

3

But the good opinion of Lady Granville, the affection of Lamartine, the admiration of Balzac, were not enough. It was during the reign of Louis-Philippe that the Napoleonic legend laid its lasting hold upon the minds and imaginations of Frenchmen. Talleyrand saw what was taking place, and he knew that in the future the brighter the fame of Napoleon appeared, the darker would appear his own infamy.

On 1st October 1836 at Valençay he drew up a solemn declaration which he wished to be read to his heirs, relations, and intimate friends after the reading of his will. It contains a brief justification of some of his actions. Passing over the part played in the Revolution, he mentions his secularisation by the Pope and expresses his belief that he was thus rendered entirely independent. He then decided that he would serve France under any Government on the ground that there was always some good to be done. 'I therefore served Bonaparte when Emperor as I had served him when Consul: I served him with devotion so long as I could believe that he himself was completely devoted to France. But when I saw the beginning of those revolutionary enterprises which ruined him I left the ministry, for which he never forgave me. . . .

'Arrived at my eighty-second year, calling back to mind the so numerous actions of my political life, which has been a long one, weighing them by the strictest measure, I find as a result—

'That of all the Governments that I have served from none have I received more than I gave;

'That I abandoned none before it abandoned itself;

'That I have not put the interests of any party, nor my own, nor those of my relations into the balance against the true interests of France, which moreover are not, in my opinion, ever in opposition to the true interests of Europe.

'This judgment that I pass on my own actions will be confirmed, I hope, by impartial men; and if this justice is denied me when I am no more, the knowledge that it is due to me will suffice to ensure the calm of my last days.'

He then went on to give orders that his memoirs should not be published until thirty years after his death. He had always timed his actions carefully. That had been his supreme art. He would continue to exercise it even from the grave. The greater part of the memoirs had been written in the early days of the Restoration, when legitimacy had been the watchword. It would not do to publish them under Louis-Philippe. But more than two volumes of them had been written while Louis-Philippe was King. Did Talleyrand foresee the future so clearly as to be aware that homage to Louis-Philippe would not be popular under the regime that should succeed him? Did he foresee already the revolution of 1848, the Second Republic, and the Second Empire? And is it possible to believe that those weary, sunken eyes saw further still? Thirty years from his death was to be the length of the interval. Thirty years would bring France to 1868, to within two years of Sedan and the downfall of the Second Empire. In 1868 the Empire was crumbling. It mattered little what was published then.

But his conduct towards Napoleon would always matter, because to the majority of Frenchmen the name of Napoleon would be always dear. A further paragraph was added to the declaration.

'Placed by Bonaparte himself in the position of having to choose between France and him, I made the choice dictated by the first of all duties, but bitterly regretting my inability to combine in one affection, as in the past, his interests and those of my country. None the less shall I remember until my last hour that he was my benefactor, for the fortune that I leave to my nephews comes to me in great part from him. My nephews ought not only never to forget this, but to teach it to their children, and they to their children so that the memory of it shall become perpetual in my family, from generation to generation in order that if ever a man bearing the name of Bonaparte shall be in a financial position where he has need of aid or assistance, he shall obtain from my immediate heirs or from their descendants every kind of assistance that it may be in their power to give him.'

Thus he justified his conduct towards Napoleon and thus with hardly human prescience he selected a date for the publication of his memoirs, when the Second Empire would be falling into greater discredit than the First had ever reached. His plan was defeated when he was no longer there to defend it, and his fame has suffered in consequence. All his papers were left to the Duchess of Dino and, failing her, to Bacourt, who had been a member of the Embassy in London and who, there is every reason to believe, was one of her lovers. She died in 1862, six years before the date fixed for the publication of the memoirs. Bacourt died three years later, and before dying he imposed upon the trustees, to whom he confided the memoirs, the prohibition to publish them until 1888. Those trustees were also dead before the time arrived and the Duke de Broglie, grandson of Madame de Staël, on whom ultimately the duty fell, did not publish the memoirs until 1891.

The moment so carefully selected by Talleyrand had been missed. In 1891 the failure of the Second Empire was forgotten, and Frenchmen looking back over a period of a hundred years saw little to arrest their admiration until they came to Waterloo. While the legend of Napoleon had soared that of Talleyrand had sunk. Those who had appreciated him in his old age, Royer-Collard, Barante, Balzac, Lamartine, Thiers, and Guizot in France, Wellington, Holland, and the Grevilles in England, were no more, and the generation that had known them and that might have contained his biographer and apologist had perished. The biography could not be written until the memoirs appeared.

The French have long memories; for them politics are the continuation of history. Royalist, Bonapartist, Republican —most French writers belong to one of these categories. Talleyrand belonged to none of them and has therefore never found his defender in France. Yet it is not for the French to decry him, for every change of allegiance that he made was made by France. Not without reason did he claim that he never conspired except when the majority of his country-men were involved in the conspiracy. Like France he responded to the ideals of 1789 and believed in the necessity of the Revolution; like France he abominated the Terror, made the best of the Directory, and welcomed Napoleon as the restorer of order and the harbinger of peace: like France he resented tyranny and grew tired of endless war and so reconciled himself to the return of the Bourbons. When Charles x proved impossible he turned rather wearily, but not without hope, to Louis-Philippe, and once again he reflected the mood of his country. Constitutional monarchy, the maintenance of order and liberty at home, peace in Europe, and the alliance with England, to these principles he was never false—and he believed that they were of greater importance than the Kings and Emperors, Directors and Demagogues, Peoples and Parliaments that he served.

He was as little concerned as ever with the opinion of his contemporaries, but as he came nearer to the end his dis-quietude concerning the judgment of history was augmented by his own dissatisfaction with himself. He could shrug his shoulders at the disapproval of George Sand who repaid hospitality at Valençay by an abusive article in the *Revue des Deux Mondes*. He knew enough about George Sand to value her opinion at its proper worth. It was his own opinion that troubled him now.

On 2nd February 1837 he wrote: 'Eighty-three years gone by! I do not know that I am satisfied when I consider how so many years have passed, how I have filled them. What useless agitations, what fruitless endeavours! tiresome complications, exaggerated emotions, spent efforts, wasted gifts, hatreds aroused, sense of proportion lost, illusions destroyed, tastes exhausted! What result in the end? Moral and physical weariness, complete discouragement and profound disgust with the past. There are a crowd of people who have the gift or the drawback of never properly understanding themselves. I possess only too much the opposite disadvantage or superiority; it increases with the gravity of old age.'

These were gloomy thoughts, but a man's brightest moments and most cheerful reflections are not those which he commits to paper. Dorothea noticed how these moods of pessimism and depression increased, 'but,' she wrote, 'as soon as there are people present, his mind takes new life, his conversation regains its vivacity and the solidity of his intellect and of his intelligence strike all who meet him.'

In the spring of this year took place the marriage of the Duke of Orleans. Talleyrand, the Duchess of Dino, and Pauline were all invited to Fontainebleau for the wedding. The château was crowded. Dorothea and Pauline had to share a bedroom, Margaret de Flahaut and her daughter shared another. The quarrel had been made up in the previous year on the melancholy occasion of the death of one of Flahaut's daughters. Even now relations though friendly were hardly satisfactory. Lady Granville writing to her brother on 29th December 1836 reported, 'Talleyrand is very well. Madame de Dino in great beauty. She and Meg meet and dine each other, but it is like the meetings in cock-and-bull fights. The night before last Dino ran into Lieven's salon, saw Meg and shrieked: "Oui, ma chère, c'était un cri épouvantable." She did not apologise or say for why. Explanations have been asked. Dino says it was a "cri de surprise," Meg says it was a "cri d'horreur." '

Perhaps this was the reason why the Flahauts did not enjoy their visit to Fontainebleau for they returned 'in a most hostile humour.' They were always quarrelling with somebody, always standing upon their dignity, and Lady Granville thought that they had resented having to share a room and had been disappointed at not receiving any special marks of favour.

Dorothea de Dino, on the other hand, thoroughly enjoyed herself. Pauline was delighted to share her mother's room and they were both pleased to notice the respect which everybody paid to Talleyrand and the strength with which he supported the long and tiring ceremonies. He left with Pauline before the last of the festivities were concluded because he considered it his duty to entertain at Valençay the Archbishop of Bourges, who was making a tour through his diocese.

Montrond was ill that summer. Talleyrand called on him every morning while he was in Paris. He could not climb the several flights of stairs to his lodging in the Rue Blanche, but he would wait at the bottom to receive a message. On one occasion, however, when he was requested by the King to convey to Montrond the announcement of the Duke of Orleans's engagement, he caused himself to be carried to the top of the house. People wondered why the King should pay such an honour to an old reprobate like Montrond, and charitably ascribed it to the fact that Montrond had information about the earlier life of the

King which it would have been a pity to publish. For
gossip of this sort we are indebted to Mr. Thomas Raikes
who, having bought his way into London society and paid
too high for the privilege, was now economising in Paris
and industriously collecting tittle-tattle about the great and
setting it down in his diary.

In August Montrond had recovered sufficiently to leave
Paris. He went to Valençay, where Dorothea had learnt to
put up with him, because she knew that Talleyrand still
preferred his conversation to that of anyone else. It was the
last autumn that the two old friends were to spend together,
and Talleyrand had an interior warning that it was so. 'It
causes me,' he wrote, 'such an excessive and extraordinary
pang of regret to tear myself away from Valençay this time,
that it seems like a presentiment.' It was.

4

At the end of 1837 there occurred the death of Reinhard
who had succeeded Talleyrand at the Ministry for Foreign
Affairs under the Directory. Subsequently he had filled
various minor diplomatic posts. Talleyrand determined to
deliver at the Academy of Moral and Political Science a
funeral oration in memory of Reinhard, and to take this
opportunity of giving to the world some of the conclusions
that he had reached as the result of his long political experience. 'It will be my farewell to the public,' he said. In vain
his friends, who were anxious for his health, attempted to
dissuade him from the effort. When his doctor said that he
would not answer for the consequences, 'Who asked you
to answer for them?' was the reply.

On the 3rd of March the ceremony took place. It was
felt to be an event of historical importance. All Paris was
present. When the ushers announced 'The Prince,' the

whole assembly rose to their feet. Supported on the arms
of two lackeys the old man slowly made his way to the place
reserved for him. In his deep voice, as firm and resonant as
ever, he began to read. He used no spectacles, and every
word was clearly audible.

He traced the not excessively distinguished career of
Reinhard from its beginnings, laying stress on the fact that
he had originally studied for the Church and insisting that
theological studies formed an excellent preparation for
diplomacy. The audience immediately understood that it
was of himself rather than of Reinhard that he was speaking.
He followed, however, the progress of the latter until it
reached its apogee in his brief tenure of the Ministry for
Foreign Affairs. He had at one time been a clerk in the
Ministry, he had filled many positions abroad, first secretary,
consul-general, minister plenipotentiary. Briefly the qualities required for each of these functions were described, and
Reinhard's possession of them noted. One gift only had
been lacking. His mind worked slowly. To express himself properly he had to be alone. Conversation did not
afford him the time that he required. The audience could
not fail to draw the contrast between Reinhard and one who
in conversation had never met his equal.

Then followed a description of the perfect Minister for
Foreign Affairs. 'A sort of instinct, always prompting him,
should prevent him from compromising himself in any discussion. He must have the faculty of appearing open, while
remaining impenetrable; of masking reserve with the manner
of careless abandon; of showing talent even in the choice of
his amusements. His conversation should be simple, varied,
unexpected, always natural and sometimes naïve; in a word,
he should never cease for an instant during the twenty-four
hours to be a Minister for Foreign Affairs.

'Yet all these qualities, rare as they are, might not suffice, if good faith did not give them the guarantee which they almost always require. Here there is one thing that I must say, in order to destroy a widely spread prejudice: no, diplomacy is not a science of deceit and duplicity. If good faith is necessary anywhere it is above all in political transactions, for it is that which makes them firm and lasting. People have made the mistake of confusing reserve with deceit. Good faith never authorises deceit but it admits of reserve; and reserve has this peculiarity that it increases confidence.'

These simple but profound truths, the manner in which they were uttered, the great age and the astonishing career of the speaker, produced a deep impression on the audience. Victor Cousin exclaimed that it was better than Voltaire, and all who were present shared his enthusiasm. The press the next morning was, with few exceptions, extremely favourable. Talleyrand was pleased, and even Dorothea, though she could not bear a word of criticism, was fain to be content.

5

Talleyrand had said his good-bye to this world, he had now to consider his reception in the next. The sands were running out. He had not three months to live. In the declaration of October 1836 he had affirmed his adherence to the Catholic faith. It has been seen how, at the time of his secularisation by the Pope, he had done his utmost to obtain a dispensation that would allow him to marry, and how completely he had failed. Since that date he had never been reconciled to the Church. At Valençay he would regularly attend mass on Sundays and festivals, but he never went to confession nor was admitted to communion.

The Duchess of Dino, who became Duchess of Talleyrand at the end of March, owing to the death of her father-in-law, Talleyrand's younger brother, was in ceaseless anxiety about the state of her uncle's soul. Brought up as a Protestant herself she had long since embraced the Catholic faith and became ever more religious as she grew older. Pauline shared to the full her mother's distress, but neither woman dared mention the subject to Talleyrand; so much awe was mingled with the affection that they bore him. They sought therefore every occasion to turn the conversation in the direction of religion, but for long they did so without success.

The following is Madame de Boigne's version of a story which she received from the Duke de Noailles, who was at one time a close friend of Dorothea's. Uncle and niece had attended mass together on some great festival of the church. As they drove away she said to him: 'It must have a curious effect on you to hear a mass.'

'No, why?'

'I don't know, it seems to me'—she became embarrassed —'I thought that you wouldn't feel quite the same as other people.'

'I? But exactly the same; and why not?'

'But after all, you have made priests.'

'Not many.'

There is another incident described by Madame de Dino herself. In August 1836 she was playing piquet with Talleyrand at Valençay during a thunderstorm. After a particularly loud clap of thunder he asked her of what she was thinking. She seized the opportunity. 'If there had been a priest in the room I should have confessed,' she said: 'I am afraid of sudden death. To die unprepared, to carry with me my heavy burden of sin terrifies me, and however careful one may be to live properly, one cannot do without reconciliation and forgiveness.' Talleyrand did not say a word, but continued to play in silence.

The Archbishop of Paris, who had been a close friend of Talleyrand's uncle, the Cardinal, believed that the latter had bequeathed to him the solemn duty of bringing his erring nephew back to the fold. He had thought that the death of Talleyrand's wife would provide a suitable occasion for opening the question and had written to him at the time suggesting an interview. Talleyrand had been pleased and touched. He had replied that unfortunately his health would not permit of an interview immediately, but that he would call in the following week. Next week, however, something else occurred to prevent the visit, and despite the influence of Dorothea, ever at his elbow, the interview did not take place.

In December of 1837 Dorothea herself fell seriously ill at Rochecotte. According to one of Lady Granville's letters she was suffering from a paralytic stroke. Talleyrand was with her at the time, and when she recovered, she reproached him with having concealed from her the gravity of her condition. Had she been aware of it, she explained, she would have sent for the local curé. 'What, that drunkard?' was, according to Madame de Boigne, Talleyrand's reply. But Madame de Dino herself says—and both versions may be true—that he merely expressed some surprise, and asked: 'You have got as far as that, have you, and how did you arrive there?' She told him, and added that among many other serious considerations she had not omitted that of her social position; she felt that her high rank imposed an obligation upon her. He interrupted her with the words: 'In truth, there is nothing less aristocratic than unbelief.'

These words should be borne in mind, when reading the account of what followed. A great change had come over the attitude of the upper classes towards religion since the French Revolution. Doubt had proved to be the friend of disorder, and atheism the parent of anarchy. The Holy

THE LAST TREATY

Alliance had not been merely a fantasy of Alexander's ill-ordered brain. Everywhere those who desired the maintenance of the existing order turned to the faith of their fathers as the safest guarantee for the future. Ethical convictions, none the less firmly held because of their political origin, appeared on the surface as a change in manners and a new tone in society. To be sceptical was no longer the fashion, and Talleyrand had been a man of fashion all his life.

Two days after the incident that has been referred to above Talleyrand himself reopened the subject of religion and asked his niece to repeat the account of her conversion. When she had ended he looked at her steadily—'You do believe then?' he asked. 'Yes, Monsieur, firmly,' she replied. He said no more at the time. She began to hope, but she realised that the task of bringing him back into the Church was not one to be entrusted to a drunken parish priest.

He was fond, during these last years, of going for long drives in Paris with Pauline. He would revisit the scenes of incidents in his past life. What sights he had witnessed in those streets of Paris! How many secret memories those old houses held for him! The girl at his side was well able to appreciate the privilege of listening to such reminiscences, but sometimes she would talk herself, and often in her conversation would occur the name of her confessor, the Abbé Dupanloup. She was at the age of hero worship and the enthusiasm of the young is infectious. Talleyrand's interest was aroused, and at last he said that he would like to meet this Abbé of whom he had heard so much.

6

Dupanloup was a man of imposing appearance, great eloquence and saintly character. He was now thirty-six years of age and he was to play a considerable part in the ecclesiastical life of France. He has left a full and detailed account of all that follows.

When he first received an invitation to the Rue St. Florentin he refused it. Like all who did not know Talleyrand, especially those who held sincere religious beliefs, he felt strongly prejudiced against him. He knew that if he were to dine there, the news would appear in all the papers on the morrow, as actually happened, and form the subject of general comment. He mistrusted Talleyrand's sincerity, feared his intellectual superiority, and had no wish to enter the great world of politics and fashion.

Talleyrand was annoyed by his refusal. 'They told me the Abbé Dupanloup was an intelligent man,' he said, 'if it were true he would come; he would have understood the importance of his entry into this house.' The invitation, however, was repeated, and could not be refused a second time. The Archbishop of Paris probably insisted on its acceptance.

The dinner took place on Sunday, 18th February. They were twenty at table. Dupanloup was conquered from the first. 'Imagine my surprise. I expected that the conversation would doubtless be seemly, it was, in fact, actually religious; I will say even ecclesiastical. M. de Talleyrand talked much of sermons and of living preachers: he quoted several fine passages and beautiful sayings of preachers he had heard in his youth. . . . I noticed particularly how apropos, with what exquisite taste and grace his quotations were introduced.'

Everything he said delighted the Abbé, whether he were praising the generosity of the Archbishop, condemning the heartlessness of the English—due to the aridity of Protestantism—or deploring the irreligion of the age; and when the good man left the house he said to himself: 'That was certainly one of the most edifying conversations that have taken place in Paris to-day; there only lacked a cross upon his chest to convince me that I was talking to one of the most venerable bishops in France.'

Talleyrand's comment upon Dupanloup, eagerly awaited by Dorothea and Pauline, was concise. 'I like your Abbé,' he said, and added the untranslatable phrase: 'Il sait vivre.' The anxious women were satisfied, for they knew how much importance he attached to the quality that the words described.

There was a passage in the speech on Reinhard which referred to 'the religion of duty.' When rehearsing the speech with Madame de Dino, Talleyrand pointed with a smile to the phrase and said: 'That bit will please the Abbé Dupanloup.' It did please him; and together with the praise of theology as a training for diplomats, emboldened the Abbé to call again at the Rue St. Florentin. He was received in private and held a long and intimate conversation with the Prince, but still hesitated to broach the subject that was in both their minds.

Encouraged by such a reception the Abbé's next step was to send a copy of a book that he had written on Fénelon, accompanied by a letter which, in admirably guarded language, faintly hinted at a parallel between the careers of Fénelon and Talleyrand. Both were noblemen who had entered the Church; both had been educated at Saint Sulpice; both had had difficulties with the Pope; Fénelon had admitted his errors.

Talleyrand sent for Dorothea when he received this letter and asked her to read it aloud to him. Towards the end, where there was a touching reference to Pauline, she was overcome by tears. 'Finish reading it,' he exclaimed, with some asperity. 'There is nothing to cry about. All this is serious.' When she had read it, he said: 'If I fell seriously ill I should send for a priest. Do you think the Abbé Dupanloup would come with pleasure?' She said that she was sure he would, but that it would serve little purpose until Talleyrand had been received back into the Church. 'Yes, yes,' he answered, 'there is something I must do with regard to Rome, I know; I have been thinking of it for some time.'

Talleyrand replied to the Abbé's letter and sent him an elzevir edition of the *Imitation of Christ*. Two more interviews took place. They were friendly, intimate, almost affectionate. The most serious matters were discussed. They skirmished round the great question but neither would open it. The Abbé was perhaps still too much in awe of the Prince, and the Prince, a diplomatist to the last, believed in placing the lead in the hand of his opponent.

One day as Madame de Dino was about to leave the house and was going to visit the Archbishop, Talleyrand took from a drawer a sheet of paper, covered on both sides with his own handwriting, and marked with many erasures. He handed it to her, remarking casually that it would ensure her a good reception where she was going. It was, in fact, his own retractation; the first draft, as it were, of his treaty with heaven. The Archbishop kept the paper, of which no copy exists, expressed his great satisfaction, but added that he would re-draft it in more canonical form.

Talleyrand's three great errors in the eyes of the Church were his acceptance of the civil constitution of the clergy, his ordination of bishops, and his marriage. He considered that he had an excuse for each of them, and while he was prepared to make a general admission of guilt, he was unwilling to subscribe to a catalogue of crimes.

7

On 12th May there were several people dining at the Rue St. Florentin—the Princess de Lieven, the Duke de Noailles, Montrond, and others. Their host complained of the cold, the fire failed to warm him, and he had his chair moved into another room where he suffered an attack of violent sickness and shivering. When it had passed he insisted on the company rejoining him, and once more took his part in the conversation.

The next day it was decided that he was suffering from anthrax in the lumbar region, and an operation was advised. This took place on the 14th. He bore it with unflinching courage. He had schooled himself to conceal physical as well as mental emotion. When the pain was most intense he exclaimed: 'Do you know that you are hurting me very much.'

That same evening he again received visitors, although he was feverish and suffering. He talked calmly and gaily, jesting about the sensation produced by the operating-knife, and delighting to tell how his dog had had to be shut out of the room to prevent him from flying at the surgeon. He had always loved dogs, and was particularly attached to the one then in his possession.

The next morning he was worse. The Abbé Dupanloup, summoned in haste, arrived early. The doctor whispered in his ear: 'If you can do anything, do it quickly. Time presses.' He brought with him the Archbishop's corrected version of the document received from Madame de Dino. It consisted now of two parts, the one a declaration and the other a letter to the Pope. These had to be signed before the penitent could be granted the consolations of religion.

When the Abbé referred to these papers he was surprised and discouraged by the firmness with which Talleyrand replied that there could be nothing to add to his original statement, over which he had deeply reflected, and which contained everything that was necessary. He was, however, not without difficulty, persuaded to read the Archbishop's version. This he did seated upon the edge of the bed, supported by cushions. The wound in his back rendered it painful for him to lie down, and he spent most of his last days in this position. 'I must say,' writes the Abbé, 'that at this moment his appearance was really imposing; his face was calm, serious, meditative; his hand supported his forehead; his eyes were fixed and thoughtful; and I, silent and motionless, watched his face, which remained unmoved.'

When he had finished reading, after a moment's silence, he raised his head. 'Monsieur the Abbé,' he said, 'I am very well satisfied with this paper.' The Abbé's heart leapt. All was well, he thought, all was settled. But he did not know his man. It was not so that the Minister for Foreign Affairs, the Grand Chamberlain, the King's Ambassador, was accustomed to conclude affairs of high importance. 'Will you be good enough to leave this paper with me,' he continued calmly. 'I desire to read it again!' The Abbé, in great distress, could not refuse and dared not protest. He remained some time, talking earnestly to the Prince of religious matters, but although their conversation was intimate and personal, the Abbé left with a heavy heart for the documents remained unsigned.

The following morning the Abbé was sent for yet earlier. The condition of the invalid was hopeless. Dorothea and Pauline were in despair. All their efforts now were concentrated on securing his reconciliation to the Church before it was too late. They knew that the hours were few and that no minute must be wasted. The account given by the Abbé of the emotion felt and the courage shown by both is extremely moving. The mother urged the daughter to use her influence. At first she seemed too overcome by misery but 'the strength of God descended into her soul,' and when she had received his blessing this 'visible angel of the old man' passed into the death chamber. When she re-appeared, after a lengthy interval, she was smiling through her tears, and she told the Abbé to go in.

The Abbé first expressed his sympathy with the sufferer. 'I thank you,' was the reply, spoken with an 'air of indescribable kindness and benevolence.' Then the Abbé grew eloquent; he felt inspired. The importance of the occasion, the urgency of the task, the sanctity of his office, the respect and the affection which he now felt for the man whose soul he held himself charged to save, all contributed to lend fervency to the words of the great preacher. 'I shall never forget the veritable outburst of gratitude depicted in his face, the blessed eagerness of his regard while he listened to me. 'Yes, yes, I am willing to do all that,' he said, offering me his hand and seizing mine with the most genuine emotion. 'I am willing—you know it, I told you so before —I said so to Madame de Dino.' He continued to talk eagerly and seemed about to enter on a general confession, when the Abbé reminded him that before doing so he must signify his formal reconciliation by signing the documents. 'That is right,' he replied, 'then I want to see Madame de Dino; I want to re-read these two documents with her; I want to add something to them; and then we will finish.'

It was another disappointment for the Abbé, a further delay. The conversation with Dorothea produced no more satisfactory result. He still maintained that he wished to add something before signing, but said that he was too tired to do so at present. When he was urged to sign while he could still hold the pen he told them not to be anxious and assured them that he would not be too late. To the Abbé, who remained by his bed most of the day in prayer, he said frequently: 'You do me good,' and once he added: 'I should have already done what I have promised you if I were not in such pain.'

Meanwhile all Paris was waiting for the news, and the anteroom was full of those who hoped to be its first bearers. They were oddly assorted, those who kept that long vigil, and representative of the society he had frequented all his life. If sometimes the murmur of their conversation reached his ears he would not have resented their presence. Old statesmen were there and political intriguers, young women and those who followed them; one lady reclining on a sofa listened to whispers which were not all concerned with the tragedy of the adjoining room; sometimes even a light laugh escaped instantly suppressed with frowns. Montrond sat apart from all in gloomy silence.

Whether he would sign was the main subject of discussion. Some maintained that to do so would be to wipe out his whole life with one stroke of the pen, and protested that it would be an unpardonable betrayal of the eighteenth century; but Royer-Collard, that stern old Christian, reassured the anxious. 'Fear nothing,' he said, 'he who has always been the peacemaker will not refuse to make his peace with God before he dies.' These words were repeated to Talleyrand. With great animation he exclaimed: 'I do not refuse, I do not refuse'; but still he delayed.

Towards eight o'clock in the evening the Abbé Dupanloup feared he was sinking. Determining to make another effort he said that he was about to visit the Archbishop, whose mind would be set at rest if the news were brought to him that the documents were signed. 'Thank Monseigneur the Archbishop,' replied the Prince, 'tell him that everything shall be done.' 'But when shall that be, good uncle?' exclaimed Pauline, who was kneeling by his side. 'To-morrow,' he replied, 'between five and six o'clock in the morning.' The Abbé began to say that he would inform the Archbishop that there was this hope, but he was sharply interrupted by the dying man—'Don't say this hope, say this certitude: it is positive.' 'These words were pronounced with such extraordinary force and firmness,' wrote the Abbé nine months later, 'that I can still feel my astonishment and that I can hear them still.'

The Abbé retired. Later that night, the doctor having expressed some uncertainty as to whether the patient would much longer retain the command of his mental faculties, Dorothea decided that it was her duty to make one more attempt. Holding a candle in one hand she gently lifted the curtain of the bed and the dying man saw Pauline standing beside him with the papers and a pen in her hands. 'Good uncle, you are calm now,' she said, 'won't you sign these two papers? You have approved of what is in them. It will comfort you.' But the old man replied with all the obstinacy of a diplomatist who has already made his ultimate concession: 'It is not yet six o'clock. I told you that I would sign to-morrow between five and six in the morning: I still promise to do so.' The young girl blushed like one reproved for an error, and the tired watchers had to face another night of torturing suspense.

8

But what was passing in the mind of the sufferer during the long hours of that night? He had been brought up to the priesthood and such early training is seldom completely eradicated. His practice of religion had been negligent but he had never professed infidelity, and we must believe the Abbé Dupanloup's testimony that his mind was now seriously occupied with spiritual matters. He had always set store by correct behaviour and it was only seemly and fitting that a Talleyrand-Périgord should die in the faith of his fathers, the faith in which he had been born and bred. Above all, it was the dearest wish of those who were dearest to him, the last service that he could render them on earth. Never can there have been stronger or more imperative reasons for the fulfilment of a simple task, never can there have been less ground for the least delay. Why then this astounding procrastination? That his intelligence was in no way darkened seems to be established by all the evidence. There was no moment of delirium, nor was it the peevishness of second childhood that made him still seek postponement and select so strange an hour for such a solemn act. To avoid haste had always been with him a rule of diplomacy, and he had always warned the young against excess of zeal. But surely haste presented no danger now and zeal could not be excessive when the salvation of his soul was at stake? It is possible that he still clung to some hope of recovery; it is even thinkable that, as he lay there, he imagined what form Montrond's mockery would take of the death-bed conversion, sarcastic references to the lost sheep, the penitent thief, the prodigal son. He may also have been reluctant to have it thought he was afraid, and that it was the fear of death which was dictating conduct which would seem to some like a betrayal of principles once held by that young Abbé who knelt at the feet of Voltaire in the age of reason, when it had been so sweet to live.

But these are only conjectures. The May morning was breaking. At half-past four Dupanloup, 'trembling with emotion,' returned to Talleyrand's bedside. He found already there 'those guardian angels whom God had given him.' They feared that he might no longer have the strength to hold the pen, an eventuality which had been foreseen by the Archbishop, who, lest there should be any doubt as to exactly what took place, had arranged for witnesses of unimpeachable integrity to be present. Carriages were despatched through the empty streets to collect them, the Duke de Poix, the Count de Sainte-Aulaire, Barante, Royer-Collard, and Molé. When they had all arrived they gathered in the doorway dividing the two rooms whence they could observe what passed.

Talleyrand was the first to speak. He greeted those who were present with a slight smile and inclination of the head, and inquired what time it was. When somebody replied that it was six the scrupulous Dupanloup felt it his duty to correct the statement and to say that it was but little past five.

There was a pause and then a little girl, dressed all in white, timidly entered the room. She was the daughter of that mysterious Charlotte whom Talleyrand had brought up in his house and had married to one of his relatives. She was going, on this morning, to her first communion, and the scene had been previously arranged by the Abbé Dupanloup. Falling on her knees by the bedside, she said: 'My uncle, I am going to pray to God for you; I ask your blessing.' 'My child,' he answered, 'I wish you much happiness in your life and if I could contribute to it in any way I would do so with all my heart.' 'You can,' said Dorothea, 'by blessing her.' He stretched out his hand and did so; the child burst into tears. As she was led away he turned to one of those who were supporting him, and said: 'There you have the two extremities of life: she is going to make her first communion— and I—' he did not finish the phrase. Was he thinking, perhaps, even in that solemn moment, of the little child's grandmother, whom he had loved so long ago and whose honour he had preserved so carefully that history does not know her name?

Soon afterwards the clock struck six: the hour had arrived. Dorothea bringing him the papers, reminded him that he knew all that they contained, and asked whether he wished that they should be read again. 'Yes, read them,' he said, and sitting on the edge of the bed, with eyes shut and one hand holding the pen aloft, he listened. The room was full and the Abbé feared lest the terms of the statement might prove too humiliating for the Prince's pride. There seems to have been little cause for his apprehension. Nothing was referred to in detail; no particular act was mentioned for which forgiveness was asked; there was no admission of specific error. He regretted the grievous sins of the Revolution and his own share in them, he deplored the harm and sorrow they had caused the Church. He had never ceased to regard himself as the son of the Church; he submitted himself entirely to the Church's discipline and doctrine.

The letter to the Pope was couched in language equally indefinite and put forward one important plea in his defence. 'The respect,' so it ran, 'that I owe to the authors of my being does not forbid me to say that all my youth was dedicated to a profession for which I was not born.' When the reading was ended he dipped his pen into the ink and firmly affixed to both documents his full signature, which he reserved for state papers of the first importance—Charles-Maurice, Prince de Talleyrand.

They asked him how the documents were to be dated. He replied: 'The week of my speech at the Academy.' This answer, says the Abbé Dupanloup, had an extraordinary effect on those present; they were overcome by admiration of the firmness of his will, the clearness of his mind, the precision of his thought which enabled him, almost in the arms of death, to decide even the details of the great affair he was engaged in. He had determined that it should not be alleged that he was no longer in possession of his senses when he signed the papers. He asked to be reminded of the date of his speech. They told him 3rd March. 'Very well, then,' he replied, 'date these the 10th so that it shall be in the same week.' It was done as he directed.

Now, at last, Dorothea and Pauline felt that their task

was accomplished. Their anxiety was at an end, only their grief remained. Dupanloup, on the other hand, had still two duties to perform, to hear the dying man's confession, and to grant him absolution.

But there came to the house of death on that spring morning one more message from the living world which even at such an hour demanded attention and seemed designed to hold down to the earth until the last moment a mind that had been so long occupied with worldly things. It was announced that the King was coming; and presently Louis-Philippe, together with Madame Adelaide, arrived.

The interview was brief, but it made a final tax on Talleyrand's failing strength. His mind was still clear; his manners were still perfect. 'It is a great honour that the King does to this house, in coming here to-day,' he said, and then, in accordance with the rules of Court procedure, he insisted on presenting all those who were in the room, including the doctor and the valet, to the King. Louis-Philippe rather awkwardly expressed his sympathy. When they withdrew Talleyrand pressed the hand of Madame Adelaide and assured her of his affection. After their departure he fell into a stupor that lasted for more than two hours.

At the end of that period the Abbé, who had been torn with anxiety lest he should die without receiving absolution after all, succeeded in rousing him. So much had passed between them at their previous interviews that the hearing of his confession was soon completed. Absolution followed. When it came to the sprinkling of the holy oil he held out his hands, closed, the palms downwards, murmuring: 'Do not forget I am a bishop'—for it is the right of bishops to receive extreme unction in this manner, and it was characteristic of him to remember such a detail at such a moment.

When these last offices had been performed he sank rapidly. He retained the sitting posture to the end. His room, as well as the anteroom, was full of relations, attendants, and friends. He died, as he had lived, in public. When they told him that the Archbishop had said that morning that he would gladly give his life for him, he replied: 'Tell him that he has a much better use for it.' This was his last civility; these were his final words. Afterwards he still listened to the prayers that were being recited and gave signs of comprehending them, until suddenly his head fell heavily forward on to his chest.

The old diplomatist had set forth upon his last mission. Some doubts he may have felt as to the country whither he was travelling, some uncertainty as to the form of government that there prevailed; but he had made inquiries of those best qualified to advise him; he had obtained the most reliable information available; he had taken, not a moment too soon, all possible precautions, and he departed with his credentials in order, his passport signed.

9

Five months later Dorothea de Dino, who had spent the interval in travel, returned to Paris. Among her first visitors was Montrond, her ancient enemy. He talked to her for some time in the old bantering spirit. He supposed that she would abandon the Orleans monarchy now, and return to her spiritual home, the aristocrats of the Faubourg St. Germain, who had never recognised the usurper. She coldly informed him that she intended to do nothing of the kind. He rose to go—but suddenly seizing her hand he begged her to be kind to him, said he was alone in the world, that he would so much like to be able to talk to her sometimes about M. de Talleyrand; and then the old sinner burst into tears and sobbed like a child.

Bibliography and Notes

ASTERISKS, marginal numerals and footnotes, which tease the eye and disfigure the page, have been dispensed with, and an effort has been made to make plain in the text, whenever possible, the source from which information is derived. The following notes, however, may be useful to those who wish to consult for themselves the original authorities in order to learn more about any particular personality or incident.

The author has been greatly assisted by the kindness of Lord Lansdowne in allowing him to inspect the important collection of unpublished documents at Bowood, and in giving him the benefit of his own wide knowledge of the period.

Works dealing with the life of Talleyrand may be classed under four headings:

(1) Collections of original documents.
(2) Books of libel and gossip.
(3) Essays.
(4) Biographies.

(1) *Original Documents.*—The most important of those included in the first category are Talleyrand's own memoirs, which were published in five volumes in 1891. They came as a disappointment to people who had been expecting sensational revelations and a feast of scandal. Lord Acton, writing in 1880, said that the reason why Talleyrand's memoirs could not even then be published was the amount of scandal they contained (see *Letters of Lord Acton to Mary Gladstone,* page 28). When they proved, on the contrary, to be concerned almost entirely with politics, some were inclined to question their authenticity; but of this there can be no doubt. More than three-fifths of the whole are taken up with official correspondence, and, except in the first volume, private life is hardly mentioned. An English translation by Mrs. Angus Hall appeared in 1892.

Éclaircissemens donnés par le C$^{en.}$ Talleyrand à ses Concitoyens, An. VII, a short pamphlet published at the time of his resignation under the Directory.

Other collections of letters that have been published are as follows:

Correspondance Inédite du Prince de Talleyrand et du Roi Louis XVIII (1888), edited by M. G. Pallain.

An English translation appeared in 1891.

These letters subsequently were included in Talleyrand's own memoirs, Vols. II and III.

La Mission de Talleyrand à Londres en 1792 (1889), edited by M. G. Pallain.

Le Ministère de Talleyrand sous le Directoire (1891), edited by M. G. Pallain.

Ambassade de Talleyrand à Londres (1891), edited by M. G. Pallain.

These letters also form part of the last two volumes of Talleyrand's memoirs.

Talleyrand à Napoléon (1889), edited by P. Bertrand.

Talleyrand Intime (1892). A small collection of letters to the Duchess of Courland.

(2) *Libel and Gossip.*—Various volumes purporting to be biographies of Talleyrand appeared in his lifetime. The earliest of these was *Memoirs of C. M. Talleyrand de Périgord*, by the author of *The Revolutionary Plutarch*, published in London in 1805. England was then at war with France, and no libel was too gross at the expense of one who was known to be Napoleon's chief Minister. Murder is the least of the crimes of which Talleyrand is accused. Neither history nor fiction, the book is hardly readable, and the portrait drawn of Talleyrand is analogous to those drawn by Gillray in his caricatures of Napoleon at this date. Talleyrand is usually in the picture in the shape of a deformed monster.

The most important of the contemporary works is *Monsieur de Talleyrand*, published anonymously in 1834 (see page 342). The author was a certain Villemarest, who had served in the Ministry for Foreign Affairs, and who, although disgraced and disgruntled, had had access to reliable sources of information. It is written from a point of view violently hostile to Talleyrand, but it does justice to some of his qualities, particularly to the affection with which he was regarded by nearly all those who worked under him, and it also acquits him of any responsibility for Napoleon's Spanish policy.

Mémoires du Prince de Talleyrand-Périgord par Madame la Comtesse O. . . . du C. . . ., published in 1838, shortly after Talleyrand's death, while less hostile, is of even inferior value. It is a mixture of second-rate melodrama and third-hand gossip.

Colmache, who had been Talleyrand's secretary, published in London in 1848 *Reminiscences of Prince Talleyrand* in two volumes, a gossipy, unreliable work, but not uninteresting.

Souvenirs Intimes sur Monsieur de Talleyrand, by Amédée Pichot (1870) is little more than a collection of anecdotes, while *L'Esprit de M. de Talleyrand*, by Louis Thomas (1909) is merely an anthology of *bons mots*.

Les Belles Amies de Talleyrand, by Mary Summer (1893), is an historical novel, but neither such good history nor such good fiction as Mr. Kipling's 'A Priest in Spite of Himself' in *Rewards and Fairies*.

(3) *Essays.*—On 8th, June 1838 Barante pronounced in the Chamber of Peers his 'Éloge de M. le Prince, Duc de Talleyrand.' It is printed in his *Études Historiques* (1857). A noble tribute in eloquent but never exaggerated language, it is by no means the ordinary funeral oration, and is well worth reading.

A year later, at the Academy of Moral and Political Science, the historian Mignet delivered a lecture, 'Sur la Vie et les Travaux de M. le Prince de Talleyrand.' It was published in his *Portraits et Notices Historiques* (1852). This is the first attempt to give an unbiassed account of Talleyrand, and while the writer finds difficulty in accepting his conduct towards Napoleon, he is scrupulously fair, and his final verdict is distinctly favourable.

Lord Brougham, in his *Historical Sketches of Statesmen* (1839-43), wrote an essay on Talleyrand, whom he had known and liked; and Capefigue, in *Diplomates Européens* (1843), does full justice to the wisdom and consistency of Talleyrand's foreign policy.

The best account of Talleyrand that appeared prior to the publication of his memoirs is that contained in Sir Henry Lytton Bulwer's *Historical Characters* (1868). The whole of the first of two volumes is concerned with Talleyrand considered as 'The Politic Man.' Bulwer was a diplomatist, had lived in the world where Talleyrand was still remembered, and must have met many who had known him. He takes the favourable view of Talleyrand that was prevalent in such circles at the time of his death.

Sainte-Beuve, in *Nouveaux Lundis* (No. 12), devoted a lengthy essay to 'M. de Talleyrand,' which was published separately in 1870. It was written largely in reply to Bulwer, and is definitely hostile to Talleyrand. Sainte-Beuve was too good a friend to the Second Empire to do justice to one who had contributed so largely to the downfall of the First. No other French writer of equal standing has written about Talleyrand, and Sainte-Beuve's views must therefore have had great influence on opinion in France. This is really the turning point in the history of the Talleyrand legend, and it is curious that this should have been the very moment that Talleyrand himself had selected for the publication of his memoirs. Had they appeared then, instead of some twenty years later, his fame would certainly have benefited.

Lord Acton's essay on 'Talleyrand's Memoirs' in his *Historical Essays* (1906) is disappointing. More interesting, though no better disposed towards Talleyrand, is Albert Sorel's article on 'Talleyrand et ses Mémoires,' published in his *Lectures Historiques* (1894). He also wrote an essay on 'Talleyrand au Congrès de Vienne' in his *Essais d'Histoire et de Critique* (1895).

In a brilliant volume entitled *Romantisme et Diplomatie*, M. Maurice Paléologue devotes more than a third of his space to Talleyrand, and traces the growth of the Talleyrand legend, rightly attributing their share of responsibility to such imaginative writers as George Sand, Chateaubriand and Victor Hugo.

In *Les Hommes de la Révolution* (1928), Louis Madelin has an essay on 'Talleyrand Révolutionnaire,' which gives an account of that period of his life. Both these works have been translated into English.

The series of *Vies des Hommes Illustres* includes a volume entitled *Talleyrand*, by Jacques Sindral—a clever essay which has no claims to be considered a biography.

An increasing appreciation among modern writers of Talleyrand's services to Europe is indicated in *Le Diplomate*, by Jules Cambon, translated into English by Christopher R. Turner (1931), and also in an excellent sketch of Talleyrand in *The Peacemakers*, by J. G. Lockart (1932).

(4) *Biographies.*—Last in date, but first in importance, of the biographies of Talleyrand, comes the work of G. Lacour-Gayet, in three volumes, published in 1928, 1930, and 1931. This is, and will probably remain, the standard work on the subject, and all present and future students of the life of Talleyrand must be indebted to it. M. Lacour-Gayet is a great admirer of Napoleon, but he tries throughout to be fair to Talleyrand with whose policy he cannot sympathise, and for whose character he can feel no affection.

A biography by Lady Blennerhasset (Gräfin Leyden), written in

German, was published in an English translation (two volumes, 1894). It is a fair and unbiassed account, more valuable for the earlier than for the later years.

Bernard de Lacombe is the author of two works, *Talleyrand Évêque d'Autun* (1903), and *La Vie Privée de Talleyrand* (1910), both of which are of great value. The latter is particularly interesting and contains a great deal of matter concerning the last years which had not previously been published.

Joseph McCabe's *Talleyrand, A Biographical Study* (1906), has the advantage, which Lady Blennerhasset lacked, of having studied the new material produced by Lacombe. It is written with insight and sympathy.

Talleyrand et la Société Française, by Frédéric Loliée (1910) is, as the title implies, concerned mainly with the lighter side of Talleyrand's life and might almost be included in the first of these categories.

Talleyrand, the Training of a Statesman, by Anna Bowman Dodd (1927), contains some interesting illustrations.

CHAPTER ONE:

Page 11.—The quotation in the first paragraph is from the memoirs of the Duke de Lauzun, which appeared in 1818. Many people, including Talleyrand, questioned their authenticity, but they bear the stamp of truth.

Page 23.—Barras, in the first volume of his memoirs, suggests that the physical resemblance of Talleyrand to Robespierre was due to similarity of character. He adds that for the same reason Napoleon resembled Marat. *Mémoires de Barras* (1895), Vol. I, page 151.

Arnault was the author of a book entitled *Souvenirs d'un Sexagénaire,* in which he describes Talleyrand as he appeared to him in 1789.

Page 26.—Talleyrand's work as Agent General of the Clergy is dealt with at length in *Talleyrand Évêque d'Autun,* by Bernard Lacombe (1903).

Page 28.—Mirabeau's letters from Berlin were published in two volumes in 1789, under the title of *Histoire Secrète de la Cour de Berlin* (à Londres—chez S. Vladon, dans Paternoster Row).

The best authority for all the diplomatic history of the period is Albert Sorel, *L'Europe et la Révolution Française,* eight volumes.

CHAPTER TWO:

Page 30.—Talleyrand's association with Pitt at Rheims in 1783 is referred to in Lord Holland's *Foreign Reminiscences* (1850). The author adds in a footnote: 'My general and long observation of Talleyrand's veracity in great and small matters makes me confident his relation is correct. He may as much, or more, than other diplomats suppress what is true; I am quite satisfied he never actually says what is false, though he may occasionally imply it.' (Page 36.)

Page 37.—The Count d'Artois confirmed Talleyrand's account of what passed between them on this occasion. He referred to the incident in conversation with Lady Elizabeth Foster at Chiswick in 1805 (see *Lord Granville Leveson Gower—Private Correspondence*, Vol. II, page 113).

Page 40.—The authority for Talleyrand's irreverent remark to Lafayette at the Feast of the Federation is Lafayette himself, as reported by Pasquier. Although they bore no good will towards Talleyrand, it is not a remark which either of them would have invented.

Mémoires du Chancelier Pasquier (1894), Vol. I.

Page 43.—*The Diary and Letters of Gouverneur Morris*. Edited by Anne Carey Morris. Two volumes, London, 1889.

Page 44.—The letter referred to from Lady Sutherland is printed in *Lord Granville Leveson Gower—Private Correspondence*, Vol. I, page 28.

Page 51.—For the mission to London see *Le Duc de Lauzun (Général Biron)* (1791-1792), *Correspondance Intime*, by Le Comte de Lort de Sérignan (1906); also *La Mission de Talleyrand à Londres en 1792*, by G. Pallain (1889).

Page 53.—Lord Holland, in his *Foreign Reminiscences*, asserts that Talleyrand complained to him that Pitt 'never had the grace to allude either during his embassy or his "emigration" to their earlier meeting at Rheims' (page 35), but in his official letter to Delessart, recounting his first interview, he states quite definitely the opposite. (*La Mission de Talleyrand à Londres*, page 55.)

Page 59.—Barère describes in his memoirs meeting Talleyrand dressed for travelling at Danton's the night of his departure. (*Mémoires de B. Barère* (1842), Vol. II, page 25.)

CHAPTER THREE:

Page 61.—Miss Burney's account of Juniper Hall will be found in Vol. v of the *Diary and Letters of Madame D'Arblay* (1904).

Page 65.—The memorandum of 25th November is printed in full in *Le Ministère de Talleyrand sous le Directoire*, by G. Pallain.

Page 68.—Talleyrand's letters to Shelburne are printed in *La Mission de Talleyrand à Londres*, by G. Pallain.

Page 69.—The fourth volume of Madame de Genlis's memoirs deals with this period in London.

Page 74.—The story of Burr calling on Talleyrand in Paris is to be found in *The Mount Vernon Papers*, by Edward Everett (1860), page 359, and is related by Mrs. Anna Bowman Dodd in *Talleyrand, the Training of a Statesman* (1927). She says that it was told her by a descendant of General Schuyler's family.

Page 75.—Mme de la Tour du Pin's memoirs are entitled *Journal d'une Femme de Cinquante Ans.*

Page 79.—Cobbett's account of the interview is contained in *Peter Porcupine.*

Page 81.—The Kipling story referred to is 'A Priest in Spite of Himself' in *Rewards and Fairies.*

CHAPTER FOUR:

Page 82.—Talleyrand recounts this incident in his memoirs, Vol. I, page 248. It is the only reference to Madame de Flahaut contained in them.

Page 88.—The best accounts of Thérèse Tallien are contained in *Notre Dame de Thermidor*, by Arsène Houssaye (favourable), *La Belle Tallien*, by Louis Gastine (unfavourable), and a recent semi-historical work entitled *Scandalous Princess*, by S. B. Whipple (1932).

Page 89.—Madame de Staël was so indignant when she heard the American story that she called on Talleyrand, expecting a denial. Having heard all she had to say he left the room without answering and did not return. She never forgave him. (*Souvenirs du Baron de Barante*, Vol. I, page 92.)

Page 89.—*Le Beau Montrond*, by Henri Malo (Paris, 1926), see also 'L'Ami de M. de Talleyrand,' by Henri Welschinger (*La Revue de Paris*, 1st February 1895).

Page 91.—*The Narrative of the Life of a Gentleman Long Resident in India*, by G. F. Grand, gives the husband's version of this affair. This book was privately printed at the Cape of Good Hope in 1814, and published by the Calcutta Historical Society in 1910. See also *Echoes from Old Calcutta*, by H. E. Busteed (Third Edition, 1897), and *Memoirs of Sir Philip Francis*, K.C.B. (Vol. II), by J. Parkes and H. Merivale (1867). Also the *Memoirs of William Hickey* (Vol. II, 1918).

Page 92.—Madame Grand's appearance is described in the *Mémoires de Madame de Rémusat* (Vol. II), and there is much gossip about her in the *Mémoires de la Comtesse de Boigne* (Vol. I), including a description of how she was attired when she had supper with Édouard Dillon, page 433.

Page 94.—The best account of the last days of the Directory is contained in *L'Avènement de Bonaparte*, by A. Vandal.

Page 113.—*Journal du Comte P. -L. Roederer* (Paris, 1909).

CHAPTER FIVE:

Page 119.—*Memoirs of Napoleon Bonaparte*, by M. de Bourrienne. London (1836), Vol. I, page 260, etc.

Page 121.—*Memoirs of Baron Hyde de Neuville* (translated and abridged by Frances Jackson, two vols). Hyde de Neuville speaks well of Talleyrand throughout his memoirs. There is an interesting passage in the second volume (page 212) recounting a chance meeting in 1827, when Talleyrand referred to this interview with Napoleon.

Page 123.—The authoritative life of Fouché is by Louis Madelin, in two volumes (1900). Memoirs of doubtful authenticity were published in 1821. See also *Joseph Fouché*, by Stefan Zweig (1930), a brilliant sketch.

Page 125.—This story is elaborated in Balzac's *Une Ténébreuse Affaire*.

Page 144.—The story told by Balzac is also referred to in the *Mémoires du Baron de Vitrolles*, Vol. I, page 236. On the other hand, in the *Mémoires de Madame de Chastenay* (1896), the authoress, who was present at the house of Madame de Luynes that evening, while confirming Talleyrand's presence and mentioning that she left him gambling when she retired, makes no reference to his dramatic statement. If it was made after she left, it is probable that she would have heard of it.

CHAPTER SIX:

Page 147.—The young Scotsman referred to was Lord John Campbell, who became 7th Duke of Argyll (see *Intimate Society Letters of the Eighteenth Century*, by the Duke of Argyll (1910), page 515).

Page 149.—The scene at Nikolsburg is described in Bismarck's *Gedanken und Erinnerungen* (1898), Vol. II, page 47.

Page 153.—The private letter from Fox to Talleyrand is in the author's possession.

Page 154.—Sorel, *Oubril et Yarmouth à Paris*, Vol. VII, Chapter I, Part VI.

Page 156.—*Mémoires de la Reine Hortense* (1927), Vol. I, page 269.

Page 161.—The question as to who betrayed the Treaty of Tilsit to England is thoroughly examined in *Four Famous Mysteries*, by Sir John Hall (1922).

Page 165.—Two recent works of importance throw fresh light on the Spanish question: *L'Espagne et Napoléon*, by Geoffroy de Grandmaison (1908), three volumes, and *Napoléon et L'Espagne*, by André Fuzier (1930), two volumes. Villemarest, in *Monsieur de Talleyrand*, though generally hostile, supports the view that Talleyrand disapproved of the Spanish policy from the first.

CHAPTER SEVEN:

Page 170.—The leading authority on transactions at Tilsit and Erfurt, and subsequent relations with Russia, is Albert Vandal's *Napoléon et Alexandre I*.

Page 184.—See *Memoirs of Prince Metternich*, translated by Mrs. Alexander Napier (1880), Vol. II, pages 183 and 193.

Page 187.—An account of the scene of 23rd January and of Talleyrand's subsequent conduct is given in Méneval's *Memoirs of Napoleon I*, translated by Robert H. Sherard (1894), Vol. II, page 200. Accounts are also given in the memoirs of Pasquier, of Madame de Chastenay, and elsewhere.

CHAPTER EIGHT:

Page 191.—See *Life and Memoirs of Count Molè*, edited by the Marquis of Noailles (translated) (1923), Vol. I, page 198.

Page 198.—See *Mémoires de la Comtesse Potocka*. Edited by Casimir Stryienski (1896).

Page 198.—A collection of Talleyrand's letters to the Duchess of Courland has been published in a volume entitled *Talleyrand Intime.*

Page 199.—For the relations of the Comte de Flahaut with the Queen Hortense, see *The First Napoleon*. Edited by the Earl of Kerry (1925). Subsequent researches that Lord Lansdowne has made among the papers at Bowood have enabled him to establish that Flahaut was also engaged in an affair with Caroline Murat, Queen of Naples. See also *Mémoires de la Reine Hortense* (1927), Vol. II, page 9.

Page 204.—*Memoiren der Gräfin Kielmannsegge über Napoleon I* Dresden, 1927.

Page 209.—*Mémoires de Aimée de Coigny*, with introduction and notes by Étienne Lamy (N.D.).

Page 212.—For Savary's evidence, see *Mémoires du Duc de Rovigo*, Vol. VI, Chapter VII and Chapter XXI.

Page 214.—See *Journal d'une Femme de Cinquante Ans*, Vol. II, Chapter XV.

CHAPTER NINE:

Page 219.—See *Mémoires et Relations Politiques du Baron de Vitrolles* (1884), three volumes.

Page 230.—The best and fairest account of Marmont and of his conduct at this crisis is given in Sainte-Beuve's *Causeries du Lundi*, Vol. VI. See also Caulaincourt's account, given in 'L'Agonie de Fontainebleau,' published in the *Revue des Deux Mondes*, January 1930.

CHAPTER TEN:

Page 245.—See *The Foreign Policy of Castlereagh, 1812-1815*, by C. K. Webster (1931), page 323.

Page 245.—*Anecdotal Recollections of the Congress of Vienna*, by the Comte A. de la Garde-Chambonas, translated by the author of *An Englishman in Paris* (1902).

CHAPTER ELEVEN:

Page 265.—See Chateaubriand's *Mémoires d'Outre-Tombe*, Part III, Book v.

Page 269.—See *Mémoires du Comte Beugnot* (1868), Vol. II, page 307 *et seq.*

Page 274.—*Le Comte Molé, 1781—sa Vie—ses Mémoires*. Edited by the Marquis de Noailles. In six volumes. The sixth volume appeared in 1930. The earlier volumes have been translated—see note on page 191.

Page 274.—*Histoire de Mon Temps*. The memoirs of Pasquier were published in 1894 in six volumes.

Page 278.—The scene of Fouché receiving intimation of his fall is minutely described by Pasquier as well as by Vitrolles, and their accounts agree. In Stefan Zweig's recent book on Fouché he asserts that it took place at an evening party before an audience of 'pretty women, court dignitaries and young folks as well.' He quotes no authority.

CHAPTER TWELVE:

Page 287.—The diary of James Gallatin was published in 1914 under the title *A Great Peacemaker*. This extremely entertaining work is not always reliable. The writer states that in March 1827 at Crockfords in London, he sat opposite Talleyrand, who 'looked more like an ape than ever' (page 268). Talleyrand was certainly not in England between the years 1794 and 1830.

Page 292.—The memoirs of Antonin Carême are contained in a volume entitled *Les Classiques de la Table*, published in 1843. A portrait of Talleyrand serves as frontispiece, and there is much interesting matter concerning his diet and habits.

Page 292.—*The Diary of Frances Lady Shelley*. Edited by Richard Edgcumbe (1912), Vol. I, page 137. Lady Shelley did not like Talleyrand, thought him 'a frightful object to look at,' and was surprised that 'the French ladies find him irresistible.'

Page 295.—The letter from Madame de Sousa referred to is at Bowood.

Page 299.—See *Souvenirs du Baron de Barante* (1890), Vol. I, page 208.

Page 308.—Morley recounts that Mr. Gladstone was deeply

shocked by Talleyrand's comment on the death of Napoleon. 'Imagine such a way,' said Mr. G., 'of taking the disappearance of that colossal man!' (Morley's *Life of Gladstone*, Vol. III, page 485). The great rhetorician could not bear to think of such an opportunity for eloquence being missed.

Page 310.—For the remark about the Duke of San Carlos, see *Journal du Maréchal de Castellane*, Vol. II, page 257.

Page 312.—For Talleyrand's conduct after Maubreuil's assault, see *Mémoires de la Comtesse de Boigne*, Vol. III, page 202.

CHAPTER THIRTEEN:

Page 316.—See *Personal Recollections of the Duc de Broglie*, translated and edited by Raphael Ledos de Beaufort (1887), Vol. II, page 193.

Page 320.—For Ferdinand von Funck's evidence, see *In the Wake of Napoleon*, by Oakley Williams (1931), page 106.

Page 322.—For the American who found London improved in 1830, see Greville's *Memoirs*, Vol. II, page 53.

Page 322.—The best account of Aberdeen and Palmerston as Foreign Secretaries is contained in *British Foreign Secretaries, 1807-1916*, by Algernon Cecil.

Page 327.—For Lord Grey's view of Talleyrand, see *Lord Grey of the Reform Bill*, by G. M. Trevelyan, page 223.

Page 332.—Lord Alvanley called on Talleyrand the morning after the incident in the House of Lords and witnessed his tears. See *Journal kept by Thomas Raikes, Esq., 1831-1847* (1856), Vol. I, page 137.

Page 332.—Cobbett, in *Peter Porcupine*, says that Talleyrand (in 1796) 'knew English as well as I did.' This is certainly an exaggeration. Very few people knew English so well as the unschooled author of *Rural Rides*.

Page 337.—The unpublished correspondence of the Count de Flahaut and his wife is at Bowood, together with a number of letters from Talleyrand to Flahaut.

Page 338.—Prosper Mérimée's letter is quoted by Lacour-Gayet, in his *Talleyrand*, Vol. III, page 259.

Page 341.—For Lady Cowper's efforts to make peace between Talleyrand and Palmerston, and for the conclusion of the mission to London, see *Chronique de 1831 à 1862*, by the Duchess of Dino.

Page 342.—The letters of the Duchess of Dino to Thiers were published in the *Revue de Paris*, July-August 1923.

CHAPTER FOURTEEN:

Page 345.—See *Leaves from the Diary of Henry Greville* (1883), Vol. I, page 19 *seq*.

Page 349.—See Balzac's *Lettres à l'Étrangère*, Vol. I, page 371, and Lamartine, *Cours Familier de Littérature*, Vol. X, page 390. Both quoted by Lacour-Gayet.

Page 350.—See *Letters of Harriet, Countess of Granville*. Edited by the Hon. F. Leveson Gower (1894), Vol. II, page 127.

Page 355.—George Sand's article entitled 'Le Prince' appeared in the *Revue des Deux Mondes* of 15th October 1834.

Page 357.—A portion of the *Journal kept by Thomas Raikes, Esq., from 1831-1847* (1856).

Page 358.—Talleyrand's speech on Reinhard is printed verbatim in French and in English in Sir Henry Lytton Bulwer's *Historical Characters*, Vol. I, page 409.

Page 363.—The Abbé Dupanlop's statement concerning the last days of Talleyrand is dated 2nd February 1839. It was first published in the *Revue des Deux Mondes*, March 1910. See also Bernard de Lacombe, *La Vie Privée de Talleyrand* (1910), and *La Conversion et La Mort de M. Talleyrand*, 'Récit de l'un des cinq témoins, le Baron de Barante, recueilli par son petit-fils, le Baron de Nervo' (1910).

ADDENDUM

CHAPTER TWELVE:

PAGE 308.—Henry Edward Fox gives a different account of how Talleyrand received the news of Napoleon's death. He says that they were dining together at the time when the report was received 'which, to his credit be it said, seemed to shock the iniquitous old traitor very much.'—*The Journal of the Hon. Henry Edward Fox*, edited by the Earl of Ilchester. Both stories may be true as the one may refer to a report and the other, given in the text, to the official confirmation. Talleyrand would thus have had time in the interval to harden his heart and to prepare his *mot*.

Index

Dupanloup, Abbé, 362-74
Dupont, General, 207-8, 307
Durham, 1st Lord, 337
Duroc, Michel, 166

Enghien, Duke of, 139-45, 187, 265

Fénelon, François de S. de la Mothe, 364
Ferdinand, King of Spain, 164-5, 268, 306
Ferrand, Count, 238
Fitzgerald, Lady Edward, 69, 82
Fitzgerald, Lord Edward, 69, 82
FitzJames, Duke of, 306
Flahaut, Countess de, 44-6, 68, 82, 295, 335-7, 355
Flahaut, Count, son of above, 45, 156, 198-200, 261, 295, 334-7, 345
Flahaut, Countess de, wife of above, 335-7, 355
Fleury, Duke of, 209
Fouché, Duke of Otranto, 107, 123-5, 137, 161, 183, 185-6, 192, 194-7, 204, 209, 272-3, 277-9, 281, 286.
Fox, Charles James, 68, 132, 153, 155, 321
Fox, Henry, 89
Fox, Mrs., 132-4
Francis, Emperor of Austria, 143, 258
Francis, Sir Philip, 91-2
Franklin, Benjamin, 333
Frederick Augustus I, King of Saxony, 196, 252-3, 256-7, 259
Frederick the Great, 156-7
Frederick William III, King of Prussia, 239-54, 256, 257, 317, 329
Frénilly, Baron, 93
Funck, Ferdinand von, 320

Gaeta, Duke of, 188-92
Gallatin, James, 287.
Garde-Chambonas, Count de la, 246
Gaudin, see Gaeta
Genlis, Madame de, 68, 82
Gentz, Friedrich von, 252
George III, 50, 53, 56, 129
George IV, 215, 263
George V, 322
Gladstone, William Ewart, 321
Godoy, Duke of Alcudia, Manuel de, 164
Gohier, Director, 106, 115
Gontaut, Duchess de, 314
Gordon, Duchess of, 68
Gouvernet, see Tour du Pin, Marquis de
Goya y Lucientes (F.), 164
Grand, Madame see Talleyrand, Princess de
Grand, Monsieur, 91-2, 169
Granville, Countess, 350-1, 355-6, 361
Granville, 1st Earl, 67, 132, 328
Gregory XVI, Pope, 366-73
Grenville, Lord, 53-4, 70-1
Greville, Charles, 318, 321, 331-3, 345, 350, 354
Greville, Henry, 345, 350, 354
Grey, Countess, 337, 340
Grey, Earl, 318, 326-7, 334, 337
Guizot, François Pierre, 235, 346, 348, 354
Gustavus III, King of Sweden, 24

Hamilton, Alexander, 73-4
Hardenberg, Prince of, 220, 249
Hastings, Warren, 91
Haugwitz, Count, 157
Hauterive, Count d', 141-2
Hawkesbury, 2nd Baron, afterwards 1st Earl of Liverpool, 131
Hénin, Princess d', 60
Henri IV, 119, 205